HIGH/SCOPE®

Survey of

Early Childhood
Software

BY
WARREN BUCKLEITNER

1989

THE HIGH/SCOPE PRESS
A Division of the High/Scope Educational Research Foundation

Other books for teachers and parents
from the High/Scope® Press:

Changed Lives:
The Effects of the Perry Preschool Program
on Youths Through Age 19

Good Beginnings:
Parenting in the Early Years

Movement Plus Rhymes,
Songs, & Singing Games

A School Administrator's Guide
to Early Childhood Programs

The Teacher's Idea Book

Young Children in Action
A Manual for Preschool Educators

Coming soon:
Young Children & Computers

High/Scope® Press

CONTENTS

Editors: Marge Senninger, Polly Neill

The following names are used throughout the *High/Scope Survey of Early Childhood Software* and are registered trademarks of the companies indicated:

Apple Computer Company: Apple II, IIe, IIc, IIGS, Macintosh, Imagewriter, Imagewriter II
Atari, Inc.: Atari 400, 800, ST
Borg-Warner Educational Sytems: Ufonic voice system
Commodore Business Machines: PET, C64/128, Amiga, Vic-20
Dunamis Corp.: PowerPad, WonderWorker
International Business Machines, Inc.: IBM Personal Computer
Koala Technologies Corporation: Koala Pad
Personal Touch Corp.: Touch Window
RC Systems: Slotbuster II
Street Electronics Corp.: Echo II, II+, IIb, Cricket
Sunburst Communications, Inc.: Muppet Learning Keys
Tandy, Inc.: Radio Shack TRS-80 Models

ISBN 0-929816-00-5
ISSN 0898-6169

Printed in the United States of America

INTRODUCTION

Welcome to the new *High/Scope Survey of Early Childhood Software*! Now in it's fifth year, the *Survey* is the result of our extensive and continuing study of computer programs for young children. It is designed to assist parents, teachers, and early childhood educators in finding developmentally appropriate software for children aged three to six years.

This year's *Survey* reviews 355 programs. These are primarily programs for the Apple, C64, IBM, and Atari computers. Each program is described and given ratings based on its (1) user friendliness, (2) educational value, and (3) instructional design. A final rating is given as well. Other components of the *Survey* include a list of names and addresses of software producers, a glossary, the rating forms used in evaluating the software, and a variety of listings of the software titles — by content area, by final rating, and by computer brand.

A glance at the *Survey* shows there's a wide range of software available for young children — everything from drill-and-practice activities to open-ended programs that stimulate creative artwork and language — but a glance at the ratings shows how widely the quality of this software varies. Experts agree that software that is easy to use, strong in content, and designed with the special qualities of a young child in mind is the key to children's enjoyment and learning at the computer. Not all that we've seen is appropriate by these measures, but we are happy to report again this year that **there's plenty of good software available** for most popular computer models and that since last year's *Survey,* the software for young children has gotten better.

Why is High/Scope reviewing computer software? Since 1962, the High/Scope Educational Research Foundation has been studying and supporting the development of young children. During the late 1970s, we began to explore the use of computers with young children, and since that time, the High/Scope Foundation has been carefully integrating computer technology into the early childhood curriculum at its demonstration school in Ypsilanti, Michigan. The result is that today's visitor sees young children at our school using computers as routinely as they use blocks and art materials. These years of experience have taught us that the success of computer-based learning for young children depends on (1) the quality of the overall preschool or kindergarten curriculum, (2) the quality of the computer software, and (3) the software's match with the goals of the curriculum. Publishing these software reviews is one way we can share our experience with others who are looking for quality in young children's software.

High/Scope, a nonprofit organization, receives no fees or monetary consideration from either publishers or distributors for reviewing their software. Our work is supported by grants where possible and by subscriber fees for our services and publications.

If you produce early childhood software and are interested in having your products and company listed in the 1990 *Survey,* contact us before September 30, 1989. If you have questions about our reviews or want information about our work with young children, write to the Survey of Early Childhood Software, High/Scope Educational Research Foundation, 600 North River Street, Ypsilanti, Michigan 48198, or phone (313)485-2000.

1

USING THE SURVEY

This chapter contains (1) an alphabetical index of software titles, indicating the page numbers of the program descriptions in Chapter 2; (2) a guide to interpreting the software descriptions in Chapter 2; and (3) a computer scan, or summary, of *Survey* information.

INDEX OF SOFTWARE TITLES

Title	Company	Date	Page
Micro-LADS	Laureate Learning Systems	1984	83
Microzine Jr. (Sept/Oct. '88)	Scholastic Software, Inc.	1988	84
Milk Bottles	Island Software	1982	84
Money Works	MECC	1987	84
Monkey Math	Artworx	1983	85
Monsters and Make-Believe	Learning Lab Software	1987	85
Moptown Parade	The Learning Company	1981	85
Mount Murdoch	Kidsview Software, Inc.	1987	86
Mr. and Mrs. Potato Head	Random House Software	1985	86
Muppet Slate	Sunburst Communications, Inc.	1988	86
Muppet Word Book	Sunburst Communications, Inc.	1986	87
Muppets On Stage	Sunburst Communications, Inc.	1984	87
Muppetville	Sunburst Communications, Inc.	1986	87
Music	Lawrence Hall of Science	1984	88
Music Maestro	Springboard	1984	88
My ABC's	Paperback Software	1984	88
My Book	BeCi Software	1984	89
My Letters, Numbers, and Words	Stone & Associates	1983	89
My Words	Hartley Courseware, Inc.	1987	89
New Talking Stickybear ABC's, The	Weekly Reader Software	1988	90
Not Too Messy, Not Too Neat	D.C. Heath & Company	1988	90
Notable Phantom, The	DesignWare, Inc.	1984	90
Now You See It, Now You Don't	Sunburst Communications, Inc.	1987	91
Number BeCi	BeCi Software	1983	91
Number Farm	DLM	1984	91
Numbers	Lawrence Hall of Science	1984	92
Numbers Count	Polarware, Inc.	1987	92
Observation and Classif.	Hartley Courseware, Inc.	1985	92
Odd One Out	Sunburst Communications, Inc.	1983	93
Ollie and Seymour	Hartley Courseware, Inc.	1984	93
Ollie Finds It	S.R.A.	1985	93
Ollie Hears and Sequences	S.R.A.	1985	94
Ollie Remembers It	S.R.A.	1985	94
Once Upon a Time . . .	Compu-Teach	1987	94
One Banana More	Data Command	1984	95
Ordering/Sequencing	Aquarius People Materials	1984	95
Paint With Words	MECC	1986	95
Pals Around Town	CBS Software	1985	96
Path-Tactics	MECC	1986	96
Patterns	MECC	1988	96
Patterns and Sequences	Hartley Courseware, Inc.	1984	97
Peanuts Maze Marathon	Random House Software	1984	97
Peanuts Picture Puzzlers	Random House Software	1984	97
Peter and the Wolf Music	Spinnaker Software Corp.	1985	98
Peter Rabbit Reading	Spinnaker Software Corp.	1985	98
Peter's Growing Patterns	Strawberry Hill Software	1985	98
Picture Dictionary	D.C. Heath & Company	1985	99
Picture Perfect	MindPlay	1984	99
Pictures, Letters, and Sounds	Hartley Courseware, Inc.	1986	99

Title	Company	Date	Page
Play Together Learn Together	Grolier Electronic Publishing	1985	100
Pockets and Her New Sneakers	World Book, Inc.	1984	100
Pockets Goes on a Picnic	World Book, Inc.	1984	100
Pockets Goes on Vacation	World Book, Inc.	1984	101
Pockets Goes to the Carnival	World Book, Inc.	1984	101
Pockets Leads the Parade	World Book, Inc.	1984	101
Preschool Disk 1	Nordic Software	1986	102
Preschool Disk 2	Nordic Software	1986	102
Preschool Fun	THESIS	1980	102
Preschool IQ Builder I	PDI Software	1982	103
Preschool IQ Builder II	PDI Software	1984	103
Primary Editor Plus	IBM Educational Systems	1988	103
Print Shop, The	Broderbund Software	1987	104
Puss in Boot	Island Software	1982	104
Puzzle Master	Springboard	1984	104
R.J.'s Switch Progressions	R.J. Cooper & Associates	1987	105
Rabbit Scanner, The	E.C.S.	1986	105
Race the Clock	MindPlay	1984	105
Rainbow Painter	Springboard	1984	106
Rainy Day Games	Baudville	1985	106
Read, Write, & Publish 1	D.C. Heath & Company	1988	106
Reader Rabbit	The Learning Company	1984	107
Reading and Me	Davidson and Associates, Inc.	1987	107
Reading Comprehension: Lev. 1	Houghton Mifflin Co.	1988	107
Reading Fun: Beg. Consonants	Troll Associates	1985	108
Reading Helpers	Houghton Mifflin Co.	1986	108
Reading Machine, The	SouthWest EdPsych Services	1982	108
Reading Starters	Houghton Mifflin Co.	1986	109
Representational Play	P.E.A.L. Software	1985	109
Rhyming to Read	Grolier Electronic Publishing	1985	109
Rosie the Counting Rabbit	D.C. Heath & Company	1988	110
Rumpelstiltskin	Troll Associates	1987	110
Run Rabbit Run	E.C.S.	1988	110
Same or Different	Learning Technologies, Inc.	1985	111
Sesame Street Print Kit	Hi Tech Expressions	1988	111
Shape & Color Rodeo	DLM	1984	111
Shape Games	BeCi Software	1983	112
Shapes & Patterns	Mindscape, Inc.	1984	112
Shutterbug's Patterns	Learning Technologies, Inc.	1985	112
Shutterbug's Pictures	Learning Technologies, Inc.	1985	113
Sight Word Spelling	E.C.S.	1987	113
Simon Says	Sunburst Communications, Inc.	1987	113
Size and Logic	Hartley Courseware, Inc.	1984	114
Sleepy Brown Cow, The	D.C. Heath & Company	1988	114
SocPix	American Guidance Service	1985	114
Sound Ideas: Consonants	Houghton Mifflin Co.	1986	115
Sound Ideas: Vowels	Houghton Mifflin Co.	1986	115
Sound Ideas: Word Attack	Houghton Mifflin Co.	1987	115
Sound Tracks	MECC	1984	116

Title	Company	Date	Page
Webster's Numbers	EduWare	1983	132
What Makes a Dinosaur Sore?	D.C. Heath & Company	1988	133
What's in a Frame?	Sunburst Communications, Inc.	1987	133
What's Next	Strawberry Hill Software	1985	133
Where Did My Toothbrush Go?	D.C. Heath & Company	1988	134
Word Factory	Island Software	1983	134
Words	Lawrence Hall of Science	1984	134
Words & Concepts	Laureate Learning Systems	1987	135
Words & Concepts II	Laureate Learning Systems	1988	135
Words & Concepts III	Laureate Learning Systems	1988	135
Writing to Read 2.0	IBM Educational Systems	1982	136

Title: **Animal Alph. and Other Things** Final Rating: 81 ★★★★★★★★
Company: Random House Software User Friendliness: 87 ★★★★★★★★★
Date: 1986 Educational Value: 87 ★★★★★★★★★
Price: $29.95 Instructional Design: 73 ★★★★★★★
Age: 3-6
Computer: Apple
Conceptual Area: LA/1,4,6
■ Letter recognition, alphabetical order

Comments: Child presses a key, e.g., A, to see that letter on the screen. Pressing A again causes the letter to turn into an alligator. Pressing spacebar causes the next letter in the alphabet to appear. There are 26 pictures on each side of the disk. Side 1 covers upper case; side 2, lower case. Easy to use.

TITLE: The program's title.

COMPANY: The program's publisher. This is not necessarily the name of a software distributor. The address and phone number of the program's publisher are given in Appendix 1: Early Childhood Software Producers.

DATE: The program's most recent copyright date.

PRICE: The publisher's list price for the version of the program evaluated. Prices often vary with the type of computer and source of software.

AGE: The publisher's recommended age-range for the users of the program. Many software packages contain more than one game or activity, and the specified age-range takes into account the difficulty levels of all the various games or activities available. We mention in our comments if the publisher's recommended age-range seems inappropriate.

COMPUTER: A listing of the computers for which versions of the program are available. A star (*) is placed after any version used in evaluating the program.

Apple — Apple II family with at least 48K of memory
IIGS — Apple IIGS
Amiga — Commodore Amiga
Atari — Atari 400, 800, or 1200
Atari ST — Atari ST
C64 — Commodore 64

IBM — IBM Personal Computer or compatible with color graphics adapter
IBM PS/2 series
IBM PCjr
Mac — Macintosh
TRS 80 — TRS 80 computer
TI — Texas Instruments

Any additional hardware a program requires or can utilize, such as a speech synthesizer, a mouse, additional memory, a printer, is listed.

If more specific computer information is required, e.g., 3.5-inch disk availability, it is safest to call the producer directly before ordering. See Appendix 1 for a listing of producers and phone numbers.

CONCEPTUAL AREA: A listing, from strongest to weakest, of the conceptual areas present in a program. The codes used refer to the lists found in Appendix 3. For example, CL/1 refers to the first item under the conceptual area of Classification, "Identifying attributes." (High/Scope Curriculum users will recognize the Appendix 3 lists as incorporating the curriculum's "key experiences.")

Title: **Animal Alph. and Other Things**
Company: Random House Software
Date: 1986
Price: $29.95
Age: 3-6
Computer: Apple
Conceptual Area: LA/1,4,6
■ Letter recognition, alphabetical order

Final Rating: **81** ★★★★★★★★
User Friendliness: **87** ★★★★★★★★★
Educational Value: **87** ★★★★★★★★★
Instructional Design: **73** ★★★★★★★

Comments: Child presses a key, e.g., A, to see that letter on the screen. Pressing A again causes the letter to turn into an alligator. Pressing spacebar causes the next letter in the alphabet to appear. There are 26 pictures on each side of the disk. Side 1 covers upper case; side 2, lower case. Easy to use.

The line under "Conceptual Area" contains a short description of the computer program's goals or objectives as stated by the producer.

COMMENTS: An overview of the program, what the child does when using the program, its strengths and weaknesses, and any special equipment requirements.

INTERPRETING THE RATINGS: The Early Childhood Software Evaluation Instrument rates each program with an *overall score,* which is the mean of nine component scores; with three *summary scores,* which are means of selected component scores; and with nine *component scores.* (Each of these elements is defined in the next two pages.) The diagram below indicates how the three levels of scoring are related.

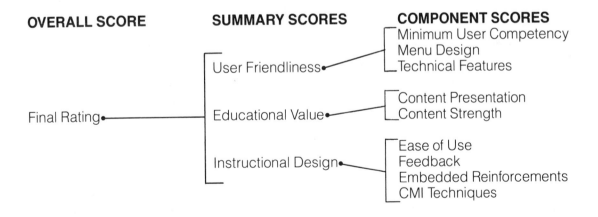

OVERALL SCORE   **SUMMARY SCORES**   **COMPONENT SCORES**

Final Rating •
— User Friendliness •
—— Minimum User Competency
—— Menu Design
—— Technical Features

— Educational Value •
—— Content Presentation
—— Content Strength

— Instructional Design •
—— Ease of Use
—— Feedback
—— Embedded Reinforcements
—— CMI Techniques

All scores are percents from 1 to 100 based on a program's performance on the evaluation instrument (Chapter 3). The scores are displayed in numerical form and as a bar graph with a row of 1 to 10 stars. The bar graph represents the score rounded to the nearest 10%. (For example, 47% = ★★★★★.) The software was evaluated with the assistance of the children and teachers in the High/Scope demonstration classroom at the High/Scope Educational Research Foundation in Ypsilanti, Michigan. Scoring was done by Warren Buckleitner.

OVERALL SCORE

FINAL RATING: The mean score of all nine component scores.

SUMMARY SCORES

Selected component scores are combined into the following scores:

USER FRIENDLINESS: The mean score of Minimum User Competency, Menu Design, and Technical Features.

EDUCATIONAL VALUE: The mean score of Content Presentation and Content Strength.

INSTRUCTIONAL DESIGN: The mean score of Ease of Use, Feedback, Embedded Reinforcements, and CMI techniques.

COMPONENT SCORES

MINIMUM USER COMPETENCY: A measure of the degree of computer skill a child needs to use the program independently. A program that allows the user to enter information via picture menus and arrow keys is more suitable for a young child than is a program that requires typing words or using SHIFT keys, the CONTROL key, or the function keys. This scale covers only the parts of the program intended for the child's use. It does not consider features designed for the teacher (e.g., setting difficulty levels). The higher the score, the easier it is for preschoolers and kindergartners to use the program.

MENU DESIGN: A rating of the ease-of-use of the menu(s). A menu is a point in the program when choices are listed and a child selects one of them and enters this choice into the computer. If the child can use and access a program menu, she or he can usually control the program without adult help. Using some menus, however, requires skills preschool children may not have, such as reading skill. The higher the score in this category, the easier the menu is for preschoolers or kindergartners to use.

Title:	**Animal Alph. and Other Things**	Final Rating:	81 ★★★★★★★★
Company:	Random House Software	User Friendliness:	87 ★★★★★★★★★
Date:	1986	Educational Value:	87 ★★★★★★★★★
Price:	$29.95	Instructional Design:	73 ★★★★★★★
Age:	3-6		
Computer:	Apple		
Conceptual Area:	LA/1,4,6		

■ Letter recognition, alphabetical order

Comments: Child presses a key, e.g., A, to see that letter on the screen. Pressing A again causes the letter to turn into an alligator. Pressing spacebar causes the next letter in the alphabet to appear. There are 26 pictures on each side of the disk. Side 1 covers upper case; side 2, lower case. Easy to use.

TECHNICAL FEATURES: A rating of technical features of the program. Does the program permit a child to experiment with *all* the keys without "locking up?" Can a teacher easily use the program in a classroom situation where there is little time to review the program instructions? Does the program make effective use of the computer's capabilities?

CONTENT PRESENTATION: A rating of how well content is presented, including whether the program maintains a level of challenge; whether a child controls the functioning of the program; whether the content is free from gender, racial, or ethnic bias; whether there are demonstrations; whether the program is free from unnecessary stimulation; and whether the central outcome is educational.

CONTENT STRENGTH: A rating of the accuracy and depth of the program's conceptual content.

EASE OF USE: A rating of the program's ease of use by a first-time user. Higher scores mean easier first-time use.

FEEDBACK: A rating of the feedback techniques employed by the program. This measures such factors as correlation between the keystrokes and screen events, appropriateness of feedback for preschool and kindergarten children, and reinforcement of content by feedback.

EMBEDDED REINFORCEMENTS: A rating of how well graphics and sounds used for rewards complement and reinforce content.

COMPUTER-MANAGED INSTRUCTION TECHNIQUES: A rating of the level of computer-managed instruction (CMI) techniques employed by the program. This score includes consideration of whether the program changes levels as the child progresses and whether the program keeps ongoing records. This score is not counted if (1) the program is completely open-ended (e.g., a drawing activity) or (2) the program permits the child or adult to set the difficulty level.

SCAN OF SOFTWARE DESCRIPTIONS

BACKGROUND INFORMATION: Some facts about the 355 programs we reviewed —

  Copyright dates range from 1982 to 1989.

  Prices range from $5.95 to $16,800.00.

  $45.53 is the average price for a one-disk package.

  63.8% is the average final rating.

  90% is the highest final rating.

  22% is the lowest final rating.

  83 companies produce early childhood software.

  75 programs are open-ended in nature or are used by a child to create a product of some kind.

  31 programs can "talk."

  22 programs utilize an Echo speech synthesizer.

  61 programs can utilize a printer.

  15 programs can utilize a color printer.

USER INTERFACE: This *Survey* contains

  93 programs that use the arrow keys.

  68 programs that can work with a joystick.

  46 programs that can work with a mouse.

  16 programs that can work with a Touch Window.

COMPUTER TYPES: Percent of reviewed software available for various brands of computers —

Apple	307/355	87.0%
C64	124/355	34.9%
IBM	115/355	32.4%
Atari	43/355	12.1%
Macintosh	23/355	6.5%
Apple IIGS	14/355	3.9%
Amiga	8/355	2.3%
TRS	6/355	1.7%

Software by Computer Brand

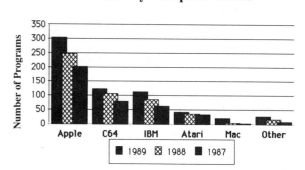

Software by Price

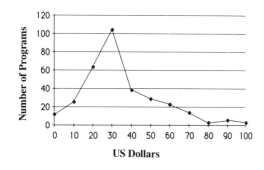

Software by Final Rating

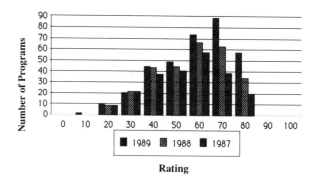

2

SOFTWARE DESCRIPTIONS

This chapter contains an alphabetical listing of software descriptions.

Title: 1-2-3 Sequence Me
Company: Sunburst Communications, Inc.
Date: 1988
Price: $65.00
Age: 5-7
Computer: Apple
Conceptual Area: TI/2,6 LA/5
■ Sequencing skills

Final Rating: 75 ********
User Friendliness: 67 *******
Educational Value: 84 ********
Instructional Design: 75 *******

Comments: Child sees three pictures or phrases that form an ordered sequence but are placed out of order, e.g., a snowman progressively melting. By putting a 1, 2, or 3 under each box, child puts the pictures back in the correct order. Some reading required. Works with Muppet Learning Keys or regular keyboard.

Title: 1st Math
Company: Stone & Associates
Date: 1986
Price: $39.95
Age: 4-8
Computer: IBM*, Atari ST
Conceptual Area: NB/3,4,7,8 SE/2 SP/1
■ Addition & subtraction equations, patterns

Final Rating: 75 ********
User Friendliness: 68 *******
Educational Value: 94 *********
Instructional Design: 69 *******

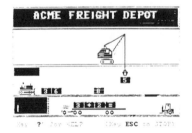

Comments: Four well-designed activities: Equations — child enters answer for equation to see answer animated. Construction — child sees equation and types answer to build a scene. Freight Depot — child uses arrow keys or joystick to load answers onto truck. Patterns — child selects next pattern element. Adult menu offers control over content.

Title: ABC's
Company: Polarware, Inc.
Date: 1986
Price: $14.95
Age: 3-up
Computer: Apple* (128K), IBM, C64
Conceptual Area: CP/1,4 SP/4
■ Coloring pictures

Final Rating: 80 ********
User Friendliness: 79 ********
Educational Value: 73 *******
Instructional Design: 84 ********

Comments: A coloring program with 26 pictures, one per letter (e.g., an acrobat for "a"). Child moves cursor with mouse, joystick, or arrow keys to fill in sections of a picture with 1 of 16 available colors. Prints in color. Mouse and color monitor recommended. Very easy to use. Prints picture with calendar.

LA = Language   CP = Creative projects   OT = Other topics   CL = Classification   SP = Spatial relations   TI = Time   NB = Number   SE = Seriation   * = Version reviewed   NA = Not applicable

Title: Adventures in Space
Company: Scandura Training Systems
Date: 1983
Price: $29.95
Age: 3-7
Computer: Apple
Conceptual Area: SP/4
■ Spatial relationships

Final Rating: 46 *****
User Friendliness: 28 ***
Educational Value: 56 ******
Instructional Design: 56 ******

Comments: Ten activities offered in spatial concepts (e.g., up and down, in and out, above and below). Sample problem: Where is the flower? (A) around the swarm of bees, (B) in the swarm, etc. No random generation or branching.

Title: Adventures of Dobot, The
Company: Educational Activities, Inc.
Date: 1986
Price: $59.95
Age: 3-7
Computer: Apple*, IBM, C64
Conceptual Area: SP/4 CL/2 SE/2 OT/1
■ Problem solving, critical thinking

Final Rating: 70 *******
User Friendliness: 77 ********
Educational Value: 87 *********
Instructional Design: 55 ******

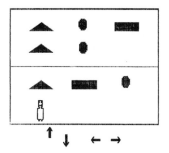

Comments: Seven simple games in which child uses arrow keys to move robot to sort letters, arrange rods according to length, match numerals, and practice with the arrow keys. Management tracks the progress of up to 50 children.

Title: Adventures of Jimmy Jumper
Company: E.C.S.
Date: 1986
Price: $29.95
Age: 2.5-5
Computer: Apple
Conceptual Area: LA/1,8 SP/4
■ Prepositional concepts

Final Rating: 69 *******
User Friendliness: 61 ******
Educational Value: 84 ********
Instructional Design: 65 *******

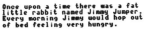

Comments: A story program of 12 screens. The story is told using an Echo speech synthesizer while the graphics show the prepositional concepts. Child uses a game paddle or spacebar to advance the story screen-by-screen.

LA = Language   CP = Creative projects   OT = Other topics   CL = Classification   SP = Spatial
relations   TI = Time   NB = Number   SE = Seriation   * = Version reviewed   NA = Not applicable

Title: Alice in Wonderland
Company: HRM Software
Date: 1985
Price: $49.00
Age: 7-12
Computer: Apple
Conceptual Area: LA/5,8 TI/5
■ Remembering a sequence of events

Final Rating: 69 *******
User Friendliness: 67 *******
Educational Value: 70 *******
Instructional Design: 69 *******

Comments: Modeled from the traditional story. Child uses arrow keys and RETURN to select two-word commands to explore Wonderland. How children proceed depends on the options they choose. Requires reading. Could be used as language experience with adult help.

Title: Alpha Build
Company: Spinnaker Software Corp.
Date: 1984
Price: $9.95
Age: 4-8
Computer: Apple*, IBM, C64 (cartridge)
Conceptual Area: LA/4,5 CL/2 SP/4
■ Upper/lower-case, alphabetical order

Final Rating: 56 ******
User Friendliness: 64 ******
Educational Value: 49 *****
Instructional Design: 54 *****

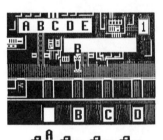

Comments: Child uses arrow keys or joystick to match letters to complete an alphabetical sequence or simple words. Eight levels, ranging from matching one letter to completing a word. Somewhat confusing graphics.

Title: Alpha Teach
Company: Aquarius People Materials
Date: 1982
Price: $39.95
Age: 3-6
Computer: Apple
Conceptual Area: LA/4
■ Alphabet, initial consonants

Final Rating: 39 ****
User Friendliness: 37 ****
Educational Value: 48 *****
Instructional Design: 37 ****

Comments: Contains three activities: (1) shows continuous alphabet with no interaction, (2) shows display for any letter chosen, and (3) child matches object shown with initial consonant in a model word. Reading required. Discontinued in 1987.

LA = Language   CP = Creative projects   OT = Other topics   CL = Classification   SP = Spatial
relations   TI = Time   NB = Number   SE = Seriation   * = Version reviewed   NA = Not applicable

Title: Alphabet Arcade, The
Company: PDI Software
Date: 1983
Price: $24.95
Age: 5-9
Computer: Apple*, C64, Atari
Conceptual Area: LA/4
■ Alphabetizing, dictionary skills

Final Rating: 42 ****
User Friendliness: 48 *****
Educational Value: 52 *****
Instructional Design: 31 ***

Comments: Consists of three games in which child puts letters and short words in correct alphabetical order. No branching. Not recommended.

```
pigeon        1. enjoy
ostrich       2.
→ turkey      3.
              4.
   ATTEMPTS  I M      TIME
      03             1:04
```

Title: Alphabet Circus
Company: DLM
Date: 1984
Price: $32.95
Age: 4-7
Computer: Apple*, IBM, C64
Conceptual Area: LA/4
■ Letter recognition, alphabet order

Final Rating: 68 *******
User Friendliness: 54 *****
Educational Value: 89 *********
Instructional Design: 69 *******

Comments: Child presses any key to move a hat and presses spacebar to select 1 of 6 letter-recognition, alphabetical order, or keyboard-skill activities. Good sound and graphics. Best for age 5. Some reading.

Title: Alphabet Recognition
Company: Micro Power & Light Company
Date: 1986
Price: $24.95
Age: 4-6
Computer: Apple
Conceptual Area: LA/4
■ Letter recognition, upper/lower-case matching

Final Rating: 46 *****
User Friendliness: 56 ******
Educational Value: 52 *****
Instructional Design: 35 ****

Comments: Child uses arrow keys to select 1 of 4 letters to match a letter carried by a swimming fish. If the match is correct, a point is earned. Can be set for upper or lower case. Limited content.

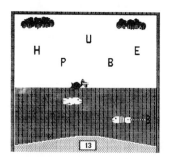

LA = Language   CP = Creative projects   OT = Other topics   CL = Classification   SP = Spatial
relations   TI = Time   NB = Number   SE = Seriation   * = Version reviewed   NA = Not applicable

Title: Alphabet Song and Count
Company: Edusoft
Date: 1983
Price: $29.95
Age: 3-7
Computer: Apple
Conceptual Area: LA/4 NB/3,4
■ Alphabet order, counting skills

Final Rating: 51 *****
User Friendliness: 35 ****
Educational Value: 57 ******
Instructional Design: 58 ******

Comments: Two games: Alphabet Song — computer plays the ABC song as each letter of the alphabet is typed. Count — a branched activity for numbers 1-57. Simple reading required (e.g., "press spacebar").

Title: Alphabet Sounds
Company: Data Command
Date: 1984
Price: $84.95
Age: 5-7
Computer: Apple
Conceptual Area: LA/6
■ Letter sounds, initial consonants

Final Rating: 29 ***
User Friendliness: 35 ****
Educational Value: 33 ***
Instructional Design: 23 **

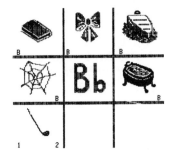

Comments: Three disks show eight pictures of each letter of the alphabet, one at a time. For vowels, a child must choose long or short (L or S); for consonants, whether the sound comes at the beginning or end (1 or 2). Smile/frown reinforcements. Low level of child-interaction. Not recommended.

Title: Alphabet Zoo
Company: Spinnaker Software Corp.
Date: 1983
Price: $29.95
Age: 3-8
Computer: Apple*, IBM, C64 ($20.95)
Conceptual Area: LA/4,5
■ Letter recognition

Final Rating: 51 *****
User Friendliness: 56 ******
Educational Value: 52 *****
Instructional Design: 48 *****

Comments: Poor menu design makes maze game difficult to use. Child uses joystick or ESDX keys to move a character through randomly generated mazes. Must find each letter in sequence of a model word given above the maze.

LA = Language   CP = Creative projects   OT = Other topics   CL = Classification   SP = Spatial
relations   TI = Time   NB = Number   SE = Seriation   * = Version reviewed   NA = Not applicable

Title: Alphabetization Sequence
Company: Milliken Publishing Co.
Date: 1980
Price: $75.00
Age: 5-13
Computer: Apple
Conceptual Area: LA/4 CL/2
- Alphabetizing, letter discrimination

Final Rating: 67 *******
User Friendliness: 54 *****
Educational Value: 76 ********
Instructional Design: 69 *******

Comments: First of two-disk Language Arts Series for K-8. Contains 63 levels of alphabetizing drills, from letter discrimination (child presses Y if two letters are the same) to alphabetizing to the seventh letter. Uses sophisticated password and record-keeping system.

Title: Alphabots
Company: D.C. Heath & Company
Date: 1985
Price: $51.00
Age: 4-7
Computer: Apple
Conceptual Area: LA/4,5
- Letter recognition

Final Rating: 54 *****
User Friendliness: 50 *****
Educational Value: 69 *******
Instructional Design: 49 *****

Comments: Consists of five letter and word activities in which child must type in letters for objects shown. Model keyboard on screen shows key location on screen for help. Uses animated "robots" as reinforcement for correctly spelled words.

Title: Alphaget
Company: Alphaphonics
Date: 1982
Price: $50.00
Age: 5-6
Computer: Apple
Conceptual Area: LA/4,5
- Letter recognition practice

Final Rating: 51 *****
User Friendliness: 47 *****
Educational Value: 63 ******
Instructional Design: 47 *****

Comments: Presents simple maze context where child moves "Astro" (using arrow keys) to arrange letters or letter symbols in alphabetical order. Upper/lower-case option available. Effective for practice with alphabetical order.

LA = Language   CP = Creative projects   OT = Other topics   CL = Classification   SP = Spatial relations   TI = Time   NB = Number   SE = Seriation   * = Version reviewed   NA = Not applicable

Title: Animal Alph. and Other Things
Company: Random House Software
Date: 1986
Price: $29.95
Age: 3-6
Computer: Apple
Conceptual Area: LA/1,4,6
- Letter recognition, alphabetical order

Final Rating: 81 ********
User Friendliness: 87 *********
Educational Value: 87 *********
Instructional Design: 73 *******

Comments: Child presses a key, e.g., A, to see that letter on the screen. Pressing A again causes the letter to turn into an alligator. Pressing spacebar causes the next letter in the alphabet to appear. There are 26 pictures on each side of the disk. Side 1 covers upper case; side 2, lower case. Easy to use.

Title: Animal Hotel
Company: Learning Technologies, Inc.
Date: 1985
Price: $24.95
Age: 4-8
Computer: Apple*, C64
Conceptual Area: OT/1
- Memory skills

Final Rating: 45 *****
User Friendliness: 55 ******
Educational Value: 38 ****
Instructional Design: 40 ****

Comments: A memory game that shows either three (easy level) or six (hard level) animals and then hides each behind a different door. When shown a door, child selects animal behind that door by pressing a number key. Menu requires reading.

Title: Animal Photo Fun
Company: DLM
Date: 1985
Price: $32.95
Age: 4-8
Computer: Apple
Conceptual Area: OT/1
- Animals and their habitats

Final Rating: 70 *******
User Friendliness: 62 ******
Educational Value: 75 ********
Instructional Design: 73 *******

Comments: Six games in which children match animals with their habitats. Includes Animal Concentration and Animal Rummy. Child uses spacebar and RETURN to play with 36 animals from six habitats. Good graphics, sounds. Color monitor recommended.

LA = Language   CP = Creative projects   OT = Other topics   CL = Classification   SP = Spatial relations   TI = Time   NB = Number   SE = Seriation   * = Version reviewed   NA = Not applicable

Title: Arithmetic Critters
Company: MECC
Date: 1986
Price: $59.00
Age: 5-7
Computer: Apple (64K)
Conceptual Area: NB/3,6,7,9
■ Counting, addition, and subtraction

Final Rating: 78 ********
User Friendliness: 64 ******
Educational Value: 98 **********
Instructional Design: 77 ********

Comments: Four well-designed games: adding groups of up to 9, subtracting up to 9 from a group of up to 18, measuring lengths using a worm as units, and counting in groups of 10. Allows teacher modification. Clear sounds and graphics aid the content.

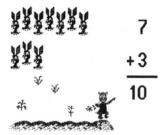

Title: Astro's ABCs
Company: Alphaphonics
Date: 1984
Price: $175.00
Age: 5-6
Computer: Apple
Conceptual Area: LA/4,5
■ Letter recognition skills

Final Rating: 62 ******
User Friendliness: 63 ******
Educational Value: 75 ********
Instructional Design: 54 *****

Comments: Consists of seven disks, each covering four letters. Lessons follow fixed sequence, showing alphabet, word pictures, and the letter drawn on the screen. Child then finds letter on keyboard and plays a game with the letter symbols. Child cannot control sequence. Offers effective practice with each letter.

Title: Astro-Grover
Company: Hi Tech Expressions
Date: 1984
Price: $29.95
Age: 3-6
Computer: Apple, IBM, C64*
Conceptual Area: NB/3,4
■ Counting, adding, and subtracting

Final Rating: 41 ****
User Friendliness: 45 *****
Educational Value: 44 ****
Instructional Design: 36 ****

Comments: Consists of five games that provide practice counting, adding, and subtracting objects in an "outer space" context. Lively graphics and sounds not related to content. Includes keyboard overlay. Apple version compatible with Muppet Learning Keys.

LA = Language   CP = Creative projects   OT = Other topics   CL = Classification   SP = Spatial
relations   TI = Time   NB = Number   SE = Seriation   * = Version reviewed   NA = Not applicable

---

Title: Balancing Bear
Company: Sunburst Communications, Inc.
Date: 1988
Price: $65.00
Age: 5-8
Computer: Apple
Conceptual Area: NB/1,2,3
■ Comparing amounts, addition, problem solving

Final Rating: 77 ********
User Friendliness: 64 ******
Educational Value: 92 *********
Instructional Design: 78 ********

Comments: Introduction to addition and inequalities. Child selects number or set that will make a scale balance. Can involve sums up to 99. Can use regular keyboard, Touch Window, or Muppet Learning keys. Includes worksheets and classroom lesson ideas.

Title: Bald-Headed Chicken, The
Company: D.C. Heath & Company
Date: 1988
Price: $75.00
Age: 5-10
Computer: Apple
Conceptual Area: LA/2,3,5,9 CP/4 SP/4,7
■ Language experience

Final Rating: 89 *********
User Friendliness: 85 *********
Educational Value: 94 *********
Instructional Design: 91 *********

Comments: Children use mouse, Koala Pad, joystick, or arrow keys to select or move objects, back grounds, words, or characters of a story. They can also add their own words. Resulting stories can be saved and printed in color. Includes four copies of the storybook. Good design. Fun to use.

Title: Bank Street Writer III, The
Company: Scholastic Software, Inc.
Date: 1986
Price: $79.95
Age: 7-up
Computer: Apple*, IBM
Conceptual Area: LA/9
■ Word processing

Final Rating: 71 *******
User Friendliness: 49 *****
Educational Value: 88 *********
Instructional Design: 80 ********

TYPE IN TEXT AT CURSOR   ESC FOR MENU
MOVE WITH ←,→,↓,↑

My dog likes to
play with me. I
will throw a stick
or a ball and she
will get it. _

Comments: Easy-to-use word processor with large (20-column) text. Effective for writing preschool experience stories. Stories can be saved, printed, and edited. Price also includes small print (40- and 80- column) version with more word processing features.

LA = Language   CP = Creative projects   OT = Other topics   CL = Classification   SP = Spatial
relations   TI = Time   NB = Number   SE = Seriation   * = Version reviewed   NA = Not applicable

Title: Beginner Reader
Company: Scandura Training Systems
Date: 1983
Price: $24.95
Age: 5-7
Computer: Apple
Conceptual Area: LA/7
- Rhyming words

Final Rating: 39 ****
User Friendliness: 20 **
Educational Value: 29 ***
Instructional Design: 50 *****

Comments: Three activities: Drill 1 — a rhyming activity using a multiple choice format. Drill 2 — child types Y or N if two words rhyme. Drill 3 — child types in rhyming word. Poorly designed program. Not recommended.

Title: Beginning Counting
Company: MicroEd, Inc.
Date: 1987
Price: $39.95
Age: 3-6
Computer: Amiga (512K)
Conceptual Area: NB/3,4,8
- Counting from 1 to 9

Final Rating: 43 ****
User Friendliness: 51 *****
Educational Value: 53 *****
Instructional Design: 32 ***

Comments: Two disks dealing with numbers 1-9. Child uses the mouse to (1) count objects, (2) identify the names of numbers upon hearing names, and (3) arrange numbers in order. Has several levels of difficulty. Requires mastery of each level to go to the next. Provides spoken feedback in a fairly clear voice.

Title: Beginning Reading Skills
Company: MicroEd, Inc.
Date: 1986
Price: $89.95
Age: 3-6
Computer: Amiga (512K)
Conceptual Area: LA/5,6
- Beginning reading skills

Final Rating: 57 ******
User Friendliness: 53 *****
Educational Value: 61 ******
Instructional Design: 57 ******

Comments: A four-disk series that presents (using computer voice) a sentence, e.g., "A man ran." Each word of the sentence also appears randomly in 1 of 9 boxes. The child identifies, in order, each word in the sentence by clicking the mouse on the appropriate word box. Contains 1000 words, as hard as "delve" and "gauze."

LA = Language   CP = Creative projects   OT = Other topics   CL = Classification   SP = Spatial relations   TI = Time   NB = Number   SE = Seriation   * = Version reviewed   NA = Not applicable

Title: Best Electronic Word Book Ever!
Company: Mindscape, Inc.
Date: 1985
Price: $29.95
Age: 5-up
Computer: Apple*, C64
Conceptual Area: LA/5 CL/2 OT/1
■ Reading readiness skills

Final Rating: 70 *******
User Friendliness: 68 *******
Educational Value: 75 ********
Instructional Design: 69 *******

Comments: Using arrow keys or joystick, child moves worm down a road that has objects, e.g., a cow, a barn, scattered along the side. Stopping at an object animates and labels it. Six scenes are available on two disks that contain both Apple and C64 formats. Harder levels ask child to find a specified object.

Title: Big Bird's Funhouse
Company: Hi Tech Expressions
Date: 1984
Price: $14.95
Age: 3-6
Computer: C64
Conceptual Area: OT/1
■ Concentration and memory

Final Rating: 49 *****
User Friendliness: 45 *****
Educational Value: 64 ******
Instructional Design: 43 ****

Comments: Five levels of memory games that use eight muppet characters who move among the windows of a house. Children can play hide-and-seek or other more advanced games. Lots of graphics and music. Uses keyboard overlay (included). No CMI.

Title: Big Bird's Special Delivery
Company: Hi Tech Expressions
Date: 1984
Price: $34.95
Age: 3-6
Computer: C64* (cartridge), IBM, Apple
Conceptual Area: CL/2
■ Object recognition

Final Rating: 31 ***
User Friendliness: 43 ****
Educational Value: 34 ***
Instructional Design: 21 **

Comments: Consists of a multiple-choice format in which child uses arrow keys to match 1 of 4 pictures according to form (easiest), class, and function (hardest). Menu requires reading. Discontinued in 1986.

LA = Language   CP = Creative projects   OT = Other topics   CL = Classification   SP = Spatial relations   TI = Time   NB = Number   SE = Seriation   * = Version reviewed   NA = Not applicable

Title: Bike Hike
Company: Learning Technologies, Inc.
Date: 1985
Price: $24.95
Age: 4-8
Computer: Apple*, C64
Conceptual Area: OT/1 NB/3
■ Memory, recall of objects

Final Rating: 41 ****
User Friendliness: 57 ******
Educational Value: 35 ****
Instructional Design: 32 ***

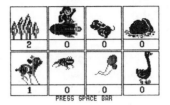

Comments: Child first watches objects pass a bicycle, then uses number keys to select objects from a list shown at the end of the ride. Reading required. Two difficulty levels available. Inflexible design allows little child-control.

Title: Bird's Eye View
Company: Hartley Courseware, Inc.
Date: 1987
Price: $49.95
Age: 5-8
Computer: Apple*, IBM
Conceptual Area: SP/3,4 LA/1
■ Perspective and positional relationships

Final Rating: 73 *******
User Friendliness: 73 *******
Educational Value: 98 **********
Instructional Design: 59 ******

Comments: A scene is shown with a bird. Views possibly seen by bird appear in a box. Child uses spacebar to select which view bird sees, based on the bird's location. Other activities allow moving the bird to correspond to a view shown. Management keeps records and allows teacher-control over the presentation.

Title: Boars Tell Time, The
Company: Random House Software
Date: 1987
Price: $29.95
Age: 3-7
Computer: Apple
Conceptual Area: TI/9 NB/4
■ Clock skills

Final Rating: 68 *******
User Friendliness: 64 ******
Educational Value: 82 ********
Instructional Design: 63 ******

Comments: Three activities: Telling Time — child sees clock and must type in the time shown. Setting The Clock — child sees a digital time and must set the clock hands to match. Time Trials — a faster version of the first activity, keeps score. Clear, colorful graphics. Some reading required.

LA = Language   CP = Creative projects   OT = Other topics   CL = Classification   SP = Spatial
relations   TI = Time   NB = Number   SE = Seriation   * = Version reviewed   NA = Not applicable

Title: Body Awareness
Company: Mindscape, Inc.
Date: 1983
Price: $49.95
Age: 3-6
Computer: Apple
Conceptual Area: SP/5 LA/5
■ Location of body parts

Final Rating: 64 ******
User Friendliness: 82 ********
Educational Value: 65 *******
Instructional Design: 50 *****

Comments: Three games on body parts. Child selects Y, N, ?, or ESCAPE for each problem. Provides practice with body part locations, names of body parts, and seasonal clothing. Provides performance summary and allows selection for number of rounds, season, and timing of cursor movement. No reading required.

Title: Bouncy Bee Learns Letters 1.0
Company: IBM Educational Systems
Date: 1985
Price: $56.00
Age: 4-8
Computer: IBM
Conceptual Area: LA/4
■ Letter recognition

Final Rating: 72 *******
User Friendliness: 42 ****
Educational Value: 97 **********
Instructional Design: 81 ********

Comments: Four games: Game 1 introduces a letter. Games 2-4 provide practice with the letter in a game context using the spacebar and arrows. Management can track up to 225 children and automatically adjusts difficulty. Independent of "Writing to Read." Speech attachment optional.

Title: Bouncy Bee Learns Words 1.0
Company: IBM Educational Systems
Date: 1985
Price: $56.00
Age: 5-10
Computer: IBM
Conceptual Area: LA/5
■ Word knowledge

Final Rating: 62 ******
User Friendliness: 44 ****
Educational Value: 87 *********
Instructional Design: 61 ******

Comments: Four activities using common words in game context. Child uses arrow keys and spacebar to match words with pictures, pick a word from one or more distractors, or identify a word as it is formed by marching ants. Management system can track 150 children. Menu requires reading. Speech synthesizer is optional.

LA = Language   CP = Creative projects   OT = Other topics   CL = Classification   SP = Spatial
relations   TI = Time   NB = Number   SE = Seriation   * = Version reviewed   NA = Not applicable

Title: Brand New View, A
Company: D.C. Heath & Company
Date: 1988
Price: $75.00
Age: 5-10
Computer: Apple
Conceptual Area: LA/2,3,5,9 CP/4 SP/4,7
■ Language experience

Final Rating: 89 ********
User Friendliness: 85 ********
Educational Value: 94 ********
Instructional Design: 91 ********

Comments: Children use mouse, Koala Pad, joystick, or arrow keys to select or move objects, backgrounds, words, or characters of a story. They can also add their own words. Resulting stories can be saved and printed in color. Includes four copies of the storybook. Good design. Fun to use.

Title: Bremen Town Musicians
Company: Troll Associates
Date: 1987
Price: $39.95
Age: 5-8
Computer: Apple
Conceptual Area: LA/5,7 SP/4
■ Homonyms, context clues, comprehension

Final Rating: 45 *****
User Friendliness: 53 *****
Educational Value: 54 *****
Instructional Design: 35 ****

THROUGH THE [ ] THE ROBBERS RAN

OUT OF THE ____.

LATER, ONE OF THE ROBBERS CREPT

BACK INTO THE ____ AND TOOK A MATCH

FILL IN THE FLASHING BLANK.
USE THE SPACE BAR TO CHOOSE
A PICTURE, THEN PRESS RETURN.

Comments: Three games: Rebus — child places pictures on blank lines in text of story to complete the tale. Stepping Stones — child moves along a path, selecting homonyms to earn moves, e.g., "Bremen was weigh/way off." Mystery — child solves rebus puzzle. Best for ages 6 and up. Includes book.

Title: Build a Book About You
Company: Scarborough Systems, Inc.
Date: 1985
Price: $39.95
Age: 2-12
Computer: Apple
Conceptual Area: LA/5,9 CP/4
■ Creating a book

Final Rating: 68 *******
User Friendliness: 44 ****
Educational Value: 89 ********
Instructional Design: 76 ********

```
FACTS ABOUT CHILD/ENTER OR EDIT
        (PRESS ? FOR HELP)
     BOY OR GIRL B
  BIRTHDAY KNOWN Y
        HAS A PET Y
       FIRST NAME ------------------
        LAST NAME ------------------
    STREET NUMBER --------
      STREET NAME ------------------
             CITY ------------------
            STATE ------------------
              ZIP --------------
   SCHOOL OR PARK ------------------
     AGE OF CHILD ----------
         BIRTHDAY --------------
         FRIEND 1 --------------
         FRIEND 2 --------------
         FRIEND 3 --------------
      NAME OF PET --------------
      KIND OF PET --------------
    BOOK GIVEN BY ------------------
       ENTER DATA FOLLOWED BY RETURN
     PRESS <-- OR RETURN TO SELECT
   PRESS ESC WHEN ALL ITEMS ARE CORRECT
```

Comments: With adult help, child enters personal information (e.g., name, hometown, favorite toy), which the computer incorporates into 1 of 4 available stories. Text can then be printed onto blank picture-book pages and made into a book. Includes two large hardcover book kits. Best for home use.

LA = Language   CP = Creative projects   OT = Other topics   CL = Classification   SP = Spatial
relations   TI = Time   NB = Number   SE = Seriation   * = Version reviewed   NA = Not applicable

---

Title: Bumble Games
Company: The Learning Company
Date: 1982
Price: $59.95 (school edition)
Age: 5-10
Computer: Apple
Conceptual Area: NB/1
- Plotting (x,y) points on a grid.

Final Rating: 49 *****
User Friendliness: 55 ******
Educational Value: 50 *****
Instructional Design: 51 *****

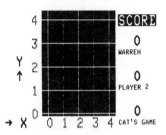

Comments: Five games from easy to hard provide practice for plotting points on grid. Whether or not content is applicable to early childhood is at issue. Menu requires reading. School edition includes curriculum materials.

Title: Castle Clobber
Company: Mindscape, Inc.
Date: 1985
Price: $29.95
Age: 5-9
Computer: Apple, IBM*, C64, Atari
Conceptual Area: CL/1,2 SP/4,6,7,8 OT/1
- Logical thinking skills

Final Rating: 56 ******
User Friendliness: 61 ******
Educational Value: 73 *******
Instructional Design: 37 ****

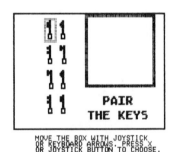

Comments: Child uses joystick or arrow keys to move "Tonk" through a 50-room castle to collect objects, play 1 of 5 memory or classification games, and try to find a hidden toy chest. Three levels are available. Simple reading required. Children enjoy exploring the rooms. Discontinued in 1988.

Title: Cat 'n Mouse
Company: MindPlay
Date: 1984
Price: $49.99
Age: 5-12
Computer: Apple*, IBM
Conceptual Area: LA/6
- Relational concepts

Final Rating: 65 *******
User Friendliness: 74 *******
Educational Value: 55 ******
Instructional Design: 63 ******

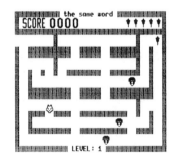

Comments: A maze game in which child earns points by moving a mouse (with joystick, mouse, or arrow keys) away from a hungry cat and correctly matching homonyms, antonyms, and picture words. Adult can add own words or change other features of the program.

LA = Language   CP = Creative projects   OT = Other topics   CL = Classification   SP = Spatial relations   TI = Time   NB = Number   SE = Seriation   * = Version reviewed   NA = Not applicable

Title: Charlie Brown's 1-2-3's
Company: Random House Software
Date: 1985
Price: $30.00
Age: 3-7
Computer: Apple
Conceptual Area: NB/3,4,8
- Numeral recognition, counting

Final Rating: 67 *******
User Friendliness: 60 ******
Educational Value: 78 ********
Instructional Design: 69 *******

Comments: Child selects a numeral and then uses spacebar or number keys to count out the number. Correct response makes 1 of 16 animated Peanuts scenes appear. Good sound and graphics. Enjoyable program.

Title: Charlie Brown's ABC's
Company: Random House Software
Date: 1984
Price: $39.95
Age: 3-7
Computer: Apple*, C64, IBM
Conceptual Area: LA/4
- Letter recognition & association

Final Rating: 64 ******
User Friendliness: 47 *****
Educational Value: 70 *******
Instructional Design: 71 *******

Comments: Child presses any letter to see tutorial screen on the letter (letter and picture). Finding and pressing the letter again on the keyboard animates the picture with Peanuts Gang characters. Disk must be turned over to access entire alphabet. Fun to use. Potential starter program.

Title: City Country Opposites
Company: Random House Software
Date: 1986
Price: $29.95
Age: 3-7
Computer: Apple
Conceptual Area: SE/1 TI/1
- Word meanings through context

Final Rating: 78 ********
User Friendliness: 74 *******
Educational Value: 87 *********
Instructional Design: 76 ********

Comments: Presents and illustrates 20 antonym pairs. Child uses left and right arrows to alternate between pictures illustrating antonyms, e.g., push/pull. Easy to use. Good level of child-control. Includes scenes from city and country environments. Limited content.

LA = Language   CP = Creative projects   OT = Other topics   CL = Classification   SP = Spatial relations   TI = Time   NB = Number   SE = Seriation   * = Version reviewed   NA = Not applicable

---

Title: Clock Works
Company: Nordic Software
Date: 1986
Price: $39.95
Age: 4-10
Computer: Mac
Conceptual Area: TI/9 NB/3
■ Clock-reading skills, units of time

Final Rating: 72 *******
User Friendliness: 80 ********
Educational Value: 83 ********
Instructional Design: 56 ******

Comments: Contains five clock lessons on analog and digital watches, using time expressions and time units. Prints worksheets to go with lessons. Offers a variety of content and lesson setups. Includes a game, called 4 in a Row, that is a strategy game played against a friend or the computer.

Title: Coin Works
Company: Nordic Software
Date: 1986
Price: $39.95
Age: 4-12
Computer: Mac
Conceptual Area: NB/3,7 TI/3,4,5
■ Value of coins

Final Rating: 71 *******
User Friendliness: 81 ********
Educational Value: 69 *******
Instructional Design: 63 ******

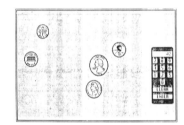

Comments: Uses a set of U.S. coins to provide practice counting money, making change, and comparing coin value. For a given coin, child can click mouse to hear computer say value. Teacher options include control over presentation and generation of worksheets. Also includes a game in which child moves mouse to deflect a bouncing ball to earn points.

Title: Color Find
Company: E.C.S.
Date: 1985
Price: $14.95
Age: 2.5-5
Computer: Apple
Conceptual Area: CL/2
■ Matching colors

Final Rating: 69 *******
User Friendliness: 77 ********
Educational Value: 69 *******
Instructional Design: 63 ******

```
COLOR SELECTION MENU

CHOOSE THE COLORS YOU WISH TO PRESENT TO
THE CHILD BY PRESSING THE APPROPRIATE
NUMBER(0 TO 9):

(0) ALL COLORS

(1) RED    (2) BLUE    (3) YELLOW

(4) GREEN  (5) BLACK   (6) WHITE

(7) ORANGE (8) PINK    (9) PURPLE

(CTRL-Z) END OF SELECTION
```

Comments: A simple drill-and-practice program on nine colors. When a color fills the screen, child presses correspondingly colored sticker on the key board. (Stickers included.) Responses are recorded. Echo speech synthesizer optional to say "press a color."

LA = Language   CP = Creative projects   OT = Other topics   CL = Classification   SP = Spatial relations   TI = Time   NB = Number   SE = Seriation   * = Version reviewed   NA = Not applicable

Title: Color Me
Company: Mindscape, Inc.
Date: 1986
Price: $29.95
Age: 3-10
Computer: Apple*, IBM, C64 ($34.95)
Conceptual Area: CP/1,4 LA/3
■ Drawing, creating

Final Rating: 89 *********
User Friendliness: 88 *********
Educational Value: 91 *********
Instructional Design: 87 *********

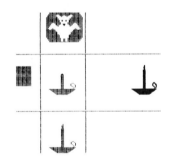

Comments: Easy-to-use program. Our youngest children could use this program with success. Requires Koala Pad, mouse, or joystick. Child can draw, select colors, or write. Pictures can be printed in color and saved. Includes book, puppet, and picture disk.

Title: Colors and Shapes
Company: Hartley Courseware, Inc.
Date: 1984
Price: $35.95
Age: 3-6
Computer: Apple
Conceptual Area: CL/1 SE/1
■ Color ID, visual discrimination

Final Rating: 76 ********
User Friendliness: 84 ********
Educational Value: 88 *********
Instructional Design: 59 ******

Comments: Consists of four activities based on matching of shapes and colors. Makes use of picture menus. Options for speed, sound, and three levels of difficulty for each activity, selected by child. Well-designed program.

Title: Come Play With Pockets
Company: World Book, Inc.
Date: 1984
Price: $39.95
Age: 3-5
Computer: IBM
Conceptual Area: CL/1,3 SP/1
■ Visual memory, tracking skills

Final Rating: 66 *******
User Friendliness: 67 *******
Educational Value: 92 *********
Instructional Design: 51 *****

Comments: Six games in which child uses spacebar and RETURN to move blocks, remember a sequence or set, play Simon Says, or find a bucket a ball landed in. No CMI. Good graphics and sounds. Effective menu gives child control.

LA = Language   CP = Creative projects   OT = Other topics   CL = Classification   SP = Spatial
relations   TI = Time   NB = Number   SE = Seriation   * = Version reviewed   NA = Not applicable

---

Title: Comparison Kitchen

Company: DLM
Date: 1985
Price: $32.95
Age: 4-8
Computer: Apple*, IBM
Conceptual Area: CL/1,2 SP/8 NB/1

- Compare and categorize pictures

Comments: Six games provide experience matching shapes, colors, and sizes. Child uses spacebar and RETURN to make selections. Menu requires reading. Color monitor recommended.

Final Rating: 72 *******
User Friendliness: 62 ******
Educational Value: 89 *********
Instructional Design: 70 *******

Title: Computergarten

Company: Scholastic Software, Inc.
Date: 1984
Price: $54.95
Age: 4-6
Computer: Apple*, C64
Conceptual Area: OT/1,2,3 LA/4

- Keyboard skills, computer terms

Comments: A workbook set, 4' by 8' keyboard-on-the-floor, teacher's edition, and game disk are designed to teach children keyboard skills, parts of the computer, and programming in LOGO and BASIC. Includes 53 lessons. Ratings apply to software only.

Final Rating: 27 ***
User Friendliness: 34 ***
Educational Value: 28 ***
Instructional Design: 21 **

Title: Concentrate

Company: Laureate Learning Systems
Date: 1988
Price: $85.00
Age: 3-up
Computer: Apple
Conceptual Area: OT/1 CL/2 LA/1,5,6

- Short-term memory skills

Comments: A simple game of Concentration, in which 6, 8, or 12 boxes appear face down on the screen. Child uses Touch Window (optional) to select two boxes with matching words, which computer reads aloud as they are selected (Echo speech synthesizer, optional). Includes 40 words. Adult setup required. Keeps records. For one or two players.

Final Rating: 80 ********
User Friendliness: 68 *******
Educational Value: 96 **********
Instructional Design: 73 *******

LA = Language   CP = Creative projects   OT = Other topics   CL = Classification   SP = Spatial relations   TI = Time   NB = Number   SE = Seriation   * = Version reviewed   NA = Not applicable

Title: Conservation and Counting

Company: Hartley Courseware, Inc.

Date: 1985

Price: $35.95

Age: 3-6

Computer: Apple

Conceptual Area: NB/1,2,3,4

■ Counting skills

Final Rating: 71 *******
User Friendliness: 78 ********
Educational Value: 81 ********
Instructional Design: 56 ******

Comments: Four games in which child uses spacebar and RETURN to match sets of objects, to match numbers with sets, and to estimate quantities, all with numbers less than 10. Three levels to each game. Child can select own level or activity, using picture menus. Limited teacher options.

Title: Copycats: ABC for Micro & Me!

Company: Educational Activities, Inc.

Date: 1984

Price: $39.95

Age: 3-7

Computer: Apple*, C64

Conceptual Area: LA/4

■ Matching, alphabet order

Final Rating: 48 *****
User Friendliness: 39 ****
Educational Value: 56 ******
Instructional Design: 50 *****

Comments: Two activities on one disk: Copycats — child matches three to five random or teacher-picked words by typing the letters and pressing RETURN. ABC — four activities to teach alphabet order. Reading required.

Title: Cotton Tales

Company: MindPlay

Date: 1987

Price: $49.99

Age: 4-8

Computer: Apple*, IBM, Mac

Conceptual Area: LA/3,4,5,8,9 CP/4

■ Word processing, language development

Final Rating: 78 ********
User Friendliness: 68 *******
Educational Value: 88 *********
Instructional Design: 81 ********

Comments: Child uses spacebar, arrow keys, RETURN and ESCAPE to manipulate menus to select pictures, select words, or type in own words to create stories. Work can be printed. Library contains 192 pictures and 616 words. Up to 168 additional words can be added. Can be used with a color printer.

LA = Language   CP = Creative projects   OT = Other topics   CL = Classification   SP = Spatial
relations   TI = Time   NB = Number   SE = Seriation   * = Version reviewed   NA = Not applicable

Title: Cotton's First Files
Company: MindPlay
Date: 1988
Price: $49.95
Age: 5-up
Computer: Apple
Conceptual Area: CL/2,3,4,5,6 CP/4
■ Beginning database management, animals

Final Rating: 77 ********
User Friendliness: 68 *******
Educational Value: 88 *********
Instructional Design: 78 ********

Comments: Four activities: Peek and Find — child sees animal (e.g., cat) and picks its category. File Hunt — child sees animal and picks which of 10 categories animal is in. Clue Search — child finds animal, using attribute clues. Custom databases (category sets) can be constructed. Instructions spoken with Echo synthesizer. Includes 200 animals. Prints "animal data cards."

Title: Counters
Company: Sunburst Communications, Inc.
Date: 1983
Price: $65.00
Age: 3-6
Computer: Apple
Conceptual Area: NB/2,3,4
■ Counting experiences

Final Rating: 69 *******
User Friendliness: 47 *****
Educational Value: 87 *********
Instructional Design: 77 ********

Comments: Consists of three counting, addition, and subtraction activities, all with numbers less than 10. Child matches sets of objects one at a time using the spacebar or all at once using a number key. Strong content. Adult help required.

Title: Counting
Company: MECC
Date: 1983
Price: $35.00
Age: 3-7
Computer: C64
Conceptual Area: NB/3,4,7 CL/1
■ Primary arithmetic skills

Final Rating: 60 ******
User Friendliness: 60 ******
Educational Value: 69 *******
Instructional Design: 54 *****

Comments: Child uses keyboard in six math games. Smile — counting from 1 to 9. Wuzzle — counting certain objects in a set. Fireworks — illustrated addition problems. Smile More — counting from 10 to 20. Return of the Wuzzle — counting objects selected from a larger set. More Fireworks — addition drill with sums between 10 and 20.

LA = Language   CP = Creative projects   OT = Other topics   CL = Classification   SP = Spatial relations   TI = Time   NB = Number   SE = Seriation   * = Version reviewed   NA = Not applicable

Title: Counting
Company: MicroEd, Inc.
Date: 1984
Price: $10.95
Age: 5-8
Computer: Apple*, C64
Conceptual Area: NB/3
■ Counting skills, basic facts

Comments: Provides counting, addition, and subtraction practice. Graphics are clearly and simply presented.

Final Rating: 53 *****
User Friendliness: 43 ****
Educational Value: 68 *******
Instructional Design: 53 *****

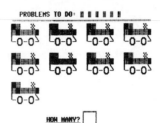

Title: Counting and Ordering
Company: Micro Power & Light Company
Date: 1986
Price: $29.95
Age: 4-6
Computer: Apple
Conceptual Area: NB/3,6
■ 1-9 counting, numeral recognition

Comments: Contains two games: Crater Jumper — child counts the height of a jump to get a spaceman out of a crater. Enjoyable game. Meteor Shower — two to four numbered meteors pass by the screen. To earn points, child must press the key for the largest of the numbers. Some reading required.

Final Rating: 56 ******
User Friendliness: 45 *****
Educational Value: 71 *******
Instructional Design: 56 ******

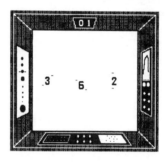

Title: Counting Critters
Company: Mindscape, Inc.
Date: 1987
Price: $39.95
Age: 4-7
Computer: Apple
Conceptual Area: NB/3,4,7
■ Counting, addition, and subtraction

Comments: Three activities. Child uses number keys to count, add, or subtract with the help of animated animal pictures, with sums all less than 12. Keeps scores for up to 20 children.

Final Rating: 62 ******
User Friendliness: 53 *****
Educational Value: 72 *******
Instructional Design: 62 ******

LA = Language   CP = Creative projects   OT = Other topics   CL = Classification   SP = Spatial relations   TI = Time   NB = Number   SE = Seriation   * = Version reviewed   NA = Not applicable

Title: Counting Critters 1.0
Company: MECC
Date: 1985
Price: $59.00
Age: 3-6
Computer: Apple (64K)
Conceptual Area: NB/3,4,7,8 CL/2
■ Counting and early math concepts

Final Rating: 81 ********
User Friendliness: 68 *******
Educational Value: 99 **********
Instructional Design: 81 ********

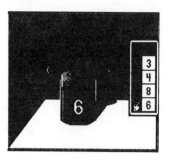

Comments: Five games on one disk. Child uses arrow keys and number keys to match numerals from 1-20, match sets with numerals, create a set corresponding to a given numeral, and use numerical order to fill in a dot-to-dot design. Clear graphics and sounds support content. Allows teacher modification.

Title: Counting Skills
Company: Aquarius People Materials
Date: 1984
Price: $260.00
Age: 3-6
Computer: Apple*, TRS 80
Conceptual Area: NB/2,3,4
■ Counting skills

Final Rating: 40 ****
User Friendliness: 73 *******
Educational Value: 49 *****
Instructional Design: 18 **

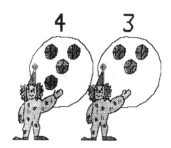

Comments: Contains nine disks covering a range of counting skills. Child needs only to press the spacebar to advance to next frame. Little interaction. Poor design.

Title: Country Combo
Company: Micro Power & Light Company
Date: 1982
Price: $29.95
Age: 3-6
Computer: Apple
Conceptual Area: CL/1,3 CP/4
■ Creative experience

Final Rating: 26 ***
User Friendliness: 25 ***
Educational Value: 29 ***
Instructional Design: 24 **

Comments: Offers a 25-square grid in which child can place 1 of 37 pieces by (1) selecting the piece and (2) typing the numeral of the location on the grid. Game too hard for young children. Reading required. Clumsy design.

LA = Language   CP = Creative projects   OT = Other topics   CL = Classification   SP = Spatial relations   TI = Time   NB = Number   SE = Seriation   * = Version reviewed   NA = Not applicable

Title: Creature Creator
Company: Designware, Inc.
Date: 1983
Price: $9.95
Age: 4-8
Computer: Apple*, IBM
Conceptual Area: TI/6 LA/10
■ Pattern matching, programming

Final Rating: 62 ******
User Friendliness: 46 *****
Educational Value: 78 ********
Instructional Design: 66 *******

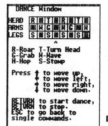

Comments: Child chooses parts of monster and makes it dance, or matches the movements of another monster. Child uses spacebar and RETURN to select monster's parts. Monster's movements can be programmed. Some reading required. Similiar in design to "Facemaker." Will not run on the Apple IIGS.

Title: Critter Count
Company: Aquarius People Materials
Date: 1982
Price: $39.00
Age: 3-6
Computer: Apple
Conceptual Area: NB/9
■ Basic math facts

Final Rating: 34 ***
User Friendliness: 39 ****
Educational Value: 34 ***
Instructional Design: 28 ***

Comments: Offers a range of addition and subtraction problems in two contexts: one that graphically shows the addends, and one that provides math drill. Pacing is rigid. Child has little control. Not recommended.

Title: Curious George in Outer Space
Company: DLM
Date: 1989
Price: $24.95
Age: 4-8
Computer: Apple
Conceptual Area: SE/1 CL/2
■ Size comparisons

Final Rating: 62 ******
User Friendliness: 62 ******
Educational Value: 78 ********
Instructional Design: 51 *****

Comments: A computerized storybook in which Curious George blasts off in a rocket for the moon, where he solves multiple-choice size comparison problems (tall and short, long and short, big and small) to get home. Includes a tutorial. Requires switching disk sides. Reading required. Limited content.

LA = Language   CP = Creative projects   OT = Other topics   CL = Classification   SP = Spatial
relations   TI = Time   NB = Number   SE = Seriation   * = Version reviewed   NA = Not applicable

Title: Delta Drawing
Company: Spinnaker Software Corp.
Date: 1983
Price: $49.95
Age: 4-up
Computer: Apple, IBM*, C64*
Conceptual Area: SP/4 CP/1,3,4
- Drawing, programming concepts

Final Rating: 78 ********
User Friendliness: 64 ******
Educational Value: 62 ******
Instructional Design: 91 *********

Comments: Offers a creative context in which single commands create pictures, e.g., D to draw, R to turn right. As picture is drawn, each command is stored as program, which can be edited. Pictures can be printed, edited. Similar to LOGO computer language.

Title: Developing Language Skills
Company: Queue, Inc.
Date: 1983
Price: $425.00 ($795.00 in Spanish)
Age: 3-6
Computer: Apple
Conceptual Area: LA/1 NB/4 SP/5
- Knowledge of words

Final Rating: 45 *****
User Friendliness: 57 ******
Educational Value: 41 ****
Instructional Design: 38 ****

RABBIT

Comments: Twelve disks and picture books, each with 32 words about toys, clothes, food, furniture, animals, transportation, body parts, action words, outside/inside, play, colors, and numbers. Child uses arrows and RETURN to match words with pictures. Keeps records. Little child-control.

Title: Dinosaurs
Company: Advanced Ideas, Inc.
Date: 1984
Price: $39.95
Age: 2.5-5
Computer: Apple*, IBM, C64 ($34.95)
Conceptual Area: CL/1,2
- Reading, math, and memory skills

Final Rating: 65 *******
User Friendliness: 77 ********
Educational Value: 72 *******
Instructional Design: 51 *****

Comments: Five games about six dinosaur breeds: matching an outline to its twin; classifying dinosaurs by what they ate, where they lived; and recognizing their written names. Uses a picture menu. Includes stickers and coloring book.

LA = Language   CP = Creative projects   OT = Other topics   CL = Classification   SP = Spatial
relations   TI = Time   NB = Number   SE = Seriation   * = Version reviewed   NA = Not applicable

Title: Dinosaurs Are Forever
Company: Polarware, Inc.
Date: 1988
Price: $29.95
Age: 3-up
Computer: Apple* (128K), IBM, C64
Conceptual Area: CP/1,4 SP/4
■ Coloring pictures

Final Rating: 80 ********
User Friendliness: 79 ********
Educational Value: 73 *******
Instructional Design: 84 ********

Comments: A coloring program with 26 blank dinosaur pictures on one disk. Child moves cursor with mouse, joystick, or arrow keys to fill in sections of a picture with 1 of 16 available colors. Prints in color. Mouse and color monitor recommended. Very easy to use. Prints picture with calendar, banner, or message.

Title: Diskovery Adding Machine
Company: Queue, Inc.
Date: 1984
Price: $39.95
Age: 4-8
Computer: Apple
Conceptual Area: NB/1,3,7,9
■ Counting, addition skills

Final Rating: 69 *******
User Friendliness: 54 *****
Educational Value: 80 ********
Instructional Design: 74 *******

Comments: Three games: Counting — child counts and combines two sets. Number Matching — child counts two uneven sets to determine the greater. Adding Facts — child practices addition problems. Some reading required. Management prints and records child's performance.

Title: Diskovery Take Away Zoo
Company: Queue, Inc.
Date: 1984
Price: $39.95
Age: 4-8
Computer: Apple
Conceptual Area: NB/3,4,9
■ Counting, subtraction practice

Final Rating: 68 *******
User Friendliness: 52 *****
Educational Value: 82 ********
Instructional Design: 73 *******

Comments: Three games on one disk. Child uses arrow keys to remove animals from sets, illustrating subtraction problems. Progresses to traditional subtraction drill, using numbers up to 9. Management prints and records child's performance.

LA = Language   CP = Creative projects   OT = Other topics   CL = Classification   SP = Spatial
relations   TI = Time   NB = Number   SE = Seriation   * = Version reviewed   NA = Not applicable

Title: Dr. Peet's Talk/Writer
Company: Hartley Courseware, Inc.
Date: 1986
Price: $69.95
Age: 3-7
Computer: Apple
Conceptual Area: LA/3,4,5,6,7,9 CL/2 CP/4
■ Language exploration and skills

Comments: Consists of two disks. Disk 1 includes the ABC song, finding and matching letters, and creating and listening to words. Disk 2 is an easy-to-use talking word processor that says whatever is typed, in robotic voice. Uses large letters. Echo speech synthesizer required. Stories can be saved and printed.

Final Rating: 79 ********
User Friendliness: 58 ******
Educational Value: 98 **********
Instructional Design: 88 *********

My dog likes to play with me. I will throw a stick or a ball and she will get it. ■

R	S	P	Q

Title: Dr. Seuss Fix-Up . . . Puzzler
Company: CBS Software
Date: 1985
Price: $29.95
Age: 4-10
Computer: Apple, C64*
Conceptual Area: SP/1
■ Problem solving

Comments: A puzzle program featuring six Dr. Seuss characters. Each puzzle is randomly designed with five difficulties to choose from. More advanced levels use smaller and/or inverted pieces. Compatible with Muppet Learning Keys.

Final Rating: 70 *******
User Friendliness: 51 *****
Educational Value: 83 ********
Instructional Design: 79 ********

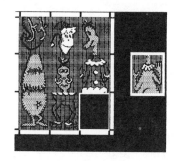

Title: Ducks Ahoy
Company: Joyce Hakansson Associates
Date: 1984
Price: $34.95
Age: 3-6
Computer: C64 (cartridge)
Conceptual Area: TI/3,5
■ Logical reasoning skills

Comments: A game in which children move a boat through canals to pick up ducks. Timing and selection of the best route to avoid a moving obstacle are required to collect all the ducks. Entertaining music and graphics. Joystick required. Discontinued in 1986.

Final Rating: 78 ********
User Friendliness: 70 *******
Educational Value: 87 *********
Instructional Design: 76 ********

LA = Language   CP = Creative projects   OT = Other topics   CL = Classification   SP = Spatial relations   TI = Time   NB = Number   SE = Seriation   * = Version reviewed   NA = Not applicable

Title: Early & Advanced Switch Games
Company: R.J. Cooper & Associates
Date: 1987
Price: Free preview copy
Age: 2-up
Computer: Apple
Conceptual Area: CL/2,4 TI/1 SP/4,8 CP/4
■ Cause/effect, matching, counting, scanning

Final Rating: 75 ********
User Friendliness: 86 *********
Educational Value: 87 *********
Instructional Design: 63 ******

Comments: Thirteen clever games. Child uses only single switch or open APPLE key to make noises or visual effects, build a scene, play music, scan, build shapes, count, match shapes and colors, move through a maze, or construct a face that can be printed. Adult setup required. Designed for children with limited motor abilities. Echo speech synthesizer optional. Good child-control.

Title: Early Childhood . . . Program
Company: Educational Activities, Inc.
Date: 1983
Price: $159.00
Age: 3-7
Computer: Apple*, C64
Conceptual Area: CP/3 SP/1 TI/3
■ Conceptual skill development

Final Rating: 53 *****
User Friendliness: 36 ****
Educational Value: 56 ******
Instructional Design: 67 *******

Comments: A series of five disks, all of which use one-key commands (e.g., F = forward) to move objects. Based on LOGO concepts. Gives open-ended context for exploration in directionality, planning, sequencing, etc. Animation is slow, limiting child's control.

Title: Early Elementary I
Company: Compu-Tations
Date: 1982
Price: $34.95
Age: 4-7
Computer: Apple*, Atari, IBM
Conceptual Area: CL/1 NB/4
■ Counting and matching

Final Rating: 27 ***
User Friendliness: 26 ***
Educational Value: 23 **
Instructional Design: 40 ****

Comments: Presents four activities: Count Shapes, Color Match, Number Drill, and Shape Match. Contains management file and password system. Uses blocky graphics. Presentation can trap child in routines. Not recommended.

LA = Language   CP = Creative projects   OT = Other topics   CL = Classification   SP = Spatial
relations   TI = Time   NB = Number   SE = Seriation   * = Version reviewed   NA = Not applicable

Title: Early Elementary II
Company: Compu-Tations
Date: 1981
Price: $34.95
Age: 5-7
Computer: Apple
Conceptual Area: LA/4 SP/4 NB/4,8
■ Letter recognition, counting

Final Rating: 28 ***
User Friendliness: 28 ***
Educational Value: 23 **
Instructional Design: 30 ***

Comments: Contains four games: Upper/Lower-case Match, Alphabet Line, Inside Out, Number Line. Includes management file. No branching. Possible to break the program. Graphics are unclear and sounds are distracting. Not recommended.

Title: Early Games
Company: Springboard
Date: 1984
Price: $31.95
Age: 2-6
Computer: Apple*, IBM, C64, Atari
Conceptual Area: CP/1 LA/4 CL/1 NB/3,8
■ Counting, letters, and drawing

Final Rating: 60 ******
User Friendliness: 44 ****
Educational Value: 72 *******
Instructional Design: 74 *******

CAN YOU MATCH THIS NUMBER?

Comments: Contains nine separate games that are strong in content. Poorly designed menu is easy to use but confusing to children. Successful in providing a variety of activities. Drawing activity pictures can be saved on disk.

Title: Early Learning Friends
Company: Spinnaker Software Corp.
Date: 1985
Price: $9.95
Age: 4-7
Computer: C64
Conceptual Area: TI/1,3 CL/1,2,5
■ Shapes, colors, sizes, and timing

Final Rating: 71 *******
User Friendliness: 69 *******
Educational Value: 89 *********
Instructional Design: 60 ******

Comments: Child uses joystick in three games: Alf — an enjoyable maze-like game in which child moves Alf through caves, avoiding "Wufflegumps." Shape shop — child makes toy's missing part, considering the color and shape of the needed part. Coney Island — child moves a penguin to match the attributes of an ice cream cone.

LA = Language   CP = Creative projects   OT = Other topics   CL = Classification   SP = Spatial relations   TI = Time   NB = Number   SE = Seriation   * = Version reviewed   NA = Not applicable

Title: Early Math
Company: MicroEd, Inc.
Date: 1987
Price: $49.95
Age: 3-6
Computer: Amiga (512K)
Conceptual Area: NB/3
■ Counting, numerical order, basic skills

Final Rating: 43 ****
User Friendliness: 43 ****
Educational Value: 69 *******
Instructional Design: 41 ****

Comments: Four programs on one disk: child counts from 1-31 objects and enters the number, completes a three-number sequence, finds the sum of two groups of 0-9 objects, or subtracts with sets of 0-9 objects. Blocky graphics. Provides verbal feedback.

Title: Early Skills
Company: Hartley Courseware, Inc.
Date: 1986
Price: $39.95
Age: 5-7
Computer: Apple
Conceptual Area: CL/2 SE/4
■ Shape and word discrimination

Final Rating: 61 ******
User Friendliness: 49 *****
Educational Value: 83 ********
Instructional Design: 58 ******

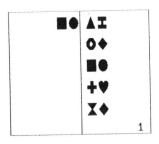

Comments: Child uses spacebar to match objects, colors, or words in this simple, matching, two-disk program. Design permits control over many aspects of the content and includes record keeping and automatic progress report. Menu requires reading.

Title: Easy as ABC
Company: Springboard
Date: 1984
Price: $39.95
Age: 3-6
Computer: Apple*, Mac, IBM, C64
Conceptual Area: LA/4,5
■ Letter recognition, alphabet order

Final Rating: 80 ********
User Friendliness: 78 ********
Educational Value: 91 *********
Instructional Design: 77 ********

Comments: Provides five games: Match Letters, Dot-to-Dot, Leapfrog, Lunar Letters, and Honey Hunt. Spacebar, JKIM keys, arrow keys, and joystick make the program easy to use. Can be used with upper- and lower-case letters. Reading not required.

LA = Language   CP = Creative projects   OT = Other topics   CL = Classification   SP = Spatial relations   TI = Time   NB = Number   SE = Seriation   * = Version reviewed   NA = Not applicable

Title: Easy Street
Company: MindPlay
Date: 1988
Price: $49.95
Age: 4-8
Computer: Apple*, IBM, Mac, IIGS
Conceptual Area: CL/2,3 SP/4,8 LA/4,5 NB/2,3 TI/3
■ Classification, matching, and counting

Final Rating: 84 ********
User Friendliness: 79 ********
Educational Value: 90 *********
Instructional Design: 84 ********

Comments: Using arrow keys, joystick, or mouse, child moves a boy down a street past various storefronts in search of special objects. "Challenge Upgrade" feature offers a wide range of challenges. Optional speech synthesis makes the program easier to use (Echo speech synthesizer). Enjoyable program.

Title: Ernie's Big Splash
Company: Hi Tech Expressions
Date: 1985
Price: $14.95
Age: 4-6
Computer: C64*, IBM, Apple
Conceptual Area: SP/4,7
■ Planning, predicting, problem solving

Final Rating: 59 ******
User Friendliness: 51 *****
Educational Value: 63 ******
Instructional Design: 60 ******

Comments: Using function keys, child builds path that transports Rubber Duckie from his soap dish to Ernie's bathtub. The path is made by choosing squares that will move Duckie to Ernie. Three levels. Program takes three minutes to load from disk. Limited content.

Title: Ernie's Magic Shapes
Company: Hi Tech Expressions
Date: 1984
Price: $19.95
Age: 3-6
Computer: C64*, Atari, IBM, Apple
Conceptual Area: CL/1,2
■ Visual discrimination practice

Final Rating: 45 *****
User Friendliness: 43 ****
Educational Value: 61 ******
Instructional Design: 37 ****

Comments: In all of the six shape- and color-matching games, child uses two arrow keys to decide if a shape or color matches one shown. Features Ernie, who nods feedback and brings new shapes. Provides little interaction or variety. Color monitor required.

LA = Language   CP = Creative projects   OT = Other topics   CL = Classification   SP = Spatial relations   TI = Time   NB = Number   SE = Seriation   * = Version reviewed   NA = Not applicable

Title: Estimation

Company: Lawrence Hall of Science
Date: 1984
Price: $34.95
Age: 4-6
Computer: Apple
Conceptual Area: TI/1,3,4 NB/5,6
■ Est. of length, area, & time units

Final Rating: 78 ********
User Friendliness: 67 *******
Educational Value: 92 *********
Instructional Design: 79 ********

Comments: Offers three activities with estimation skills: Choo-Choo — child guesses when a train is over an arrow by pressing spacebar. Junk Jar — child estimates area. Bugs — presents units of "bugs" for child to estimate a line's length.

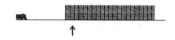

Title: Expl. Your World: The Weather

Company: Grolier Electronic Publishing
Date: 1985
Price: $24.95
Age: 4-7
Computer: Apple*, C64
Conceptual Area: LA/5 SP/2,4,5
■ Body parts, weather words

Final Rating: 51 *****
User Friendliness: 46 *****
Educational Value: 75 ********
Instructional Design: 43 ****

Comments: Two activities on one disk: (1) An open activity. Child uses joystick or arrow keys to pick a weather picture (e.g., sun, rain) and moves it to a scene. (2) Child dresses man or woman figure by selecting clothes and moving them to the appropriate body part. Menu requires reading.

Title: Exploratory Play

Company: P.E.A.L. Software
Date: 1985
Price: $150.00
Age: 1.5-3
Computer: Apple (64K)
Conceptual Area: LA/1,5 SP/7
■ Early language acquisition

Final Rating: 71 *******
User Friendliness: 62 ******
Educational Value: 69 *******
Instructional Design: 84 ********

Comments: Provides two overlays for the Muppet Learning Keys (required). Child first plays with real toys, then presses their pictures on the overlay to hear the associated words in a robotic voice. (Toy kit purchased separately for $54.) Requires Echo speech synthesizer. Covers 24 words. Adult setup required.

LA = Language   CP = Creative projects   OT = Other topics   CL = Classification   SP = Spatial
relations   TI = Time   NB = Number   SE = Seriation   * = Version reviewed   NA = Not applicable

Title: Extrateletactograph, The
Company: DIL International
Date: 1986
Price: $69.95
Age: 4-12
Computer: Apple II + or IIe (not IIc)
Conceptual Area: CP/1,4 LA/3
■ Drawing and writing stories

Final Rating: 73 *******
User Friendliness: 67 *******
Educational Value: 80 ********
Instructional Design: 72 *******

Comments: A drawing and writing program. Child touches graphic tablet with overlay (requires WonderWorker) to draw or to change colors. Text can be added to the picture. Work can be saved and printed. Includes supplementary materials.

Title: EZ Logo
Company: MECC
Date: 1985
Price: $59.00
Age: 4-8
Computer: Apple (64K)
Conceptual Area: CP/1,3 SP/4,1,7,8 NB/1,3,5
■ Problem solving, directionality

Final Rating: 74 *******
User Friendliness: 45 *****
Educational Value: 94 *********
Instructional Design: 89 *********

Comments: Two levels on one disk. In level 1, child can draw using one-letter commands (e.g., F = Forward). Seventeen commands available. In level 2, child can create simple procedures and incorporate them into pictures. Five colors available. Work can be saved and printed. Manual includes many ideas and two keyboard sticker sets.

```
EZ Logo

Programs:

   1. EZ Logo 1
   2. EZ Logo 2

Options:

   3. General Information
   4. Printer Support
   5. End

Which number? ▓
```

Title: Facemaker
Company: Spinnaker Software Corp.
Date: 1982
Price: $29.95
Age: 3-8
Computer: Apple, IBM*, C64, Atari
Conceptual Area: CP/2,3,4 TI/6
■ Pattern matching, creative activity

Final Rating: 54 *****
User Friendliness: 41 ****
Educational Value: 58 ******
Instructional Design: 63 ******

Comments: Children use spacebar and RETURN to select elements of a face: eyes, ears, nose, mouth, hair. The face can then be made to wink, cry, etc., and a sequence activity can be done (like Simon Says). Simple reading required. Discontinued in 1986. See Facemaker Golden Edition.

LA = Language CP = Creative projects OT = Other topics CL = Classification SP = Spatial relations TI = Time NB = Number SE = Seriation * = Version reviewed NA· = Not applicable

Title: Facemaker Golden Edition
Company: Spinnaker Software Corp.
Date: 1986
Price: $39.95
Age: 3-8
Computer: Apple*, Amiga ($49.95), IBM (3.5)
Conceptual Area: SP/5 CP/3,4 LA/4,9 OT/1
■ Creativity, memory, and concentration

Final Rating: 61 ******
User Friendliness: 43 ****
Educational Value: 77 ********
Instructional Design: 66 *******

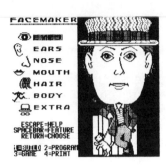

Comments: Child uses spacebar to select features for a face (eyes, ears, nose, mouth, hair) as well as a body, hats, or glasses. Face can then be programmed to move or be used in a memory game. It can then be printed along with up to 1/2 page of text. Difficult for 3-year-olds to operate.

Title: Fantastic Animals
Company: Firebird Licensees, Inc.
Date: 1985
Price: $9.99
Age: 4-9
Computer: Apple*, IBM, C64 ($7.99)
Conceptual Area: SP/1,5 CL/2
■ Part/whole relationships

Final Rating: 70 *******
User Friendliness: 63 ******
Educational Value: 78 ********
Instructional Design: 72 *******

Comments: Three games use parts of 20 animals. Child uses spacebar and RETURN to create an animal from the mixed parts of many or to make a matching animal when shown a model. Each animal has a song. Enjoyable program. Discontinued from publisher, may still be available in stores.

Title: First "R": Kindergarten, The
Company: Milliken Publishing Co.
Date: 1987
Price: $95.00
Age: 5-8
Computer: Apple
Conceptual Area: LA/4,5,6
■ Letter recognition; initial, ending sounds of words

Final Rating: 74 *******
User Friendliness: 68 *******
Educational Value: 83 ********
Instructional Design: 72 *******

Comments: Four activities — child types the first or last letter of a given word, selects letter to complete a word, selects a picture that goes with a partial word, or sees a partial word and picture and selects missing letter. Keeps records. Includes alphabet and tutorial disks, an alphabet book, and classroom materials.

LA = Language   CP = Creative projects   OT = Other topics   CL = Classification   SP = Spatial
relations   TI = Time   NB = Number   SE = Seriation   * = Version reviewed   NA = Not applicable

Title: First Encounters
Company: Educational Activities, Inc.
Date: 1983
Price: $98.00
Age: 4-6
Computer: Apple
Conceptual Area: OT/1
■ Computer literacy skills

Final Rating: 32 ***
User Friendliness: 41 ****
Educational Value: 21 **
Instructional Design: 29 ***

Comments: A "computer literacy" package designed to teach kindergarten children computer terms, computer operation, and writing of programs. Includes flashcards for memorizing terms, worksheets, keyboard models, workdisk with games. Reading required. Ratings apply only to programs.

Title: First Letter Fun
Company: MECC
Date: 1985
Price: $59.99
Age: 3-6
Computer: Apple (64K)
Conceptual Area: LA/1,4,6
■ Letter recognition

Final Rating: 82 ********
User Friendliness: 67 *******
Educational Value: 98 **********
Instructional Design: 86 *********

Comments: Four pictures stories: Farm, Circus, Park, and Magic Show introduce all the letters except Q and X. Child sees an object from a story and must use the spacebar or arrow keys to select its initial letter. Teacher options allow selection of upper/lower-case display. Clear graphics. Good design.

Title: First Letters and Words
Company: First Byte, Inc.
Date: 1987
Price: $49.95
Age: 3-8
Computer: Apple IIGS*, Mac, Amiga, Atari ST
Conceptual Area: LA/4,5,8 SP/5
■ Letters & words, dinosaurs

Final Rating: 74 *******
User Friendliness: 80 ********
Educational Value: 80 ********
Instructional Design: 62 ******

Comments: Four games: (1) Introduces upper- and lower-case letters. (2) Shows a picture and says word when any letter is typed. (3) Says body parts as a child colors in a dinosaur. (4) Presents animal riddles for which child types the answer. Talks in a primitive voice. Options give teacher control.

LA = Language CP = Creative projects OT = Other topics CL = Classification SP = Spatial relations TI = Time NB = Number SE = Seriation * = Version reviewed NA = Not applicable

Title: First Numbers: First Words
Company: Educational Activities, Inc.
Date: 1984
Price: $39.95
Age: 3-7
Computer: Apple*, C64
Conceptual Area: LA/4 NB/2,3 OT/1
■ 1-to-1 correspondence, visual memory

Final Rating: 41 ****
User Friendliness: 39 ****
Educational Value: 67 *******
Instructional Design: 38 ****

Comments: Two activities on one disk: First Numbers — matching sets 1-5, 1-10. Child sees five dots and duplicates set. Child sees set and types numeral. First Words — child copies model word, e.g., "cat." Harder level requires remembering the word after it has been flashed for two seconds.

Title: First Shapes
Company: First Byte, Inc.
Date: 1987
Price: $49.95
Age: 3-8
Computer: Apple IIGS*, Mac, Amiga, Atari ST
Conceptual Area: CL/1 SP/8 SE/1 OT/1
■ Five basic shapes

Final Rating: 75 ********
User Friendliness: 81 ********
Educational Value: 88 *********
Instructional Design: 64 ******

Comments: Four games: Child can (1) change the size of a shape by clicking the mouse, (2) design a toy out of shapes, (3) play Concentration by matching pairs of shapes, or (4) find a shape such as "the smallest circle" among three shapes presented. Gives design options. Toys can be printed and saved. Voice is hard to understand.

Title: First Steps to Reading
Company: Grolier Electronic Publishing
Date: 1985
Price: $49.95
Age: 4-7
Computer: Apple*, C64
Conceptual Area: LA/6
■ Initial consonants

Final Rating: 43 ****
User Friendliness: 49 *****
Educational Value: 55 ******
Instructional Design: 31 ***

Comments: Three activities on one disk: (1) Shows object. Child presses the first letter of object shown. (2) Shows letter. Child uses spacebar to select a corresponding object. (3) Shows letter and six objects. Child uses arrow keys to move a crane to the object corresponding to letter. Joystick is optional.

LA = Language   CP = Creative projects   OT = Other topics   CL = Classification   SP = Spatial relations   TI = Time   NB = Number   SE = Seriation   * = Version reviewed   NA = Not applicable

Title: FirstWriter
Company: Houghton Mifflin Co.
Date: 1988
Price: $117.00
Age: 5-8
Computer: Apple
Conceptual Area: LA/1,3,4,5,6,9 CP/4
■ Creative writing

Final Rating: 76 ********
User Friendliness: 59 ******
Educational Value: 96 **********
Instructional Design: 78 ********

Comments: A large-letter word processor with features that include spoken instructions (Echo speech synthesizer optional), choice of five colors for text, a built-in dictionary, 125 pictures. Stories can be saved or printed in color. Words can be added to the dictionary. Print is somewhat blocky.

Title: Fish Scales
Company: DLM
Date: 1985
Price: $32.95
Age: 4-8
Computer: Apple
Conceptual Area: NB/1,3,4,6
■ Measurement

Final Rating: 78 ********
User Friendliness: 67 *******
Educational Value: 92 *********
Instructional Design: 79 ********

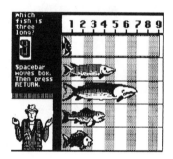

Comments: Six games in which child uses spacebar, arrow keys, or RETURN to input answers, e.g., the height of a fish jump, the longest or shortest fish, and other measurement concepts. Games encourage using units of measurement. Menu requires reading.

Title: Flodd, the Bad Guy
Company: Tom Snyder Productions, Inc.
Date: 1988
Price: $34.95
Age: 2-6
Computer: Apple*, IBM, Mac
Conceptual Area: LA/3,4,5
■ Letter and word recognition, reading stories

Final Rating: 70 *******
User Friendliness: 64 ******
Educational Value: 79 ********
Instructional Design: 73 *******

Comments: Child and adult read through a fairy-tale-like story, pressing any key to change the screen. Every five or six pages, a choice is offered, e.g., to go into a cave or not. Reading required for independent use, although clever graphics and sounds help to guide child through the story.

LA = Language   CP = Creative projects   OT = Other topics   CL = Classification   SP = Spatial
relations   TI = Time   NB = Number   SE = Seriation   * = Version reviewed   NA = Not applicable

Title: Flying Carpet, The
Company: Learning Technologies, Inc.
Date: 1985
Price: $24.95
Age: 4-8
Computer: Apple*, C64
Conceptual Area: SP/8
■ Shape recognition

Final Rating: 44 ****
User Friendliness: 65 *******
Educational Value: 52 *****
Instructional Design: 28 ***

Comments: Child uses spacebar and RETURN to count the number of a given shape contained in 1 of 12 sets of shapes presented. A flying genie provides feedback. No branching. No reading required. Rigid format permits little child-control.

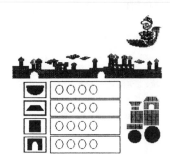

Title: Fruit Tree/Gumball
Company: BeCi Software
Date: 1983
Price: $19.95
Age: 2-6
Computer: C64*, VIC 20
Conceptual Area: NB/3,4
■ Counting, adding, and subtracting

Final Rating: 28 ***
User Friendliness: 29 ***
Educational Value: 38 ****
Instructional Design: 22 **

Comments: Two activities on same disk: Gumball — child counts from 10 to 35 gumballs and enters number. Fruit Tree — child solves addition and subtraction problems. Blocky graphics. Poor design.

Title: Fun From A to Z
Company: MECC
Date: 1985
Price: $59.00
Age: 3-6
Computer: Apple (64K)
Conceptual Area: LA/4
■ Alphabet skills practice

Final Rating: 81 ********
User Friendliness: 68 *******
Educational Value: 92 *********
Instructional Design: 85 *********

Comments: Child uses arrow keys to play three games: Birds — child matches letters. Dots — child completes a dot-to-dot picture by selecting next alphabet letter. Runners — child sees sequence (K,L,M,__,O) and must select missing letter. Management allows selection of upper/lower-case. Well-designed.

LA = Language   CP = Creative projects   OT = Other topics   CL = Classification   SP = Spatial
relations   TI = Time   NB = Number   SE = Seriation   * = Version reviewed   NA = Not applicable

Title: Fun on the Farm
Company: Polarware, Inc.
Date: 1986
Price: $14.95
Age: 3-up
Computer: Apple* (128K), IBM, C64
Conceptual Area: CP/1,4 SP/4
▪ Coloring pictures

Final Rating: 80 ********
User Friendliness: 79 ********
Educational Value: 73 *******
Instructional Design: 84 ********

Comments: A coloring program with 30 blank farm scenes. Child moves cursor with mouse, joystick, or arrow keys to fill in sections of a picture with 1 of 16 available colors. Prints in color. Mouse and color monitor recommended. Very easy to use. Prints picture with calendar.

Title: Fun With Directions
Company: Mindscape, Inc.
Date: 1984
Price: $49.95
Age: 3-6
Computer: Apple
Conceptual Area: SP/4 TI/6
▪ Perceptual and cognitive skills

Final Rating: 62 ******
User Friendliness: 81 ********
Educational Value: 69 *******
Instructional Design: 44 ****

Comments: Child selects a nodding (yes) or shaking (no) head to indicate if objects are in line, are facing same direction, or are in sequence, e.g., egg/chick/chicken. Allows for selection of difficulty level, performance feedback. No reading required.

Title: Fun With Letters and Words
Company: Wescott Software
Date: 1987
Price: $20.00
Age: 2-6
Computer: IBM
Conceptual Area: LA/4,5
▪ Letter recognition

Final Rating: 76 ********
User Friendliness: 73 *******
Educational Value: 86 *********
Instructional Design: 70 *******

Comments: Child can press any letter key to see a picture and word related to the letter, e.g., a bike for B. Six levels allow the addition of more words, with up to 147 possible. "Custom" words, such as a child's name, can be added.

LA = Language CP = Creative projects OT = Other topics CL = Classification SP = Spatial relations TI = Time NB = Number SE = Seriation * = Version reviewed NA = Not applicable

Title: Fun With Memory

Company: Wescott Software

Date: 1987

Price: $20.00

Age: 2-6

Computer: IBM

Conceptual Area: OT/1 LA/4,5 NB/4 CL/2

■ Memory

Final Rating: 77 ********
User Friendliness: 65 *******
Educational Value: 87 *********
Instructional Design: 83 ********

Comments: A seven-level Concentration game in which child uses the arrow keys, spacebar and ENTER to select a card. Child can match numerals, objects, or words. Options allow for control over the number of cards shown in a game. Can be played by one or two players.

Title: Fun With Numbers

Company: Wescott Software

Date: 1987

Price: $20.00

Age: 2-6

Computer: IBM

Conceptual Area: NB/3,4,8

■ Numeral recognition, adding and subtracting

Final Rating: 59 ******
User Friendliness: 64 ******
Educational Value: 78 ********
Instructional Design: 46 *****

How Many?

Comments: Five games provide experiences in counting, adding with objects, or subtracting, all with sums less than 18. Nine skill levels determine the difficulty of the game. Adult options permit control over the difficulty level and pacing of the game.

Title: Gertrude's Secrets

Company: The Learning Company

Date: 1982

Price: $59.95 (school edition)

Age: 4-10

Computer: Apple*, IBM*, C64 ($29.95)

Conceptual Area: CL/1,5 SP/4

■ Classifying and seriating

Final Rating: 84 ********
User Friendliness: 78 ********
Educational Value: 91 *********
Instructional Design: 86 ********

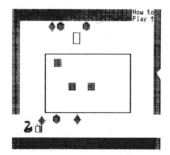

Comments: Consists of seven attribute puzzles of varying difficulty. Child uses arrow keys or joystick to move through 25 rooms (screens). Children as young as age 3 can do easiest puzzle, but lose interest quickly. Content is best for ages 5 and up. School edition contains additional curriculum materials.

LA = Language   CP = Creative projects   OT = Other topics   CL = Classification   SP = Spatial relations   TI = Time   NB = Number   SE = Seriation   * = Version reviewed   NA = Not applicable

Title: Getting Ready to Read and Add
Company: Sunburst Communications, Inc.
Date: 1984
Price: $65.00
Age: 3-6
Computer: Apple, IBM*, Atari, C64*
Conceptual Area: LA/4 CL/2 NB/3,4
■ Numerals, U/L- case letters

Final Rating: 63 ******
User Friendliness: 56 ******
Educational Value: 77 ********
Instructional Design: 80 ********

Comments: Six activities based on a matching format. Practice with shapes, letters, and numerals. Child presses any key when a match is shown for shapes, letters, and numerals. Options included for control of speed and number of problems.

Title: Grabbit Factory, The
Company: D.C. Heath & Company:
Date: 1983
Price: $45.00
Age: 3-8
Computer: Apple*, C64
Conceptual Area: NB/4,9
■ Numerals, basic math facts

Final Rating: 52 *****
User Friendliness: 81 ********
Educational Value: 46 *****
Instructional Design: 31 ***

Comments: Child uses arrow keys, joystick, to move crane and make selections of numerals. No branching. Easy to use. No reading required.

Title: Grandma's House
Company: Spinnaker Software Corp.
Date: 1983
Price: $9.95
Age: 4-8
Computer: Apple*, C64, Atari
Conceptual Area: SP/2
■ Exploring and arranging

Final Rating: 68 *******
User Friendliness: 78 ********
Educational Value: 57 ******
Instructional Design: 65 *******

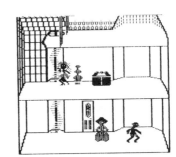

Comments: Child uses mouse or joystick (required) to move to and explore 1 of 6 different scenes. By pressing key, objects (e.g., a fish from the seashore) can be carried from scenes and collected in "Grandma's House." Easy to use but not strong in any content area.

LA = Language   CP = Creative projects   OT = Other topics   CL = Classification   SP = Spatial
relations   TI = Time   NB = Number   SE = Seriation   * = Version reviewed   NA = Not applicable

Title: Great Gonzo in WordRider, The
Company: Joyce Hakansson Associates
Date: 1985
Price: $19.95
Age: 6-up
Computer: Apple
Conceptual Area: TI/1,3,5 SP/2 LA/8
■ Fun with words, timing, and strategy

Final Rating: 73 *******
User Friendliness: 77 ********
Educational Value: 70 *******
Instructional Design: 71 *******

Comments: An adventure game in which child uses joystick (recommended) or arrow keys to move Gonzo through obstacles to earn points and rescue a chicken. On the way, Gonzo constructs machines that will get him through the dangers. An enjoyable program. Includes a Muppet storybook.

Title: Great Leap, A
Company: D.C. Heath & Company:
Date: 1988
Price: $75.00
Age: 5-10
Computer: Apple (128K)
Conceptual Area: LA/1,2,3,5,8,9 SP/4,7 CP/1,4
■ Language experience

Final Rating: 89 *********
User Friendliness: 85 *********
Educational Value: 94 *********
Instructional Design: 91 *********

Comments: Children use mouse, Koala Pad, joystick, or arrow keys to select and move objects, words, or characters in a story. Children can also type their own words. Stories can be saved and printed in color. Package includes four copies of storybook. Colorful graphics, good child-control. Mouse recommended.

Title: Grover's Animal Adventures
Company: Hi Tech Expressions
Date: 1985
Price: $14.95
Age: 4-6
Computer: C64*, IBM, Apple
Conceptual Area: CL/2
■ Classifying animals

Final Rating: 76 ********
User Friendliness: 75 ********
Educational Value: 73 *******
Instructional Design: 79 ********

Comments: Child uses joystick to move Grover to 1 of 4 environments. Pressing joystick button adds animals or objects. Each environment is divided into land, sky, and water areas. Child must place animal in appropriate area.

LA = Language   CP = Creative projects   OT = Other topics   CL = Classification   SP = Spatial relations   TI = Time   NB = Number   SE = Seriation   * = Version reviewed   NA = Not applicable

Title: Grownup and Small
Company: Mindscape, Inc.
Date: 1987
Price: $39.95
Age: 3-8
Computer: Apple
Conceptual Area: SE/1 CL/2 LA/4
■ Adult and baby names

Final Rating: 68 *******
User Friendliness: 77 ********
Educational Value: 76 ********
Instructional Design: 55 ******

Comments: Shows adult (or baby) with its name. Child presses spacebar to see the corresponding baby (or adult), which starts an animated sequence. A second activity shows an adult or baby along with four names. Child must select (with spacebar) the corresponding name. Easy to use. Includes 20 matching sets.

Title: Happy Birthday, Pockets
Company: World Book, Inc.
Date: 1984
Price: $39.95
Age: 3-5
Computer: IBM
Conceptual Area: CL/2
■ Visual discrimination

Final Rating: 71 *******
User Friendliness: 69 *******
Educational Value: 86 *********
Instructional Design: 63 ******

Comments: Eight child-controlled options in which child uses spacebar and RETURN to select upper- or lower-case letters, numerals, or the letter keys to design the wrapping for a present. Is successful in providing child-control. Good graphics, sound, and content.

Title: Hey Diddle Diddle
Company: Spinnaker Software Corp.
Date: 1983
Price: $9.95
Age: 3-10
Computer: Apple*, C64, Atari, IBM
Conceptual Area: LA/7,9
■ Rhyming words and phrases

Final Rating: 47 *****
User Friendliness: 46 *****
Educational Value: 56 ******
Instructional Design: 42 ****

THE RHYME GAME
1890
I had a little nut tree
And a golden pear
Nothing would it bear
But a silver nutmeg

Comments: Three activities based on 30 classic nursery rhymes. The first two activities illustrate the rhymes while an adult reads them. In the third, the phrases that rhyme are scrambled, and the child must put them in correct order. Joystick optional. Reading required.

LA = Language   CP = Creative projects   OT = Other topics   CL = Classification   SP = Spatial relations   TI = Time   NB = Number   SE = Seriation   * = Version reviewed   NA = Not applicable

Title: Hobo's Luck

Company: Strawberry Hill Software

Date: 1985

Price: $55.00

Age: 5-up

Computer: Apple*, C64

Conceptual Area: NB/1,3,4,6 SP/2

■ Counting and probability

Final Rating: 54 *****
User Friendliness: 54 *****
Educational Value: 73 *******
Instructional Design: 44 ****

Comments: A computerized board game in which one to four players take turns rolling dice to earn jumps. The first one reaching the end of the course wins a bag of money. Includes 13 worksheet activities for practice in probability, counting, and statistical recording.

Title: Hodge Podge

Company: Artworx

Date: 1982

Price: $14.95

Age: 1.5-6

Computer: Apple*, C64, IBM, Atari

Conceptual Area: LA/4

■ Letter recognition

Final Rating: 51 *****
User Friendliness: 75 ********
Educational Value: 55 ******
Instructional Design: 50 *****

PRISM

Comments: Child presses any key to get a response: a picture, a song, or both. Screen displays are blocky and not always appropriate for the letter pressed, e.g., P = Prism. Easy to use program, but its value is limited.

Title: Holidays & Seasons

Company: Polarware, Inc.

Date: 1988

Price: $29.95

Age: 3-up

Computer: Apple* (128K), IBM, C64

Conceptual Area: CP/1,4 SP/4

■ Coloring pictures

Final Rating: 80 ********
User Friendliness: 79 ********
Educational Value: 73 *******
Instructional Design: 84 ********

Comments: A coloring program with 30 seasonal pictures on one disk. Child moves cursor with mouse, joystick, or arrow keys to fill in sections of a picture with 1 of 16 available colors. Prints in color. Mouse and color monitor recommended. Very easy to use. Prints picture with calendar, banner, or message.

LA = Language   CP = Creative projects   OT = Other topics   CL = Classification   SP = Spatial
relations   TI = Time   NB = Number   SE = Seriation   * = Version reviewed   NA = Not applicable

---

Title: How to Weigh an Elephant
Company: Learning Technologies, Inc.
Date: 1985
Price: $24.95
Age: 4-8
Computer: Apple*, C64
Conceptual Area: NB/1 CP/3
■ Estimation of weight.

Final Rating: 42 ****
User Friendliness: 49 *****
Educational Value: 59 ******
Instructional Design: 27 ***

Comments: Three activities in which a child observes how far a boat sinks and then must select the heaviest animal, guesses which juice glass has the most, or programs a dancer, using the number keys and RETURN. Reading required.

Title: I Can Count
Company: Troll Associates
Date: 1987
Price: $39.95
Age: 5-8
Computer: Apple
Conceptual Area: NB/2,3,4,8
■ Counting up to 10

Final Rating: 40 ****
User Friendliness: 53 *****
Educational Value: 45 *****
Instructional Design: 26 ***

Comments: Eight activities based around counting, matching numbers with sets, typing the number that comes next, finding a missing number in a sequence, recognizing zero, and concepts of greater or less than. Colorful graphics but poor design. Reading is required.

Title: I Love My Alphabet
Company: First Star Software
Date: 1984
Price: $34.95
Age: 2-7
Computer: Apple*, C64, Atari
Conceptual Area: LA/4
■ Letters, alphabetical order

Final Rating: 59 ******
User Friendliness: 51 *****
Educational Value: 80 ********
Instructional Design: 55 ******

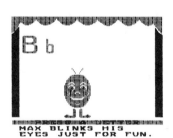

Comments: Entertaining program presents "Max" with four activities of differing difficulty. Well-programmed. Good sounds and graphics. Letter associations are limited and design requires adult or reader help.

LA = Language   CP = Creative projects   OT = Other topics   CL = Classification   SP = Spatial relations   TI = Time   NB = Number   SE = Seriation   * = Version reviewed   NA = Not applicable

Title: Inside Outside Opposites
Company: Random House Software
Date: 1986
Price: $29.95
Age: 3-7
Computer: Apple
Conceptual Area: SE/1 SP/4 LA/1
- Opposites

Comments: Contains 20 antonym pairs (in/out, high/low) that can be illustrated using the arrow keys. Pressing the spacebar brings up the next antonym pair. Easy to use. Similar to "Stickybear Opposites." Colorful graphics.

Final Rating: 72 *******
User Friendliness: 80 ********
Educational Value: 84 ********
Instructional Design: 62 ******

Title: Inside Outside Shapes
Company: Random House Software
Date: 1986
Price: $29.95
Age: 3-7
Computer: Apple
Conceptual Area: SP/8 CL/1,2
- Six shapes and corresponding words

Comments: Using arrow keys and spacebar, child must find a shape hidden in a picture. A correct response animates the picture and plays music. Pressing the spacebar brings up the next picture. Good graphics. Contains 18 pictures. Similar to "Stickybear Shapes."

Final Rating: 76 ********
User Friendliness: 70 *******
Educational Value: 90 *********
Instructional Design: 72 *******

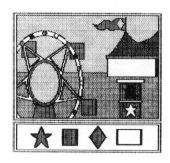

Title: Integrated Learning System
Company: Education Systems Corp.
Date: 1987
Price: Starts at $16,800
Age: 5-up
Computer: Apple IIGS, IBM*, Mac
Conceptual Area: LA/4-8 CL/1-6 NB/1-8 OT/1 CP/1
- Math and reading K-9

Comments: A networked computerized math and reading curriculum containing 1800 separate lessons stored on a laser disk which can be accessed by up to 40 stations at once. Employs the use of headphones, speech synthesis, and speech input. Keeps and prints records, and automatically adapts to each child. Good design, sound and graphics.

Final Rating: 79 ********
User Friendliness: 71 *******
Educational Value: 94 *********
Instructional Design: 79 ********

LA = Language   CP = Creative projects   OT = Other topics   CL = Classification   SP = Spatial
relations   TI = Time   NB = Number   SE = Seriation   * = Version reviewed   NA = Not applicable

Title: Introduction to Counting
Company: EduWare
Date: 1981
Price: $39.95
Age: 4-7
Computer: Apple*, IBM, Atari
Conceptual Area: NB/3 CL/1 SE/1
■ Counting

Comments: A regimented sequence of eight counting activities. Begins with selecting a set to correspond with a given number and progresses all the way to subtraction. Management keeps score and controls presentation, which allows individualization. Requires adult setup with each use.

Final Rating: 66 *******
User Friendliness: 60 ******
Educational Value: 90 *********
Instructional Design: 53 *****

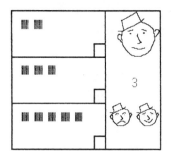

Title: It's No Game
Company: Educational Activities, Inc.
Date: 1986
Price: $49.95
Age: 5-11
Computer: Apple
Conceptual Area: LA/2,3
■ Personal safety skills

Comments: A simulation in which the child is put in a potentially dangerous situation and must make a choice. Each "wise decision" is rewarded with moves on a gameboard. Topics are trusting one's own feelings, saying no to bribes, telephone skills, dealing with strange adults, and asking for help. Reading required.

Final Rating: 62 ******
User Friendliness: 58 ******
Educational Value: 67 *******
Instructional Design: 61 ******

Title: Jack and the Beanstalk
Company: HRM Software
Date: 1985
Price: $49.00
Age: 7-12
Computer: Apple
Conceptual Area: LA/5,8 TI/5
■ Word recognition, event sequence

Comments: Children explore their own version of traditional folk tale by playing the role of Jack, making decisions by selecting two-word commands, e.g., "trade cow." Reading required. Could be used as language experience with younger children. A Spanish version is available. Available in a lab package (10 disks) for $147.00.

Final Rating: 69 *******
User Friendliness: 70 *******
Educational Value: 71 *******
Instructional Design: 66 *******

LA = Language   CP = Creative projects   OT = Other topics   CL = Classification   SP = Spatial
relations   TI = Time   NB = Number   SE = Seriation   * = Version reviewed   NA = Not applicable

Title: Jack and the Beanstalk
Company: Tom Snyder Productions, Inc.
Date: 1988
Price: $34.95
Age: 2-6
Computer: Apple*, IBM, Mac
Conceptual Area: LA/3,4,5
■ Letter and word recognition, reading stories

Final Rating: 70 ******
User Friendliness: 64 ******
Educational Value: 79 ********
Instructional Design: 73 *******

Comments: Child and adult read through a space-age version of Jack and the Beanstalk, pressing any key to change the page. Every five or six pages, a choice is offered, e.g., to continue climbing the beanstalk or not. Reading required for independent use, although graphics and sounds help guide child through the story.

Title: Jr. Typer
Company: Aquarius People Materials
Date: 1985
Price: $45.00
Age: 5-up
Computer: Apple*, TRS 80
Conceptual Area: LA/4 OT/3
■ Touch typing

Final Rating: 41 ****
User Friendliness: 33 ***
Educational Value: 49 *****
Instructional Design: 44 ****

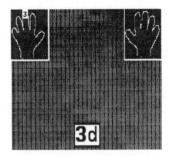

Comments: Presents a fixed series of typing problems. As a child types, graphics or words accumulate on the screen. Helpful graphic hands point out finger positions. Contains 54 combinations on two disks. Inflexible design allows little child-control.

Title: Juggle's Rainbow
Company: The Learning Company
Date: 1982
Price: $29.95
Age: 3-6
Computer: Apple, IBM*, C64
Conceptual Area: SP/4
■ Spatial relationships

Final Rating: 62 ******
User Friendliness: 65 *******
Educational Value: 74 *******
Instructional Design: 54 *****

Comments: Keyboard is a plane on which location of keys corresponds to spatial answers, e.g., above, right, below. However, pressing spacebar advances program to next segment, which children often unwittingly do. Discontinued in 1987.

LA = Language   CP = Creative projects   OT = Other topics   CL = Classification   SP = Spatial relations   TI = Time   NB = Number   SE = Seriation   * = Version reviewed   NA = Not applicable

Title: Just Around the Block
Company: D.C. Heath & Company
Date: 1988
Price: $75.00
Age: 5-10
Computer: Apple
Conceptual Area: LA/2,3,5,9 CP/4 SP/4,7
■ Language experience

Final Rating: 89 *********
User Friendliness: 85 *********
Educational Value: 94 **********
Instructional Design: 91 *********

Comments: Children use mouse, Koala Pad, joystick, or arrow keys to select or move objects, backgrounds, words, or characters of a story. Children can also add their own words. Resulting stories can be saved and printed in color. Includes four copies of the storybook. Good design. Fun to use.

Title: Kermit's Electronic Storymaker
Company: Joyce Hakansson Associates
Date: 1984
Price: $5.95
Age: 4-up
Computer: C64
Conceptual Area: LA/6,8,9 CP/4 TI/6
■ Words and their meaning

Final Rating: 77 ********
User Friendliness: 67 *******
Educational Value: 86 *********
Instructional Design: 82 ********

Comments: Child uses joystick to select the elements of a sentence, which are illustrated with clever animation and music. There are 14 different sentence forms, each on one screen. Resulting stories can be up to 14 pages long, and can be saved. Some reading required. Available in software stores only.

Title: Keytalk
Company: P.E.A.L. Software
Date: 1987
Price: $99.00
Age: 3-8
Computer: Apple (64K)
Conceptual Area: LA/3,4,5,9 CP/4
■ A beginning literacy activity

Final Rating: 76 ********
User Friendliness: 58 ******
Educational Value: 88 *********
Instructional Design: 84 ********

My pet dog is nice! He chases my cat
sometimes, however.

Comments: A talking word processor that says in a robotic voice anything that is typed. Uses regular or Muppet keyboard. Says each letter word, and sentence. Allows stories up to one page in 40-column text. Stories can be printed and saved. Includes on-screen word list. Pronunciation exceptions can be added.

```
ESC to: Talk      Save
        Print     Find
        Dictionary New
```

LA = Language   CP = Creative projects   OT = Other topics   CL = Classification   SP = Spatial
relations   TI = Time   NB = Number   SE = Seriation   * = Version reviewed   NA = Not applicable

Title: Kid Talk
Company: First Byte, Inc.
Date: 1988
Price: $49.95
Age: 3-10
Computer: Mac*, IIGS, Atari ST, Amiga
Conceptual Area: LA/3,4,5,6,8,9
■ Language experience

Final Rating: 89 *********
User Friendliness: 81 ********
Educational Value: 95 **********
Instructional Design: 94 *********

Comments: An easy-to-use word processor that will say what is typed. Makes features such as moving text, selecting sizes of type, changing sounds of words, and printing stories easy to use through clear picture menus. Uses built-in speech synthesizer. Best talking word processor available.

Title: Kid's Stuff
Company: Stone & Associates
Date: 1984
Price: $39.95
Age: 3-8
Computer: IBM*, Apple, Atari ST
Conceptual Area: LA/4,5 SE/4,5
■ Counting skills, letter recognition

Final Rating: 76 ********
User Friendliness: 64 ******
Educational Value: 86 *********
Instructional Design: 80 ********

Spell OBJECT shown   ESC for menu

Comments: Offers three activities accessible by a picture menu. In the letter recognition activity, child types in letters of a word, which creates animation and sounds. An entertaining program that provides options for the child.

Title: Kids on Keys
Company: Spinnaker Software Corp.
Date: 1983
Price: $29.95
Age: 4-9
Computer: Apple*, IBM, C64 ($20.95), Atari
Conceptual Area: LA/4 CL/1 OT/3
■ Letter recognition

Final Rating: 62 ******
User Friendliness: 38 ****
Educational Value: 63 ******
Instructional Design: 79 ********

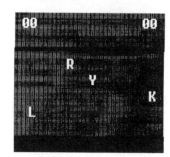

Comments: Presents three games in which letters, pictures, or words rain down the screen. Child stops them and scores points by typing in the appropriate letter or word. Three levels of difficulty. Good keyboard practice, but requires skills that few three- or four-year-olds have.

LA = Language   CP = Creative projects   OT = Other topics   CL = Classification   SP = Spatial
relations   TI = Time   NB = Number   SE = Seriation   * = Version reviewed   NA = Not applicable

Title: KidsTime
Company: Great Wave Software
Date: 1987
Price: $49.95
Age: 3-8
Computer: Mac
Conceptual Area: LA/4,9 CP/2 CL/2 NB/3 OT/1 SE/1
■ Letters, numbers, matching, writing, music

Comments: Five games in which child uses mouse to play a piano, record and play back melodies, match letters or pictures, use or create dot-to-dot pictures, find letters on the keyboard in upper or lower case, or write stories and have them read back using Mac's built-in speech. Nice range of activities. Good child-control.

Final Rating: 82 ********
User Friendliness: 80 ********
Educational Value: 91 *********
Instructional Design: 77 ********

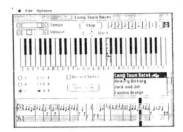

Title: Kidwriter
Company: Spinnaker Software Corp.
Date: 1984
Price: $29.95
Age: 6-10
Computer: Apple*, C64*, IBM (3.5)
Conceptual Area: LA/9 CP/4
■ Creating computer storybooks

Comments: Child creates picture, selecting from 100 objects that can be moved and changed in size or color. Text can be typed on the lower third of the screen. Stories can be saved on disk and have several pages. Reading required. Good design.

Final Rating: 73 *******
User Friendliness: 48 *****
Educational Value: 97 **********
Instructional Design: 81 ********

Title: Kieran
Company: Ohm Software Company
Date: 1986
Price: $39.95
Age: 3-6
Computer: Mac
Conceptual Area: LA/1 NB/3 TI/9 SP/2
■ Letters, numbers, clocks, upper/lower case

Comments: An easy-to-use program with 8 activities. Child uses mouse to choose a letter and see associated picture, to choose a number and see associated set, and to choose a clockface and hear the time. There is also an upper/lower case matching activity, a sliding square puzzle, a calculator, a typewriter, and a mystery picture. Uses Macintosh's internal speech.

Final Rating: 70 *******
User Friendliness: 79 ********
Educational Value: 79 ********
Instructional Design: 57 ******

LA = Language   CP = Creative projects   OT = Other topics   CL = Classification   SP = Spatial relations   TI = Time   NB = Number   SE = Seriation   * = Version reviewed   NA = Not applicable

Title: Kinder Koncepts MATH

Company: Queue, Inc.
Date: 1985
Price: $65.00
Age: 4-7
Computer: Apple*
Conceptual Area: NB/1,2,3,4,5,6,7,8
■ Number and math skills

Final Rating: 57 *****
User Friendliness: 46 *****
Educational Value: 93 *********
Instructional Design: 44 ****

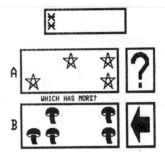

Comments: Fifteen well-designed math games cover various number concepts, e.g., estimating length, using units of measurement, counting, numeral recognition. All games follow same drill-and-practice format. Menu designed for adults, which limits child-control.

Title: Kinder Koncepts Reading

Company: Queue, Inc.
Date: 1985
Price: $65.00
Age: 4-8
Computer: Apple
Conceptual Area: LA/4 CL/1 OT/1
■ Reading readiness

Final Rating: 44 ****
User Friendliness: 44 ****
Educational Value: 56 ******
Instructional Design: 37 ****

Comments: Fifteen activites on three disks each present 10 problems concerning a specific reading concept including matching letters and shapes, upper/lower case, alphabetical order, and memory. Keeps track of progress. Offers a wide range of content. Some reading required, especially for main menu.

Title: Kindercomp

Company: Spinnaker Software Corp.
Date: 1982
Price: $29.95
Age: 3-8
Computer: Apple, IBM*, C64, Atari
Conceptual Area: CP/1 CL/2 LA/4
■ Matching, U/L-case practice, drawing

Final Rating: 68 *******
User Friendliness: 77 ********
Educational Value: 72 *******
Instructional Design: 83 ********

Comments: Offers six games of varying difficulty, including a simple drawing (move cursor with arrow keys) and matching activity that in creases in difficulty as child improves. Offers variety of content, which lengthens the life of the program. Menu requires reading.

LA = Language   CP = Creative projects   OT = Other topics   CL = Classification   SP = Spatial relations   TI = Time   NB = Number   SE = Seriation   * = Version reviewed   NA = Not applicable

Title: Kindercomp Golden Edition
Company: Spinnaker Software Corp.
Date: 1986
Price: $39.95
Age: 3-7
Computer: Apple*, IBM 3.5
Conceptual Area: NB/3 LA/4 CL/2 CP/1
■ Counting, letters, matching, and drawing

Final Rating: 70 *******
User Friendliness: 56 ******
Educational Value: 90 *********
Instructional Design: 70 *******

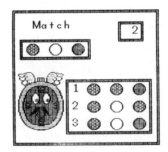

Comments: Eight activities: Draw, Name, Match, Letters, Alphabet, Count, Sequence, and Add. Provides practice with the alphabet, upper- and lower-case letters, counting (as high as 30), number sequence, counting by twos, threes, etc., and addition (sums up to 18). Offers good range in content and level of challenge.

Title: Kindermath II
Company: Houghton Mifflin Co.
Date: 1988
Price: $276.00
Age: 4-7
Computer: Apple (64K)
Conceptual Area: NB/1,2,3,4,5,8 CL/2 SP/8
■ Math fundamentals

Final Rating: 57 ******
User Friendliness: 65 *******
Educational Value: 70 *******
Instructional Design: 45 *****

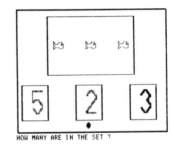

Comments: Ten disks cover 90 separate objectives, starting with "same" and "different" and ending with addition and subtraction problems with sums less than 10. Child uses joystick (required) to move cursor to correct answer. Keeps records. Requires adult setup and Echo synthesizer. Dry presentation.

Title: Knowing Numbers
Company: Mindscape, Inc.
Date: 1983
Price: $49.95
Age: 3-6
Computer: Apple
Conceptual Area: NB/1,3,7
■ Fundamental math skill practice

Final Rating: 67 *******
User Friendliness: 79 ********
Educational Value: 77 ********
Instructional Design: 53 *****

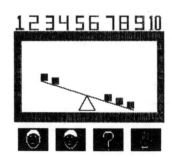

Comments: Presents counting, addition, and subtraction activities. Child uses nodding or shaking heads to decide (1) if a group matches a numeral, (2) which group has "more," and (3) if the sum of two groups equals a third. No reading. Some management.

LA = Language   CP = Creative projects   OT = Other topics   CL = Classification   SP = Spatial
relations   TI = Time   NB = Number   SE = Seriation   * = Version reviewed   NA = Not applicable

Title: Koala Pad Graphics Exhibitor
Company: PTI/Koala Industries
Date: 1983
Price: $139.50
Age: 5-up
Computer: Apple IIe*, II+, IBM
Conceptual Area: CP/1,4 SP/7
■ Drawing

Final Rating: 76 ********
User Friendliness: 85 *********
Educational Value: 74 *******
Instructional Design: 68 *******

Comments: This is the software that comes with the Koala Pad, which hooks into a joystick port. By moving finger or pointer across a pad surface, a child can draw lines, circles, or squares and fill or magnify shapes, using many available colors. Picture menu is usable but complex for young children. Price includes Koala Pad and program.

Title: Language
Company: Aquarius People Materials
Date: 1984
Price: $145.00
Age: 3-6
Computer: Apple*, TRS 80
Conceptual Area: LA/6
■ Language recognition

Final Rating: 37 ****
User Friendliness: 65 *******
Educational Value: 45 *****
Instructional Design: 18 **

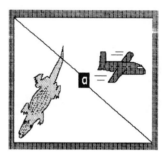

Comments: Child presses spacebar to advance through a fixed series of frames based on one to five language skills. Contains five disks. Easy to use, nice graphics. However, task allows no interaction except to proceed to next frame by pressing the spacebar.

Title: Language Experience Recorder Plus
Company: Teacher Support Software
Date: 1987
Price: $99.00
Age: 5-up
Computer: Apple
Conceptual Area: LA/1,2,3,4,5,9 OT/4
■ Word processing

Final Rating: 55 ******
User Friendliness: 33 ***
Educational Value: 75 ********
Instructional Design: 63 ******

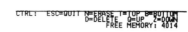

Comments: A large-print (20-column) word processor. Stories can be saved, analyzed for readability level, printed, or read back through an Echo or Slotbuster speech synthesizer. Two small-print (40- and 80-column) versions are included. Adult help required to use menus.

LA = Language   CP = Creative projects   OT = Other topics   CL = Classification   SP = Spatial relations   TI = Time   NB = Number   SE = Seriation   * = Version reviewed   NA = Not applicable

Title: Learn the Alphabet

Company: Spinnaker Software Corp.

Date: 1985

Price: $9.95

Age: 4-8

Computer: Apple*, IBM, C64 (cartridge)

Conceptual Area: LA/4,5 CL/2 SP/4

■ Upper/lower case, alphabetical order

Final Rating: 56 ****
User Friendliness: 64 ******
Educational Value: 49 *****
Instructional Design: 54 *******

Comments: Child uses arrow keys or joystick to match letters to complete an alphabetical sequence or simple words. Eight levels, ranging from matching one letter to completing a word. Somewhat confusing graphics.

Title: Learning About Numbers

Company: C&C Software

Date: 1983

Price: $50.00

Age: 3-6

Computer: Apple

Conceptual Area: NB/8 TI/9

■ Counting, clocks, basic math facts

Final Rating: 78 ******
User Friendliness: 56 ******
Educational Value: 86 *********
Instructional Design: 91 ***********

Comments: Provides a variety of number experiences. Let's Count, Let's Tell Time, and Arithmetic Fun, all with varying difficulty levels. Many aspects of this program can be managed by an adult, due to a well-designed management system.

Title: Learning Line, The

Company: D.C. Heath & Company

Date: 1983

Price: $45.00

Age: 3-6

Computer: Apple

Conceptual Area: CL/1,2 LA/4

■ Matching

Final Rating: 62 ****
User Friendliness: 82 ********
Educational Value: 73 *******
Instructional Design: 39 ****

Comments: Child uses joystick or arrow keys to move monkey to correct option, either by direct match or by correct association (e.g., rain — umbrella). Limited amount of content. Easy to use. No reading required.

LA = Language   CP = Creative projects   OT = Other topics   CL = Classification   SP = Spatial relations   TI = Time   NB = Number   SE = Seriation   * = Version reviewed   NA = Not applicable

---

Title: Learning the Alphabet
Company: MicroEd, Inc.
Date: 1987
Price: $29.95
Age: 3-6
Computer: Amiga (512K)
Conceptual Area: LA/4
■ Matching letters, alphabetical order

Final Rating: 50 *****
User Friendliness: 49 *****
Educational Value: 52 *****
Instructional Design: 50 *****

Comments: Child is shown portion of the alphabet. By clicking the mouse, child selects matching letters, in order, from letters scattered on the screen. The computer says each letter and gives a feedback message in a fairly clear voice. Repetitive format causes children to lose interest.

Title: Learning With Fuzzywomp
Company: Sierra On-Line
Date: 1984
Price: $29.95
Age: 3-6
Computer: Apple*, C64
Conceptual Area: NB/3,4 CL/2
■ Counting, matching, num. order

Final Rating: 73 *******
User Friendliness: 80 ********
Educational Value: 79 ********
Instructional Design: 64 ******

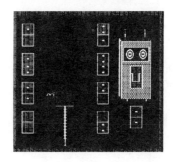

Comments: To make selections, child moves joystick to move "Fuzzywomp." Four entertaining games provide counting and matching experience. Three of the activities have multiple difficulty levels. No reading is required. Joystick required.

Title: Learning With Leeper
Company: Sierra On-Line
Date: 1983
Price: $29.95
Age: 3-6
Computer: Apple*, C64, Atari
Conceptual Area: CP/1 CL/2 NB/4
■ Counting, matching, drawing

Final Rating: 69 *******
User Friendliness: 78 ********
Educational Value: 82 ********
Instructional Design: 56 ******

Comments: Consists of four games based on matching, counting, and hand-eye coordination. A joystick is required to move "Leeper" around the screen to make selections. Designed to entertain and teach. Similar in format to "Learning With Fuzzywomp."

LA = Language   CP = Creative projects   OT = Other topics   CL = Classification   SP = Spatial
relations   TI = Time   NB = Number   SE = Seriation   * = Version reviewed   NA = Not applicable

Title: Let's Go Fishing
Company: Learning Technologies, Inc.
Date: 1985
Price: $24.95
Age: 3-6
Computer: Apple*, C64
Conceptual Area: NB/3 CL/2
- Counting and addition skills

Final Rating: 36 ****
User Friendliness: 51 *****
Educational Value: 51 *****
Instructional Design: 18 **

Comments: Two activities in which child uses A and Z keys and arrow keys to string pearls by moving a needle or to fish by lowering a line to fish swimming by. A specific number must be strung or caught. Design offers no escape from activities. Not recommended.

Title: Letter Games
Company: Island Software
Date: 1982
Price: $25.00
Age: 3-6
Computer: Apple
Conceptual Area: LA/4 CL/2
- Letter recognition

Final Rating: 34 ***
User Friendliness: 24 **
Educational Value: 40 ****
Instructional Design: 49 *****

Comments: Three drill games for letter discrimination. Upper- and lower-case options are available. No branching. Has errors if used without light pen. Not recommended.

Title: Letter Recognition
Company: Hartley Courseware, Inc.
Date: 1983
Price: $29.95
Age: 5-7
Computer: Apple
Conceptual Area: LA/4
- Location of letters on keyboard

Final Rating: 48 *****
User Friendliness: 40 ****
Educational Value: 62 ******
Instructional Design: 47 *****

Comments: A single letter is presented for child to find on keyboard. Model keyboard appears as help if needed, showing letter location. Options include upper/lower-case and number words. Records are kept.

LA = Language   CP = Creative projects   OT = Other topics   CL = Classification   SP = Spatial relations   TI = Time   NB = Number   SE = Seriation   * = Version reviewed   NA = Not applicable

---

Title: Letter-Go-Round
Company: Hi Tech Expressions
Date: 1984
Price: $34.95
Age: 3-7
Computer: C64* (cartridge), Atari
Conceptual Area: LA/4,5 TI/1,3
- Letter matching

Final Rating: 56 ******
User Friendliness: 61 ******
Educational Value: 71 *******
Instructional Design: 43 ****

Comments: Child presses spacebar to stop and start ferris wheel to match upper- and lower-case letters or to spell three-letter words. Good graphics and sounds. Menu requires reading. Includes keyboard overlay. Discontinued in 1986.

Title: Letters and First Words
Company: C&C Software
Date: 1984
Price: $60.00
Age: 3-6
Computer: Apple
Conceptual Area: LA/4,5,6
- Letters, initial consonants

Final Rating: 68 *******
User Friendliness: 55 ******
Educational Value: 72 *******
Instructional Design: 75 ********

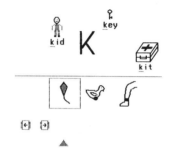

Comments: Three games: ABC, Letter Sounds, and Building Words. Management system allows for records for up to 50 children. Child makes selections by moving box cursor. Offers wide range of content and effective design features.

Title: Letters and Words
Company: Mindscape, Inc.
Date: 1983
Price: $39.95
Age: 3-6
Computer: Apple
Conceptual Area: LA/4,5
- Letter recognition, alphabet order

Final Rating: 68 *******
User Friendliness: 79 ********
Educational Value: 68 *******
Instructional Design: 60 ******

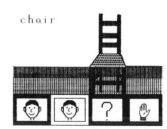

Comments: Three games on letters and words. Child selects Y, N, ?, or ESCAPE for each problem. Provides drill on alphabet order by asking what letter fits into a missing series. Management features: selection of number of rounds, performance summary, selection of timing of cursor movement, and new word list.

LA = Language   CP = Creative projects   OT = Other topics   CL = Classification   SP = Spatial
relations   TI = Time   NB = Number   SE = Seriation   * = Version reviewed   NA = Not applicable

Title: Letters for You
Company: Polarware, Inc.
Date: 1987
Price: $14.95
Age: 3-up
Computer: Apple* (128K), IBM, C64
Conceptual Area: CP/1,4 SP/4
■ Coloring pictures

Final Rating: 80 ********
User Friendliness: 79 ********
Educational Value: 73 *******
Instructional Design: 84 ********

Comments: A coloring program with 30 blank Muppets scenes. Child moves cursor with mouse, joystick, or arrow keys to fill in sections of a picture with 1 of 16 available colors. Prints in color. Mouse and color monitor recommended. Very easy to use. Prints picture with calendar.

Title: Lion's Workshop
Company: Learning Technologies, Inc.
Date: 1985
Price: $24.95
Age: 4-8
Computer: Apple*, C64
Conceptual Area: CL/2
■ Visual discrimination

Final Rating: 49 *****
User Friendliness: 49 *****
Educational Value: 54 *****
Instructional Design: 45 *****

PRESS SPACE BAR TO CHOOSE

Comments: Two activities: (1) Child uses A and Z keys to move conveyer belt to select an object that goes with another (e.g., thread/needle). (2) Child selects missing piece of a given object. Limited content. Confusing graphics.

Title: LOGO Power
Company: Mindscape, Inc.
Date: 1986
Price: $49.95
Age: 7-10
Computer: Apple
Conceptual Area: CP/3
■ Teach 12 basic LOGO commands

Final Rating: 59 ******
User Friendliness: 44 ****
Educational Value: 69 *******
Instructional Design: 65 *******

GIVE LOGO A COMMAND
TO FINISH THE BOX.
TYPE G TO GO ON   S TO STOP

Comments: One disk teaches a series of 11 step-by-step tutorial lessons and games designed to introduce and give practice with 12 LOGO commands, e.g., forward, right, repeat. A LOGO program disk is not included or needed to use this program.

LA = Language   CP = Creative projects   OT = Other topics   CL = Classification   SP = Spatial
relations   TI = Time   NB = Number   SE = Seriation   * = Version reviewed   NA = Not applicable

Title: Magic Crayon
Company: C&C Software
Date: 1983
Price: $45.00
Age: 4-6
Computer: Apple
Conceptual Area: CP/1,3,4 SP/11
▪ Drawing with arrow keys

Comments: A simple drawing program in 16 colors and 3 difficulty levels. Good recordkeeping and management are available to the teacher or parent. Stickers are included to label the keys.

Final Rating: 75 ********
User Friendliness: 53 *****
Educational Value: 67 *******
Instructional Design: 95 **********

Title: Magic Melody Box
Company: Human Touch, Inc.
Date: 1988
Price: $19.95
Age: 3-6
Computer: Atari
Conceptual Area: CP/2 SE/1
▪ Creating music

Comments: Child uses joystick to draw a melody line, to which the computer adds chords and replays. A three-octave major scale is available. A basic cartridge is required. Some reading required.

Final Rating: 59 ******
User Friendliness: 45 *****
Educational Value: 64 ******
Instructional Design: 64 ******

Title: Magic Slate
Company: Sunburst Communications, Inc.
Date: 1984
Price: $99.95
Age: 7-up
Computer: Apple
Conceptual Area: LA/4,9 CP/4 OT/3,4
▪ Word processing

Comments: Easy-to-use word processor with large (20-column) text and picture menu. Effective for experience stories for preschool level. Stories can be saved, printed, and edited. Graphics printer desirable.

Final Rating: 81 ********
User Friendliness: 70 *******
Educational Value: 92 *********
Instructional Design: 85 *********

```
Page 1 of DOG
---↓---|---1---↓---|---2
My dog likes to
play with me.  I
will throw a stick
or a ball and she
will get it.□
```

```
TYPEOVER
```

LA = Language   CP = Creative projects   OT = Other topics   CL = Classification   SP = Spatial
relations   TI = Time   NB = Number   SE = Seriation   * = Version reviewed   NA = Not applicable

Title: Magic String, The
Company: Troll Associates
Date: 1985
Price: $39.95
Age: 5-6
Computer: Apple
Conceptual Area: LA/11
■ Reading skills

Final Rating: 46 *****
User Friendliness: 52 *****
Educational Value: 46 *****
Instructional Design: 41 ****

Comments: Three activities: (1) Shows six words. Using spacebar, child arranges words in alphabetical order. (2) Child selects word that doesn't belong, e.g., "swan, duck, fail." (3) Child arranges letters to make words. Menus require reading, limiting child-control.

Title: Make a Match
Company: Springboard
Date: 1984
Price: $29.95
Age: 2.5-6
Computer: Apple*, IBM*, Atari
Conceptual Area: CL/1,2
■ Matching

Final Rating: 75 ********
User Friendliness: 82 ********
Educational Value: 73 *******
Instructional Design: 72 *******

Comments: Four matching activities in which the child presses spacebar to indicate when a match in color, shape. or size is made. Strong in content. Poor in presentation.

Title: Many Ways to Say I Love You
Company: Mindscape, Inc.
Date: 1985
Price: $29.95
Age: 4-up
Computer: Apple, C64*
Conceptual Area: CP/2,4 LA/3,4
■ Creative design

Final Rating: 69 *******
User Friendliness: 69 *******
Educational Value: 65 *******
Instructional Design: 69 *******

Comments: Child uses arrow keys or spacebar to select elements of own "greeting card," including text, background, borders, and characters. When finished, card message can be displayed with animation and music, then saved on disk.

LA = Language   CP = Creative projects   OT = Other topics   CL = Classification   SP = Spatial relations   TI = Time   NB = Number   SE = Seriation   * = Version reviewed   NA = Not applicable

Title: Mary Marvel . . . Costume Ball
Company: DIL International
Date: 1986
Price: $188.00
Age: 2-8
Computer: Apple
Conceptual Area: CL/2 SP/5 OT/1
■ Variety of basic skills

Final Rating: 62 ******
User Friendliness: 76 ********
Educational Value: 76 ********
Instructional Design: 43 ****

Comments: Six disks: Hot and Cold Food, Treasure Hunt/Voyage in Space, Sharp/Not Sharp, Occupations/Transportation, Ricochet's Costume, and Dress Ricochet. Provides simple, limited activities. Includes overlays to use with WonderWorker touch tablet (recommended).

Title: Mary Marvel . . . the Garden
Company: DIL International
Date: 1986
Price: $289.00
Age: 2-8
Computer: Apple
Conceptual Area: CL/1,2 SP/7 TI/6 OT/1
■ Functional intelligence, social skills

Final Rating: 62 ******
User Friendliness: 76 ********
Educational Value: 76 ********
Instructional Design: 43 ****

Comments: Ten disks — My Own Garden, Trees & Seasons, Gardening Tools, Parts of a Flower, Pollination, Water, Gardening, Growing a Bean Seed, Vegetables, and Flowers. Child presses overlay on WonderWorker touch tablet (recommended) to select answers, e.g., touches the autumn background when shown an autumn tree.

Title: Mask Parade
Company: Springboard
Date: 1984
Price: $39.95
Age: 4-12
Computer: Apple*, IBM, C64
Conceptual Area: CP/1,4 SP/5,7
■ Creative design

Final Rating: 77 ********
User Friendliness: 75 ********
Educational Value: 86 *********
Instructional Design: 69 *******

Comments: Child can design and print masks and other cutouts. The design part requires choosing the components of the mask (eyes, nose, etc.). Easy to print, once printer is set up. Pictures can be saved on disk. No reading required. Will not print on the II GS.

LA = Language   CP = Creative projects   OT = Other topics   CL = Classification   SP = Spatial
relations   TI = Time   NB = Number   SE = Seriation   * = Version reviewed   NA = Not applicable

Title: Match-On-A-Mac
Company: Teach Yourself by Computer
Date: 1986
Price: $39.95
Age: 3-7
Computer: Mac
Conceptual Area: CL/2 NB/1,3,4 LA/4,5 SP/8
- Matching letters, shapes, numbers, words; mouse practice

Final Rating: 79 ********
User Friendliness: 82 ********
Educational Value: 83 ********
Instructional Design: 75 ********

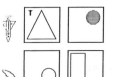

Comments: A multiple-choice program in which child matches shapes, upper- or lower-case letters, short words, the letters b and d, quantities, and numbers with quantities. Also has a game for practicing mouse use. Keeps records. Has a "lesson plan" feature whereby adult can determine the activities that appear. Easy to use.

Title: Math and Me
Company: Davidson and Associates, Inc.
Date: 1987
Price: $39.95
Age: 3-6
Computer: Apple* (128K), IBM, IIGS ($49.95)
Conceptual Area: NB/1,3,4,7 CL/2 SE/4
- Shapes, patterns, numbers, and addition

Final Rating: 78 ********
User Friendliness: 80 ********
Educational Value: 94 *********
Instructional Design: 67 *******

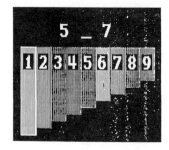

Comments: Twelve activities covering shape matching, number recognition, patterns, numerical order, and addition with objects or numbers. In each activity, child uses mouse (optional) or arrow keys to select 1 of 4 boxes in a multiple-choice format. Good design and graphics. Good range of content. Talking version for the IIGS gives verbal feedback.

Title: Math Concepts Level P
Company: IBM Educational Systems
Date: 1987
Price: $76.00
Age: 4-5
Computer: IBM
Conceptual Area: NB/1,3,4,6,7,8 CL/2 SE/3 SP/8
- Math concepts and symbols

Final Rating: 73 *******
User Friendliness: 43 ****
Educational Value: 88 *********
Instructional Design: 86 *********

Comments: The first in IBM's Math Concepts series, this program offers 4 units and 18 lessons that range from comparing sizes (child uses arrows to select largest picture to identify shapes.) Child first types in password for custom lesson. Keeps records. Offers many setup and teacher options. Wide range of content. Some reading required.

LA = Language   CP = Creative projects   OT = Other topics   CL = Classification   SP = Spatial relations   TI = Time   NB = Number   SE = Seriation   * = Version reviewed   NA = Not applicable

Title: Math Facts Level 1
Company: THESIS
Date: 1980
Price: $25.00
Age: 5-7
Computer: Apple
Conceptual Area: NB/1,4,5,8
■ Counting, numeral recognition

Comments: Presents a "workbook" context to the child, based on numerals and numeral words. Poorly designed. Not recommended.

Final Rating: 38 ****
User Friendliness: 41 ****
Educational Value: 33 ***
Instructional Design: 25 ***

Title: Math Magic
Company: MindPlay
Date: 1984
Price: $49.95
Age: 4-9
Computer: Apple*, IBM
Conceptual Area: NB/3
■ Math facts (add, sub., mult., div.)

Comments: A math game in which player deflects bouncing ball to break down a wall while periodically answering math problems to score points. Design options include paddle size, level and number of problems, and speed of ball.

Final Rating: 53 *****
User Friendliness: 53 *****
Educational Value: 67 *******
Instructional Design: 43 ****

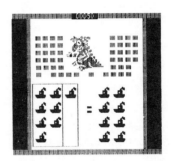

Title: Math Maze
Company: D.C. Heath & Company
Date: 1983
Price: $51.00
Age: 6-10
Computer: Apple*, IBM, Atari ($19.95), C64
Conceptual Area: NB/9
■ Basic math facts

Comments: Child moves fly through 1 of 40 simple mazes (can design own) to the correct answer, using a basic addition, subtraction, division, or multiplication fact. Available option turns spider loose in maze. A well-designed activity for basic facts practice.

Final Rating: 52 *****
User Friendliness: 47 *****
Educational Value: 62 ******
Instructional Design: 50 *****

LA = Language   CP = Creative projects   OT = Other topics   CL = Classification   SP = Spatial relations   TI = Time   NB = Number   SE = Seriation   * = Version reviewed   NA = Not applicable

Title: Math Rabbit
Company: The Learning Company
Date: 1986
Price: $39.95
Age: 5-7
Computer: Apple*, IBM
Conceptual Area: NB/1,3,4,8 OT/1
- Counting, matching sets, addition, subtraction

Comments: Enjoyable activities: child uses arrow keys, spacebar, and RETURN to count using a number line and musical scale; to match numerals; to match a set of objects or a math problem to a given number; to solve math problems to create number patterns; and to match sets of objects, numbers, and math problems. Four levels of play.

Final Rating: **78** ********
User Friendliness: **67** *******
Educational Value: **92** *********
Instructional Design: **79** ********

Title: Math Sequences
Company: Milliken Publishing Co.
Date: 1985
Price: $60.00
Age: 5-6
Computer: Apple
Conceptual Area: NB/3,8
- Number readiness

Comments: First of a 17-disk sequence spanning grades K-10 ($495 for all). Uses a flexible, powerful password system that can control content and keep records for up to 100 children. Children start by using number keys to count objects and can work up to numerical order, e.g., (6,___,8).

Final Rating: **69** *******
User Friendliness: **62** ******
Educational Value: **74** *******
Instructional Design: **69** *******

Title: Maze-o
Company: D.C. Heath & Company
Date: 1985
Price: $45.00
Age: 6-10
Computer: Apple
Conceptual Area: LA/5
- Spelling words

Comments: A spelling game that presents 10 out of 720 words at a time. Child earns points by moving a man (with joy stick, arrow keys) to incorrectly spelled words, thus working through simple maze. Moving through maze is slow. Content best-suited for grades 1 to 6.

Final Rating: **55** ******
User Friendliness: **55** ******
Educational Value: **57** ******
Instructional Design: **52** *****

LA = Language   CP = Creative projects   OT = Other topics   CL = Classification   SP = Spatial relations   TI = Time   NB = Number   SE = Seriation   * = Version reviewed   NA = Not applicable

Title: Memory Building Blocks
Company: Sunburst Communications, Inc.
Date: 1986
Price: $65.00
Age: 5-adult
Computer: Apple
Conceptual Area: OT/1 CL/2
■ Visual and auditory memory skills

Final Rating: 83 ********
User Friendliness: 83 ********
Educational Value: 85 *********
Instructional Design: 80 ********

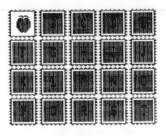

Box A and Box ?

Comments: Five Concentration-type games on one disk: Pictures, Words, Letters, Shapes, and Tunes. An easy-to-use management system allows use of own words or control over game difficulty. Minimal reading required. Operates with regular keyboard, Muppet keyboard, or Touch Window.

Title: Memory Master
Company: Stone & Associates
Date: 1985
Price: $39.95
Age: 2-6
Computer: IBM*, Atari ST
Conceptual Area: LA/5 OT/1
■ Memory skills

Final Rating: 56 ******
User Friendliness: 58 ******
Educational Value: 83 ********
Instructional Design: 41 ****

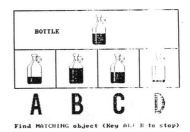

Find MATCHING object (Key A,/ B to stop)

Comments: Consists of three games in which child matches object with object, object with related object, or word with object. Also includes a picture Concentration game. Good graphics.

Title: Micro-LADS
Company: Laureate Learning Systems
Date: 1984
Price: $650.00
Age: 2-up
Computer: Apple
Conceptual Area: LA/1,8
■ Syntactic comprehension

Final Rating: 75 ********
User Friendliness: 85 *********
Educational Value: 65 *******
Instructional Design: 75 ********

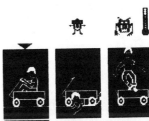

He is in the wagon.

Comments: Six disks covering grammatical constructions. Child hears sentence, e.g., "The dogs walk," and must pick correct picture (using spacebar). Keeps complete records. Adult must set up a lesson. Designed for learning disabled children. Requires an Echo speech synthesizer.

LA = Language   CP = Creative projects   OT = Other topics   CL = Classification   SP = Spatial
relations   TI = Time   NB = Number   SE = Seriation   * = Version reviewed   NA = Not applicable

Title: Microzine Jr. (Sept/Oct.'88)
Company: Scholastic Software, Inc.
Date: 1988
Price: $169.00 ($10 shipping)
Age: 6-9
Computer: Apple
Conceptual Area: CP/3,4 OT/1 CL/1 SP/5
■ Habitats, making masks, programming

Final Rating: 81 ********
User Friendliness: 73 *******
Educational Value: 87 *********
Instructional Design: 84 ********

Comments: A subscription series (five issues per year). Disks can be copied. This issue has five activities: Mask Maker — child makes masks which can be printed. Safari — child's decisions help animals survive. Eye Spy — a "which doesn't belong" activity. B.E.R.T. — child plays a question-and-answer game. Good design. Reading required.

Title: Milk Bottles
Company: Island Software
Date: 1982
Price: $25.00
Age: 3-6
Computer: Apple
Conceptual Area: NB/1
■ Comparing amounts

Final Rating: 39 ****
User Friendliness: 30 ***
Educational Value: 41 ****
Instructional Design: 45 *****

Comments: Four numbered areas with differing amounts of white represent milk in bottles. Child types number of cylinder or touches bottle with light pen to answer question that is written below, e.g., "Which is full?" Not recommended.

Title: Money Works
Company: MECC
Date: 1987
Price: $59.00
Age: 6-8
Computer: Apple (128K)
Conceptual Area: NB/1,3
■ Money skills

Final Rating: 76 ********
User Friendliness: 55 ******
Educational Value: 91 *********
Instructional Design: 88 *********

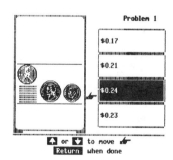

Comments: Four activities on one disk. Child uses arrows keys, ESCAPE, and RETURN to decide how much money is in a safe, count out an amount with a change machine, or make and print currency. Offers many teacher options. Correlates with many textbooks. Good child-control. The best money program we've seen.

LA = Language   CP = Creative projects   OT = Other topics   CL = Classification   SP = Spatial
relations   TI = Time   NB = Number   SE = Seriation   * = Version reviewed   NA = Not applicable

Title: Monkey Math
Company: Artworx
Date: 1983
Price: $19.95
Age: 4-10
Computer: Apple*, C64, Atari
Conceptual Area: NB/4
■ Basic math facts, numerical order

Final Rating: 49 *****
User Friendliness: 38 ****
Educational Value: 53 *****
Instructional Design: 43 ****

Comments: Provides drill and practice with math facts. Monkey knocks out correct answers on an assembly line to earn bananas and beat the clock. Practice with basic math facts (four operations) available at three levels.

Title: Monsters and Make-Believe
Company: Learning Lab Software
Date: 1987
Price: $39.95
Age: 6-up
Computer: Apple*, Mac, IBM
Conceptual Area: CP/1 SP/4,5,7 LA/9
■ Creative writing, matching, spatial relations

Final Rating: 71 *******
User Friendliness: 59 ******
Educational Value: 74 *******
Instructional Design: 81 ********

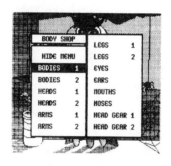

Comments: Using single-word menus to select background, head, body, arms, legs, mouth, nose, and hair, child uses spacebar and RETURN to build a monster. Half page of small print (40-column) can be created as well. Stories and monsters can be saved or printed. A talking version with many more features will be released soon.

Title: Moptown Parade
Company: The Learning Company
Date: 1981
Price: $59.95 (school edition)
Age: 6-10
Computer: Apple*, IBM*, C64
Conceptual Area: CL/1,2,4 SE/4
■ Classification and seriation

Final Rating: 55 ******
User Friendliness: 51 *****
Educational Value: 81 ********
Instructional Design: 45 *****

TALL, FAT
RED OR BLUE? (R OR B)

Comments: Contains seven progressively harder attribute games. Effective in focusing child's attention on attributes and the logic of sets. Strong in content. However, requires reading for independent use. Color monitor required. School edition includes back-up disk, teacher's guide, blackline masters, and activity ideas.

LA = Language CP = Creative projects OT = Other topics CL = Classification SP = Spatial
relations TI = Time NB = Number SE = Seriation * = Version reviewed NA = Not applicable

Title: Mount Murdoch

Company: Kidsview Software, Inc.
Date: 1987
Price: $49.95 ($39.95 for C64)
Age: 5-up
Computer: Apple*, IBM, C64
Conceptual Area: LA/10
- Adventure game and word processor

Comments: An adventure game where child types simple commands (e.g., look, help, up) to get to Mount Murdoch. Uses large letters (19 across the screen). Permits the creation of custom games. Reading required.

Final Rating: 45 *****
User Friendliness: 40 ****
Educational Value: 34 ***
Instructional Design: 53 *****

R03

```
DENSE FOREST

THE TREES CLOSE IN
ON YOU AND ALL
DIRECTIONS LOOK THE
SAME.  A CHILLING
MIST SEEMS TO CLAW
AT YOU - IT IS
GETTING DARK.
```

Title: Mr. and Mrs. Potato Head

Company: Random House Software
Date: 1985
Price: $29.95
Age: 3-8
Computer: Apple
Conceptual Area: SP/1,2,5 CP/3,4 OT/1
- Creative projects, imagination, memory skills

Comments: Child uses arrow keys or joystick to animate an existing potato character. Also can create own potato character. A Simon-Says memory game is included on the back of the disk. Attractive graphics. Minimal reading required, e.g., "press return." Color monitor recommended. No printing capacity.

Final Rating: 71 *******
User Friendliness: 58 ******
Educational Value: 84 ********
Instructional Design: 73 *******

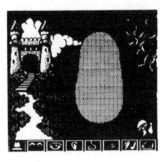

Title: Muppet Slate

Company: Sunburst Communications, Inc.
Date: 1988
Price: $65.00
Age: 5-7
Computer: Apple
Conceptual Area: LA/9 OT/4
- Language experiences

Comments: A large-letter word processor with 126 pictures that can be added to the story. Stories can be saved and printed with 10 borders. Not good for long stories. Options allow teacher control. Can be used with Muppet Learning Keys.

Final Rating: 88 *********
User Friendliness: 73 *******
Educational Value: 93 *********
Instructional Design: 98 **********

WARREN

I like to run
with my 🐕. It
is fun to run!

LA = Language   CP = Creative projects   OT = Other topics   CL = Classification   SP = Spatial
relations   TI = Time   NB = Number   SE = Seriation   * = Version reviewed   NA = Not applicable

Title: Muppet Word Book
Company: Sunburst Communications, Inc.
Date: 1986
Price: $65.00
Age: 3-6
Computer: Apple
Conceptual Area: LA/4,6 CL/1,2
■ Letters and words

Final Rating: 82 ********
User Friendliness: 85 *********
Educational Value: 92 *********
Instructional Design: 73 *******

Comments: Six games on one disk provide
practice with letters, upper/lower-case matching,
beginning consonants, and word endings. The
final activity is a simple word processor using
large letters that can be printed. Can be used
with a mouse, Touch Window, Muppet Learning
Keys, or regular keyboard.

Title: Muppets On Stage
Company: Sunburst Communications, Inc.
Date: 1984
Price: $65.00
Age: 3-6
Computer: Apple*, IBM, C64
Conceptual Area: LA/4 NB/4
■ Counting skills, letter recognition

Final Rating: 73 *******
User Friendliness: 73 *******
Educational Value: 77 ********
Instructional Design: 69 *******

Comments: Three games: Discovery, Letters, and
Numbers. Provides experience with letters, colors,
numerals, and number. Well-designed. Is effective
in giving child-control. This is the program that
comes with the Muppet Learning Keys, although
it can be used with a regular keyboard.

Title: Muppetville
Company: Sunburst Communications, Inc.
Date: 1986
Price: $65.00
Age: 4-6
Computer: Apple
Conceptual Area: CL/2 NB/3,4 OT/1
■ Classifying, memory skills

Final Rating: 87 *********
User Friendliness: 94 *********
Educational Value: 95 **********
Instructional Design: 75 ********

Comments: Six activities on one disk, starring
the Muppets. Menu design allows child-control.
Supports Touch Window (used for review), Muppet
Learning Keys, mouse, or keyboard. Gives practice
with shapes, colors, and numbers. Options allow for
several difficulty settings.

LA = Language   CP = Creative projects   OT = Other topics   CL = Classification   SP = Spatial
relations   TI = Time   NB = Number   SE = Seriation   * = Version reviewed   NA = Not applicable

Title: Music
Company: Lawrence Hall of Science
Date: 1984
Price: $34.95
Age: 4-6
Computer: Apple
Conceptual Area: CP/2 SE/1,4
■ Seriation of pitch

Final Rating: 59 ******
User Friendliness: 63 ******
Educational Value: 70 *******
Instructional Design: 51 *****

Comments: Make Music, Note Sandwich, and Play a Tune give experience with an eight-tone C-scale, associating notes with numbers and colored bars of correlated lengths. Limited in content. Design is effective in giving child-control.

Title: Music Maestro
Company: Springboard
Date: 1984
Price: $34.95
Age: 4-10
Computer: Apple*, IBM, C64, Atari
Conceptual Area: CP/2 SE/1 TI/4
■ Practice with musical notation

Final Rating: 73 *******
User Friendliness: 68 *******
Educational Value: 83 ********
Instructional Design: 71 *******

Comments: Four games in which children play and record tunes, using number keys on keyboard, thus building a correlation between numbers and notes. Kaleidoscope (game 4) adds random color to the notes.

Title: My ABC's
Company: Paperback Software
Date: 1984
Price: $24.95
Age: 3-7
Computer: IBM
Conceptual Area: LA/4 NB/3 OT/1
■ Letter and numeral recognition

Final Rating: 63 ******
User Friendliness: 67 *******
Educational Value: 91 *********
Instructional Design: 45 *****

Comments: Six activities: First Letter, Match Letters, Dancing Letters (any key pressed makes pictures dance on the screen), Counting Objects, and a multilevel game of Concentration. Good child-control. Good graphics. A good all-purpose program for IBM PC owners.

LA = Language   CP = Creative projects   OT = Other topics   CL = Classification   SP = Spatial relations   TI = Time   NB = Number   SE = Seriation   * = Version reviewed   NA = Not applicable

Title: My Book
Company: BeCi Software
Date: 1984
Price: $34.95
Age: 4-up
Computer: C64*, Atari
Conceptual Area: LA/9
▪ Writing stories

Final Rating: 38 ****
User Friendliness: 27 ***
Educational Value: 39 ****
Instructional Design: 46 *****

Comments: A picture- and text-creation program. Child uses joystick to move a balloon to select objects and options. Text is added using keyboard. Stories can be saved and printed. Reading required to select options. Joystick required.

Title: My Letters, Numbers, and Words
Company: Stone & Associates
Date: 1983
Price: $39.95
Age: 2-6
Computer: IBM*, Apple, Atari ST
Conceptual Area: LA/5
▪ Letter recognition

Final Rating: 46 *****
User Friendliness: 35 ****
Educational Value: 79 ********
Instructional Design: 38 ****

Comments: Practice with words, the numbers 1-10, key location, and letters, all reinforced through well-designed graphics and sounds. Design requires adult to start and stop the program, however. This program has later version called "Kid's Stuff" with better design features.

Title: My Words
Company: Hartley Courseware, Inc.
Date: 1987
Price: $69.95
Age: 5-8
Computer: Apple (64K)
Conceptual Area: LA/2,3,4,5,9 CP/4
▪ Language experience

Final Rating: 78 ********
User Friendliness: 60 ******
Educational Value: 92 *********
Instructional Design: 89 *********

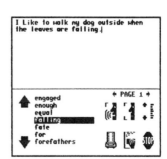

Comments: A talking word processor that keeps a list of every word used in a story. Lists can be stored, printed, and used again for other writing activities. While words are typed, they are also spoken in robotic voice (Echo speech synthesizer required). A mouse is recommended. Uses small (40-column) print.

LA = Language   CP = Creative projects   OT = Other topics   CL = Classification   SP = Spatial relations   TI = Time   NB = Number   SE = Seriation   * = Version reviewed   NA = Not applicable

Title: New Talking Stickybear ABC's, The
Company: Weekly Reader Software
Date: 1988
Price: $49.95
Age: 3-6
Computer: IIGS (512K)
Conceptual Area: LA/4,5
■ Letter recognition

Final Rating: 64 ******
User Friendliness: 46 *****
Educational Value: 73 *******
Instructional Design: 74 *******

Comments: Three activities come on two 3.5-inch disks: Alphabet — press any letter key to hear the letter and see an animated letter-related scene. There are 52 scenes available. Letter Hunt — child hears letter and must find it to see a picture. Fast Letters — press any letter key to hear the name. Uses internal IIGS speech synthesizer. Clear graphics.

Title: Not Too Messy, Not Too Neat
Company: D.C. Heath & Company
Date: 1988
Price: $75.00
Age: 5-10
Computer: Apple
Conceptual Area: LA/2,3,5,9 CP/4 SP/4,7
■ Language experience

Final Rating: 89 *********
User Friendliness: 85 *********
Educational Value: 94 *********
Instructional Design: 91 *********

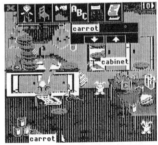

Comments: Children use mouse, Koala Pad, joystick, or arrow keys to select or move objects, backgrounds, words, or characters of a story. They can also add their own words. Resulting stories can be saved and printed in color. Includes four copies of the storybook. Good design. Fun to use.

Title: Notable Phantom, The
Company: DesignWare, Inc.
Date: 1984
Price: $9.95
Age: 5-10
Computer: Apple*, IBM, C64
Conceptual Area: SE/1 CP/2
■ Musical notation, pitch recognition

Final Rating: 66 *******
User Friendliness: 68 *******
Educational Value: 80 ********
Instructional Design: 56 ******

Comments: Uses a plastic overlay to simulate a full 1½ octave keyboard for use with three activities. Effective in teaching note names and for playing and recording songs in a game context. Main menu is confusing, may require adult help to start younger child.

LA = Language CP = Creative projects OT = Other topics CL = Classification SP = Spatial relations TI = Time NB = Number SE = Seriation * = Version reviewed NA = Not applicable

Title: Now You See It, Now You Don't
Company: Sunburst Communications, Inc.
Date: 1987
Price: $75.00
Age: 8-11
Computer: Apple
Conceptual Area: OT/1 CL/2,4,5 SP/4,8
■ Memory skills

Final Rating: 79 ********
User Friendliness: 72 *******
Educational Value: 91 *********
Instructional Design: 77 ********

Comments: Child uses keyboard, Touch Window, or Muppet keyboard to select answers. On disk 1, child is shown a set of objects to memorize, and then must identify one of the objects on disk 2, child sees picture with, then without, one or more of its objects, and must identify what's missing. Some reading required.

Study the picture.
Touch HERE to go on.

Title: Number BeCi
Company: BeCi Software
Date: 1983
Price: $19.95
Age: 3-6
Computer: C64*, VIC 20
Conceptual Area: NB/3
■ Grouping and counting

Final Rating: 29 ***
User Friendliness: 34 ***
Educational Value: 40 ****
Instructional Design: 20 **

Comments: Consists of a timed counting activity in which a child counts like or unlike objects. Three levels of difficulty available. Designed for low capacity (memory) computers. Available on cassette.

Title: Number Farm
Company: DLM
Date: 1984
Price: $32.95
Age: 3-6
Computer: Apple*, C64, IBM
Conceptual Area: NB/3,4,5,8
■ Counting skills

Final Rating: 78 ********
User Friendliness: 67 *******
Educational Value: 92 *********
Instructional Design: 79 ********

Comments: Six entertaining games present multiple counting experiences. Feedback is effective. One game presents counting in a unique way by having child count sounds. Provides good number practice.

LA = Language   CP = Creative projects   OT = Other topics   CL = Classification   SP = Spatial relations   TI = Time   NB = Number   SE = Seriation   * = Version reviewed   NA = Not applicable

Title: Numbers
Company: Lawrence Hall of Science
Date: 1984
Price: $34.95
Age: 4-6
Computer: Apple
Conceptual Area: NB/3,4,8
- Numeral disc., counting

Final Rating: 58 ******
User Friendliness: 65 *******
Educational Value: 79 ********
Instructional Design: 41 ****

Comments: Provides two activities: Balloons — lets the child pop balloons in relation to a number on the keyboard, using spacebar and RETURN. Secret Numbers — reveals parts of numerals for the child to identify. Well-designed. Best for kindergarten.

Title: Numbers Count
Company: Polarware, Inc.
Date: 1987
Price: $14.95
Age: 3-up
Computer: Apple* (128K), IBM, C64
Conceptual Area: CP/1,4 SP/4
- Coloring pictures

Final Rating: 80 ********
User Friendliness: 79 ********
Educational Value: 73 *******
Instructional Design: 84 ********

Comments: A coloring program with 30 number pictures. Child moves cursor with mouse, joystick, or arrow keys to fill in sections of a picture with 1 of 16 available colors. Prints in color. Mouse and color monitor recommended. Very easy to use. Prints picture with calendar.

Title: Observation and Classif.
Company: Hartley Courseware, Inc.
Date: 1985
Price: $35.95
Age: 3-5
Computer: Apple
Conceptual Area: CL/1,2,4
- Classification skills

Final Rating: 80 ********
User Friendliness: 70 *******
Educational Value: 86 *********
Instructional Design: 86 *********

Comments: Three activities. Child selects which object is different from others, which is the same size as one shown, or which belongs to the same class as a group shown, e.g., "all animals." Teacher options allow control over sound, movement of cursor, and number of plays per game. Child selects own difficulty level.

LA = Language   CP = Creative projects   OT = Other topics   CL = Classification   SP = Spatial
relations   TI = Time   NB = Number   SE = Seriation   * = Version reviewed   NA = Not applicable

Title: Odd One Out
Company: Sunburst Communications, Inc.
Date: 1983
Price: $65.00
Age: 3-10
Computer: Apple*, C64
Conceptual Area: CL/1,2,4
■ Matching/discrimination

Comments: Consists of five games based on format of selecting 1 of 4 boxes that doesn't belong. Child presses first letter of the color of the box containing the odd shape, e.g., B for blue. Content accessible to teacher.

Final Rating: 74 *******
User Friendliness: 58 ******
Educational Value: 84 ********
Instructional Design: 83 ********

Which one?
Please type: P for ☐   G for ☐
B for ☐   O for ☐

Title: Ollie and Seymour
Company: Hartley Courseware, Inc.
Date: 1984
Price: $49.95
Age: 3-up
Computer: Apple
Conceptual Area: CL/2 SP/4,6,8 TI/1 OT/1
■ Pedestrian safety, readiness skills

Comments: A unique simulation in which child uses arrow keys to move "Ollie" around a park and through the streets, where he can practice safe street crossings, obeying traffic signals, or games. Games involve shape and color matching, Concentration with traffic signs, and stacking and counting blocks.

Final Rating: 77 ********
User Friendliness: 85 *********
Educational Value: 75 ********
Instructional Design: 71 *******

Title: Ollie Finds It
Company: S.R.A.
Date: 1985
Price: $49.95
Age: 3-6
Computer: Apple
Conceptual Area: CL/2 LA/4
■ Matching shapes, letters, and words

Comments: One disk, eight worksheets, and a certificate of completion. Four lessons arranged from easy to hard. Child uses arrows to move a cursor to match objects. Criteria for success can be adjusted. Clear graphics, no sounds. Rather dry presentation. Keeps records.

Final Rating: 64 ******
User Friendliness: 54 *****
Educational Value: 82 ********
Instructional Design: 62 ******

LA = Language   CP = Creative projects   OT = Other topics   CL = Classification   SP = Spatial
relations   TI = Time   NB = Number   SE = Seriation   * = Version reviewed   NA = Not applicable

SOFTWARE DESCRIPTIONS

Title: Ollie Hears and Sequences
Company: S.R.A.
Date: 1985
Price: $49.95
Age: 3-up
Computer: Apple
Conceptual Area: CL/2 OT/1
■ Auditory memory skills

Final Rating: 64 ******
User Friendliness: 54 *****
Educational Value: 82 ********
Instructional Design: 62 ******

Comments: Two or three objects or letters are named (e.g., pair and lightbulb) and child uses arrows and RETURN to select the corresponding pictures in correct order. Adult can select criteria for success. Records if a child passes or fails. Contains 30 pictures. Uses a clear voice. Echo speech synthesizer is required. Dry presentation.

Title: Ollie Remembers It
Company: S.R.A.
Date: 1985
Price: $49.95
Age: 3-6
Computer: Apple
Conceptual Area: OT/1 CL/2
■ Visual Memory

Final Rating: 64 ******
User Friendliness: 54 *****
Educational Value: 82 ********
Instructional Design: 62 ******

Comments: Shows child up to three objects or letters for 1–10 seconds, then covers them up. Child must use the arrows to select those same objects from another set. Keeps success/failure records. Dry presentation. Adult can set difficulty level. Includes demonstration, practice, and test modes.

Title: Once Upon a Time . . .
Company: Compu-Teach
Date: 1987
Price: $39.95
Age: 6-12
Computer: IBM* (256K), Apple (128K), Mac
Conceptual Area: LA/1,3,4,5,8,9
■ Language experience, creation of storybooks

Final Rating: 59 ******
User Friendliness: 29 ***
Educational Value: 62 ******
Instructional Design: 85 *********

Comments: Consists of three sets of about 30 objects from the farm, safari, or main street. Child creates picture by typing the names of objects and moving them with the arrow keys). Pictures can be printed or saved. Reading required. Includes colored pencil set. Design could be improved.

LA = Language   CP = Creative projects   OT = Other topics   CL = Classification   SP = Spatial relations   TI = Time   NB = Number   SE = Seriation   * = Version reviewed   NA = Not applicable

Title: One Banana More
Company: Data Command
Date: 1984
Price: $39.95
Age: 5-6
Computer: Apple
Conceptual Area: CL/2 NB/1 LA/4,5
■ Reading readiness, counting

Final Rating: 34 ***
User Friendliness: 37 ****
Educational Value: 42 ****
Instructional Design: 26 ***

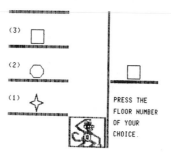

Comments: Six multiple-choice activities in which a child sees an object and presses the numeral of a matching shape, letter, size, word, number, or set, depending on the level selected. Bananas are rewards. No escape. Menu requires reading.

Title: Ordering/Sequencing
Company: Aquarius People Materials
Date: 1984
Price: $115.00
Age: 3-6
Computer: Apple*, TRS80
Conceptual Area: SE/2
■ Seriation concepts

Final Rating: 38 ****
User Friendliness: 69 *******
Educational Value: 41 ****
Instructional Design: 20 **

Comments: Set of four disks. Good graphics, content. However, design is similar to book format. Child presses spacebar to advance to next display with no interaction. No random generation or branching.

Title: Paint With Words
Company: MECC
Date: 1986
Price: $59.00
Age: 3-7
Computer: Apple (64K)
Conceptual Area: LA/5 CP/1,4
■ Word recognition

Final Rating: 73 *******
User Friendliness: 63 ******
Educational Value: 91 *********
Instructional Design: 69 *******

Comments: Using mouse, joystick, or keyboard, child creates a scene by moving 1 of 8 words to a spot on the screen, where it becomes a picture that is a part of the scene. Scenes can be printed, saved, or changed. Twelve word-sets can be created from 124 words. Ufonic speech synthesizer (optional) will say words.

LA = Language   CP = Creative projects   OT = Other topics   CL = Classification   SP = Spatial
relations   TI = Time   NB = Number   SE = Seriation   * = Version reviewed   NA = Not applicable

Title: Pals Around Town
Company: CBS Software
Date: 1985
Price: $14.95
Age: 4-6
Computer: C64*, IBM, Apple
Conceptual Area: SP/4,6,7
■ Community Exploration

Final Rating: 73 *******
User Friendliness: 76 ********
Educational Value: 73 *******
Instructional Design: 69 *******

Comments: Child uses joystick (required) and function keys to explore and add objects to 1 of 5 scenes, e.g., a playground, a schoolroom, Sesame Street, Bert and Ernie's house, and downtown. Good graphics and sound. Disk version takes about three minutes to load. Color monitor recommended.

Title: Path-Tactics
Company: MECC
Date: 1986
Price: $59.00
Age: 5-11
Computer: Apple*, IBM, C64
Conceptual Area: NB/3,5,6
■ Counting, basic math facts

Final Rating: 69 *******
User Friendliness: 50 *****
Educational Value: 91 *********
Instructional Design: 72 *******

Comments: A strategy game in which child does a math problem to decide how many steps a robot must move to get to a finish point in the least amount of steps. Levels range from counting to division (e.g., 63 / __ = 7). Teacher options allow control over presentation of content. Child can play against partner or computer. Enjoyable program.

Title: Patterns
Company: MECC
Date: 1988
Price: $59.00
Age: 5-6
Computer: Apple
Conceptual Area: CL/1,2 SE/1,2 CP/1
■ Pattern recognition: shapes, sounds, movements

Final Rating: 79 ********
User Friendliness: 73 *******
Educational Value: 94 *********
Instructional Design: 75 ********

Comments: Three activities that give practice with static, sound, or animated patterns. A fourth activity allows the creation of pattern designs. Teacher options allow modification of content. Good design, child-control, and range of content.

LA = Language   CP = Creative projects   OT = Other topics   CL = Classification   SP = Spatial relations   TI = Time   NB = Number   SE = Seriation   * = Version reviewed   NA = Not applicable

Title: Patterns and Sequences
Company: Hartley Courseware, Inc.
Date: 1984
Price: $35.95
Age: 3-6
Computer: Apple
Conceptual Area: CL/1 SE/1
■ Matching/discrimination

Final Rating: 72 *******
User Friendliness: 87 *********
Educational Value: 83 ********
Instructional Design: 48 *****

Comments: Contains four clearly designed activities that provide large objects, positive feedback, and multiple skill levels. No reading required.

Title: Peanuts Maze Marathon
Company: Random House Software
Date: 1984
Price: $39.95
Age: 4-8
Computer: Apple*, C64, IBM
Conceptual Area: TI/4 SP/4
■ Problem solving (mazes)

Final Rating: 46 *****
User Friendliness: 45 *****
Educational Value: 50 *****
Instructional Design: 46 *****

Comments: Peanuts cartoons animate themselves after the completion of simple maze. Use with the keyboard is not smooth; a joystick is recommended. Time is kept for each maze.

Title: Peanuts Picture Puzzlers
Company: Random House Software
Date: 1984
Price: $39.95
Age: 4-8
Computer: Apple*, C64, IBM
Conceptual Area: SP/1
■ Problem solving (puzzles)

Final Rating: 59 ******
User Friendliness: 44 ****
Educational Value: 51 *****
Instructional Design: 74 *******

Comments: Presents a picture to the child, then makes a puzzle by dividing it into sections. After the child puts all the pieces into the puzzle, the picture becomes animated. Entertaining program. Could be difficult for 4-year-olds to operate, however.

LA = Language   CP = Creative projects   OT = Other topics   CL = Classification   SP = Spatial relations   TI = Time   NB = Number   SE = Seriation   * = Version reviewed   NA = Not applicable

Title: Peter and the Wolf Music
Company: Spinnaker Software Corp.
Date: 1985
Price: $39.95
Age: 3-7
Computer: Apple*, C64 ($24.95)
Conceptual Area: CL/2 SE/1,2,4 OT/1
■ Music skills: pitch and melody

Final Rating: 77 ********
User Friendliness: 83 ********
Educational Value: 95 **********
Instructional Design: 62 ******

Comments: Child uses joystick or arrows keys in six music games and one exploratory activity. Gives practice distinguishing tones, ordering notes according to pitch, and re-creating simple melodies. Good design. Fun to use.

Title: Peter Rabbit Reading
Company: Spinnaker Software Corp.
Date: 1985
Price: $39.95
Age: 3-6
Computer: Apple*, C64
Conceptual Area: LA/4,5,6 TI/6
■ Letters, letter sounds, and words

Final Rating: 79 ********
User Friendliness: 70 *******
Educational Value: 94 *********
Instructional Design: 76 ********

Comments: Child uses arrows keys or joystick to move Peter to his home. On the way, Peter matches letters, sounds, and vowels. Contains four levels. Clear graphics, enjoyable activities. In some games, words are "spoken," but voice is hard to understand (extra synthesizer not required).

Title: Peter's Growing Patterns
Company: Strawberry Hill Software
Date: 1985
Price: $19.00
Age: 5-up
Computer: Apple
Conceptual Area: SE/1,2,3,4 CL/6 SP/9 NB/5 CP/4
■ Pattern recognition

Final Rating: 73 *******
User Friendliness: 69 *******
Educational Value: 91 *********
Instructional Design: 64 ******

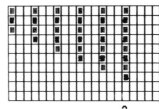

Comments: Six activities that range in difficulty and present visual and numerical patterns. Child uses joystick or keyboard to select or construct the next member of a given sequence. Teacher's edition ($55.00) includes many classroom activities. "U-Design-It" feature allows creation of new pattern problems.

LA = Language   CP = Creative projects   OT = Other topics   CL = Classification   SP = Spatial
relations   TI = Time   NB = Number   SE = Seriation   * = Version reviewed   NA = Not applicable

Title: Picture Dictionary
Company: D.C. Heath & Company
Date: 1985
Price: $45.00
Age: 5-7
Computer: Apple
Conceptual Area: LA/4 OT/1
■ Word recall and memory

Final Rating: 53 *****
User Friendliness: 63 ******
Educational Value: 73 *******
Instructional Design: 35 ****

Comments: Allows the association of pictures with words, based on initial consonants. Child can choose picture or type word. Own pictures and words can be added, although the process is difficult. Uses lower-case letters only. Discontinued in 1988.

Title: Picture Perfect
Company: MindPlay
Date: 1984
Price: $49.95
Age: 4-up
Computer: Apple*, IBM
Conceptual Area: CP/1 LA/3
■ Draw, color, and write

Final Rating: 79 ********
User Friendliness: 82 ********
Educational Value: 77 ********
Instructional Design: 75 ********

Comments: Child uses joystick or mouse to draw points, lines, or boxes and to write text. Features include a 72-picture library, five color selections, and drawing tool options. Drawing requires going between two screens, which is difficult for young children. Pictures can be saved and printed.

Title: Pictures, Letters, and Sounds
Company: Hartley Courseware, Inc.
Date: 1986
Price: $35.95
Age: 5-6
Computer: Apple
Conceptual Area: LA/4,5
■ Letter recognition

Final Rating: 78 ********
User Friendliness: 63 ******
Educational Value: 91 *********
Instructional Design: 82 ********

Comments: Five games offer a range of activity. Child can type using picture symbols for letters (e.g., Saw-S), pop balloons, or position X's or O's in a game of Tick-Tack-Toe. Design allows child-control.

LA = Language   CP = Creative projects   OT = Other topics   CL = Classification   SP = Spatial
relations   TI = Time   NB = Number   SE = Seriation   * = Version reviewed   NA = Not applicable

---

Title: Play Together Learn Together
Company: Grolier Electronic Publishing
Date: 1985
Price: $29.95
Age: 4-7
Computer: Apple*, IBM, C64
Conceptual Area: OT/2
■ Introduction to computer use

Final Rating: 44 ****
User Friendliness: 45 *****
Educational Value: 53 *****
Instructional Design: 38 ****

Comments: A 182-page book and disk designed for parents to use with their child to help both learn more about the computer. Has 36 activities covering such topics as the keyboard, moving the cursor, and simple programs written in BASIC. Ratings apply to the programs on the disk.

Title: Pockets and Her New Sneakers
Company: World Book, Inc.
Date: 1984
Price: $39.95
Age: 3-5
Computer: IBM
Conceptual Area: CL/2
■ Sorting and classification skills

Final Rating: 62 ******
User Friendliness: 70 *******
Educational Value: 84 ********
Instructional Design: 44 ****

Comments: Eight simple games in which children use spacebar, arrow keys and RETURN to match flowers, buttons, fish, toys, or shoes. Good sounds, graphics. Effective in giving child control. No CMI.

Title: Pockets Goes on a Picnic
Company: World Book, Inc.
Date: 1984
Price: $39.95
Age: 3-5
Computer: IBM
Conceptual Area: CL/2 SP/1
■ Classification, part/whole rel.

Final Rating: 61 ******
User Friendliness: 68 *******
Educational Value: 87 *********
Instructional Design: 43 ****

Comments: Six simple activities in which child uses spacebar and RETURN to put things together by category (e.g., food, toys) or to match parts of insects to make a whole. Successful in providing child-control. Good sounds and graphics. No CMI.

LA = Language   CP = Creative projects   OT = Other topics   CL = Classification   SP = Spatial relations   TI = Time   NB = Number   SE = Seriation   * = Version reviewed   NA = Not applicable

Title: Pockets Goes on Vacation
Company: World Book, Inc.
Date: 1984
Price: $39.95
Age: 3-5
Computer: IBM
Conceptual Area: SP/4
■ Positional relationships

Final Rating: 63 ******
User Friendliness: 74 *******
Educational Value: 80 ********
Instructional Design: 47 *****

Comments: Consists of one free-play and
five structured activities on positional relations.
Child uses arrow keys to move objects in/out,
above/below, left/right, etc. Menu gives
child-control.

Title: Pockets Goes to the Carnival
Company: World Book, Inc.
Date: 1984
Price: $39.95
Age: 3-5
Computer: IBM
Conceptual Area: NB/2,3 CP/2
■ Counting, 1-1 correspondence

Final Rating: 68 *******
User Friendliness: 81 ********
Educational Value: 85 *********
Instructional Design: 49 *****

Comments: Six simple games in which child uses
spacebar and RETURN to match balloons with
animals or count objects on the screen. One activity
allows a child to create tones with the number keys.
No CMI. Effective in permitting child-control.

Title: Pockets Leads the Parade
Company: World Book, Inc.
Date: 1984
Price: $39.95
Age: 3-5
Computer: IBM
Conceptual Area: CL/2 SE/2
■ Pattern recognition

Final Rating: 75 ********
User Friendliness: 81 ********
Educational Value: 96 **********
Instructional Design: 58 ******

Comments: Six games featuring (1) a dancing
bear whose movements can be controlled by
pressing any letter key and (2) various games
copying and recognizing patterns, using
spacebar and RETURN. Good graphics,
sound, content. Well-designed.

LA = Language   CP = Creative projects   OT = Other topics   CL = Classification   SP = Spatial
relations   TI = Time   NB = Number   SE = Seriation   * = Version reviewed   NA = Not applicable

Title: Preschool Disk 1
Company: Nordic Software
Date: 1986
Price: $39.95
Age: 3-7
Computer: Mac
Conceptual Area: LA/4 NB/3,8 CP/1
■ Letters, counting, alphabetical order

Final Rating: 62 ******
User Friendliness: 77 ********
Educational Value: 80 ********
Instructional Design: 40 ****

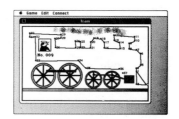

Comments: Three games: Alphaworks — child sees picture, hears the picture name and starting letter, and must press the letter key. Counting — shows up to 10 objects and number line. Child clicks the mouse on the number shown. Connect the Dots — child uses mouse to connect dots, using numbers or letters. Possible to create own puzzles. Gives verbal feedback.

Title: Preschool Disk 2
Company: Nordic Software
Date: 1986
Price: $39.95
Age: 3-7
Computer: Mac
Conceptual Area: CL/2 NB/3,7 OT/1
■ Matching, counting, adding, memory skills

Final Rating: 75 ********
User Friendliness: 82 ********
Educational Value: 86 *********
Instructional Design: 60 ******

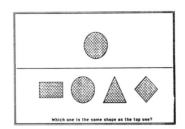

Comments: Four games: Shape Works — child clicks mouse to match shape shown. Can print worksheets. Bar Math — child counts two sets to get a total. A voice helps count. Tic-tac-toe — child plays against computer or another person. Concentration — a memory game with a 30- to 88-box grid. Many setup options available.

Title: Preschool Fun
Company: THESIS
Date: 1980
Price: $25.00
Age: 3-6
Computer: Apple
Conceptual Area: LA/4 CL/2 SP/4 NB/3
■ Counting, letters, & matching

Final Rating: 44 ****
User Friendliness: 38 ****
Educational Value: 45 *****
Instructional Design: 48 *****

Comments: Presents 11 games in which child must press Y or N to indicate a match. Offers a wide variety of content through simple graphics and sounds. Limited design offers little interaction.

LA = Language   CP = Creative projects   OT = Other topics   CL = Classification   SP = Spatial relations   TI = Time   NB = Number   SE = Seriation   * = Version reviewed   NA = Not applicable

Title: Preschool IQ Builder I
Company: PDI Software
Date: 1982
Price: $24.95
Age: 3-6
Computer: Apple*, C64, Atari, PET*
Conceptual Area: CL/2 LA/4
■ Concepts of same and different

Comments: Contains seven lessons in which the child presses the S or L key to indicate if the two objects on the screen are the same or different. Lessons range from colors (color monitor required) to letters. Provides little range of challenge or child-control.

Final Rating: 38 ****
User Friendliness: 35 ****
Educational Value: 51 *****
Instructional Design: 33 ***

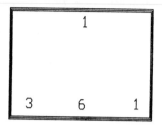

Title: Preschool IQ Builder II
Company: PDI Software
Date: 1984
Price: $24.95
Age: 3-6
Computer: Apple*, C64, PET, TI
Conceptual Area: CL/2 LA/5
■ Matching, shapes, numbers, letters

Comments: Contains six lessons all using same format of having model object at top of screen. To receive smile face, child uses spacebar and arrow keys to move model object to a matching mate at the screen bottom. Records are kept.

Final Rating: 43 ****
User Friendliness: 41 ****
Educational Value: 48 *****
Instructional Design: 42 ****

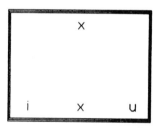

Title: Primary Editor Plus
Company: IBM Educational Systems
Date: 1988
Price: $100.00
Age: 5-up
Computer: IBM PS/2
Conceptual Area: LA/9 CP/1,4 OT/4
■ Word processing, drawing, making banners

Comments: Three programs: Picture Editor allows a child to draw in color, using arrows or mouse. Banner Maker prints banners in three different sizes of type. Primary Editor is a 40- or 80-column word processor with spell checker, eight screen colors, block move, copy and others. Menus and stories can be read aloud using the PS/2's built-in speech synthesizer.

Final Rating: 74 *******
User Friendliness: 60 ******
Educational Value: 83 ********
Instructional Design: 81 ********

LA = Language   CP = Creative projects   OT = Other topics   CL = Classification   SP = Spatial relations   TI = Time   NB = Number   SE = Seriation   * = Version reviewed   NA = Not applicable

Title: Print Shop, The
Company: Broderbund Software
Date: 1987
Price: $49.95 ($59.95 for IIGS)
Age: na
Computer: Apple, Mac, IBM, C64, Atari, IIGS*
Conceptual Area: CP/1,4
■ Creation of printed materials

Final Rating: 85 *********
User Friendliness: 88 *********
Educational Value: 66 *******
Instructional Design: 96 **********

Comments: An easy-to-use printing program that allows the creation of greeting cards, signs, letterheads, or banners. Includes 120 graphic elements. Includes 6 envelopes and 20 sheets of colored paper. Four Print Shop Graphics Libraries can be purchased separately for $24.95. Prints in color.

Title: Puss in Boot
Company: Island Software
Date: 1982
Price: $25.00
Age: 3-6
Computer: Apple
Conceptual Area: SP/4
■ Spatial concepts

Final Rating: 34 ***
User Friendliness: 33 ***
Educational Value: 33 ***
Instructional Design: 35 ****

Comments: Gives practice with 14 "positional concepts," such as below, above, in, out. Some concepts not presented accurately in a two-dimensional presentation. Limited content. Poorly designed. Not recommended.

Title: Puzzle Master
Company: Springboard
Date: 1984
Price: $34.95
Age: 4-up
Computer: Apple*, IBM, C64
Conceptual Area: SP/1,2 CP/1,4
■ Problem solving (puzzles)

Final Rating: 79 ********
User Friendliness: 72 *******
Educational Value: 91 *********
Instructional Design: 77 ********

Comments: Child uses joystick or arrow keys either to select 1 of 30 pictures or to create own, which can be scrambled and reassembled using icons. Offers hints if needed. Puzzles can be saved on disk. Child can select puzzles of varying difficulty (2-800 pieces). No reading required.

LA = Language   CP = Creative projects   OT = Other topics   CL = Classification   SP = Spatial
relations   TI = Time   NB = Number   SE = Seriation   * = Version reviewed   NA = Not applicable

Title: R.J.'s Switch Progressions
Company: R.J. Cooper & Associates
Date: 1987
Price: Free preview copy
Age: 2-up
Computer: Apple
Conceptual Area: TI/1,6
- Cause and effect, progressions

Final Rating: 65 *******
User Friendliness: 59 ******
Educational Value: 65 *******
Instructional Design: 69 *******

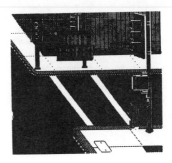

Comments: Child controls an eight-step animated sequence, such as crossing the street, by pressing a single switch or the open APPLE key. Sequences are getting up, a bird feeding, crossing the street, fireworks, making faces, catching the bus, and changing channels on a TV. Offers setup options. Menu requires reading.

Title: Rabbit Scanner, The
Company: E.C.S.
Date: 1986
Price: $29.95
Age: 2-5
Computer: Apple
Conceptual Area: TI/1,3 CL/2
- Eye tracking, matching

Final Rating: 67 *******
User Friendliness: 58 ******
Educational Value: 83 ********
Instructional Design: 64 ******

Comments: A simple program designed to provide practice scanning. Child watches a rabbit move across the screen and presses spacebar when the rabbit is over a carrot. Level of challenge can be adjusted by changing distractors, speed of rabbit, starting position. Requires adult setup.

Title: Race the Clock
Company: MindPlay
Date: 1984
Price: $49.95
Age: 5-12
Computer: Apple*, IBM
Conceptual Area: LA/5 OT/1
- Memory

Final Rating: 69 *******
User Friendliness: 57 ******
Educational Value: 72 *******
Instructional Design: 77 ********

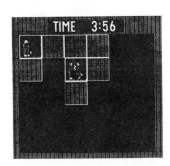

Comments: Concentration game with animated pictures. Child is given an amount of time to use joystick, mouse, paddles, or arrow keys to match pairs: picture/picture, picture/word, or word/word. Flexible design allows control of difficulty.

LA = Language   CP = Creative projects   OT = Other topics   CL = Classification   SP = Spatial
relations   TI = Time   NB = Number   SE = Seriation   * = Version reviewed   NA = Not applicable

Title: Rainbow Painter
Company: Springboard
Date: 1984
Price: $29.95
Age: 4-12
Computer: Apple*, C64
Conceptual Area: CP/1 SP/9
■ Drawing

Comments: Presents an electronic coloring book in which the colors can be selected and filled in. Menus are easy to use. A free-draw option contains "mirror drawing" activity. Offers range of activities that child can control.

Final Rating: 80 *******
User Friendliness: 80 *******
Educational Value: 73 *******
Instructional Design: 86 ********

Title: Rainy Day Games
Company: Baudville
Date: 1985
Price: $29.95
Age: 4-up
Computer: Apple*, C64, Atari, Mac
Conceptual Area: OT/1 CL/1,2
■ Memory practice

Comments: Contains three card games on one disk: Concentration, Old Maid, and Go Fish. Child uses mouse, joystick, arrow keys, or Koala Pad to move cards. Three difficulty levels offer a range in content. Well designed. Offers good level of child-control. Up to three players can play against the computer.

Final Rating: 83 *******
User Friendliness: 82 *******
Educational Value: 92 ********
Instructional Design: 79 *******

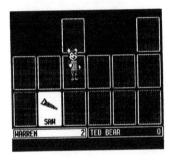

Title: Read, Write, & Publish 1
Company: D.C. Heath & Company
Date: 1988
Price: $99.00
Age: 6-up
Computer: Apple (128K)
Conceptual Area: LA/1,2,3,4,5,9 CP/1,4 SP/1,4
■ Word processing and story illustrating

Comments: Child uses keyboard or mouse to select and move objects, words, or characters and then write about them. Three two-sided disks contain eight story topics with pull-down menus that contain word files and over 35 theme-related objects each. Stories and pictures can be saved or printed in color. Story disks can be copied. Mouse recommended.

Final Rating: 81 *******
User Friendliness: 66 *******
Educational Value: 97 *********
Instructional Design: 87 ********

LA = Language   CP = Creative projects   OT = Other topics   CL = Classification   SP = Spatial
relations   TI = Time   NB = Number   SE = Seriation   * = Version reviewed   NA = Not applicable

Title: Reader Rabbit
Company: The Learning Company
Date: 1984
Price: $39.95
Age: 5-7
Computer: Apple*, IBM, C64, Apple IIGS
($59.95)
Conceptual Area: LA/4,5 OT/1
■ Basic reading skills/comprehension

Final Rating: 71 *******
User Friendliness: 59 ******
Educational Value: 87 *********
Instructional Design: 71 *******

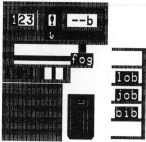

Comments: Four activities in which child uses spacebar, joystick, or paddles to match letters of C-V-C words, unscramble letters to create words, create word ladders, or play 1 of 7 levels of Concentration. Uses over 200 lower-case three-letter words. Apple IIGS version says words.

Title: Reading and Me
Company: Davidson and Associates, Inc.
Date: 1987
Price: $39.95
Age: 4-7
Computer: Apple* (128K), IBM, IIGS ($49.95)
Conceptual Area: CL/2,4 LA/4,5,6,7
■ Matching, classifying, recognizing letters & words

Final Rating: 79 ********
User Friendliness: 82 ********
Educational Value: 92 *********
Instructional Design: 65 *******

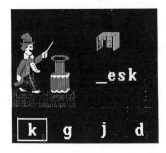

Comments: Twelve activities include matching shapes, letter recognition, upper/lower case, alphabetical order, rhyming words, picture/word matching and completing a sentence. In each, child uses mouse or arrow keys to select 1 of 4 boxes in a multiple-choice format. Good design. Talking version for IIGS gives spoken feedback.

Title: Reading Comprehension: Lev. 1
Company: Houghton Mifflin Co.
Date: 1988
Price: $174.00
Age: 6-7
Computer: Apple (64K)
Conceptual Area: LA/5,6,8
■ Reading comprehension skills

Final Rating: 82 ********
User Friendliness: 60 ******
Educational Value: 95 **********
Instructional Design: 86 *********

Comments: Child uses spacebar, arrow keys, and RETURN to page through a story in which comprehension questions are asked through an Echo speech synthesizer (required). Uses clear voice. To assist reading, child can select and listen to any word in the story. Sixteen stories come on eight disks. Keeps records. Good design.

LA = Language   CP = Creative projects   OT = Other topics   CL = Classification   SP = Spatial relations   TI = Time   NB = Number   SE = Seriation   * = Version reviewed   NA = Not applicable

Title: Reading Fun: Beg. Consonants
Company: Troll Associates
Date: 1985
Price: $39.95
Age: 5-6
Computer: Apple
Conceptual Area: LA/4,6
■ Beginning consonants

Final Rating: 56 ******
User Friendliness: 55 ******
Educational Value: 74 *******
Instructional Design: 44 ****

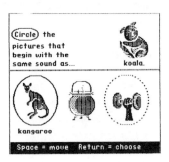

Comments: Child uses spacebar and RETURN to identify objects that start with the same sound, start with different sounds, or start with a given letter. Offers little child-control. Allows teacher to select letters, set the difficulty level, and set the number of problems.

Title: Reading Helpers
Company: Houghton Mifflin Co.
Date: 1986
Price: $135.00
Age: 5-6
Computer: Apple (64K)
Conceptual Area: LA/1,4,6,8 CL/2
■ Reading skills

Final Rating: 69 *******
User Friendliness: 53 *****
Educational Value: 88 *********
Instructional Design: 70 *******

Comments: Five disks. Child presses any key to make selections in 11 games based around decoding and encoding, sight vocabulary, letter recognition, memory, thinking skills, matching, words in context, and alphabetical order of words. Content best for grade 1 and above. Initial adult help required.

Title: Reading Machine, The
Company: SouthWest EdPsych Services
Date: 1982
Price: $59.95
Age: 5-8
Computer: Apple
Conceptual Area: LA/4
■ Various language skills

Final Rating: 65 *******
User Friendliness: 56 ******
Educational Value: 69 *******
Instructional Design: 67 *******

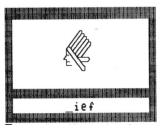

Comments: Separate activities (28) that range from matching letters to phonics practice (cassette interface available). Good management options allow teacher to set up lessons, diagnose progress, or keep records for up to 60 children. Blocky graphics.

LA = Language   CP = Creative projects   OT = Other topics   CL = Classification   SP = Spatial relations   TI = Time   NB = Number   SE = Seriation   * = Version reviewed   NA = Not applicable

Title: Reading Starters
Company: Houghton Mifflin Co.
Date: 1986
Price: $135.00
Age: 5-6
Computer: Apple (64K)
Conceptual Area: LA/4,5,6,7,8 CL/2 SP/4
■ Reading skills

Final Rating: 63 ******
User Friendliness: 51 *****
Educational Value: 84 ********
Instructional Design: 70 *******

Comments: Child uses six animals' names, Deb, Jip, Sam, Ben, Meg, and Tim, to play games based on encoding and decoding, sight vocabulary, letter recognition, memory, matching, alphabetizing, and positional words. Eighteen games on five disks offer a broad range in content. Keeps score. Initial adult help required.

Title: Representational Play
Company: P.E.A.L. Software
Date: 1985
Price: $150.00
Age: 2-5
Computer: Apple (64K)
Conceptual Area: LA/1,5 SP/7
■ Early language acquisition

Final Rating: 71 *******
User Friendliness: 62 ******
Educational Value: 69 *******
Instructional Design: 84 ********

Comments: Two overlays for the Muppet Learning Keys (required). Child first plays with real toys, then presses their pictures on the overlay to hear the associated words in a robotic voice. Requires Echo speech synthesizer. Covers 24 words. Adult setup required.

Title: Rhyming to Read
Company: Grolier Electronic Publishing
Date: 1985
Price: $189.00
Age: 4-8
Computer: Apple* C64
Conceptual Area: LA/7
■ Rhyming words

Final Rating: 37 ****
User Friendliness: 32 ***
Educational Value: 52 *****
Instructional Design: 32 ***

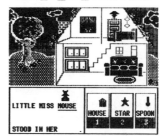

Comments: Five disks introducing 60 words in the context of several activites: matching words to pictures, determining if two words rhyme (Y/N keys), finding a rhyming word for a given word. Menus require reading. Little child interactivity.

LA = Language   CP = Creative projects   OT = Other topics   CL = Classification   SP = Spatial
relations   TI = Time   NB = Number   SE = Seriation   * = Version reviewed   NA = Not applicable

Title: Rosie the Counting Rabbit
Company: D.C. Heath & Company
Date: 1988
Price: $75.00
Age: 5-10
Computer: Apple
Conceptual Area: LA/2,3,5,9 NB/3 CP/4 SP/4,7
■ Language experience

Comments: Children use mouse, Koala Pad, joystick, or arrow keys to select or move objects, backgrounds, words, or characters of a story. Children can also add their own words. Resulting stories can be saved and printed in color. Includes four copies of the storybook. Good design. Fun to use.

Final Rating: 89 ********
User Friendliness: 85 ********
Educational Value: 94 *********
Instructional Design: 91 ********

Title: Rumpelstiltskin
Company: Troll Associates
Date: 1987
Price: $39.95
Age: 5-8
Computer: Apple
Conceptual Area: LA/10 SP/4
■ Reading comprehension

Comments: Three games: Sequencing — child puts eight sentences from "Rumpelstiltskin" in 1-2-3 order. Tic-tac-toe — child answers T/F question to win a square. Following Directions — child moves a marker in a scene, according to written directions, then creates a pattern. Best for ages 6 and up. Includes book.

Final Rating: 43 ****
User Friendliness: 51 *****
Educational Value: 48 *****
Instructional Design: 35 ****

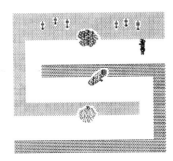

Title: Run Rabbit Run
Company: E.C.S.
Date: 1988
Price: $39.95
Age: 4-8
Computer: Apple
Conceptual Area: TI/1,3,5
■ Scanning, directionality, and attention

Comments: Child practices visual skills and timing by helping a rabbit through an obstacle course. Correct timing is required to jump over obstacles. Teacher options permit control of rabbit's speed, length of course, and number of obstacles. Can be used with joystick, paddle switches, or keyboard.

Final Rating: 70 *******
User Friendliness: 69 *******
Educational Value: 86 *********
Instructional Design: 60 ******

LA = Language   CP = Creative projects   OT = Other topics   CL = Classification   SP = Spatial
relations   TI = Time   NB = Number   SE = Seriation   * = Version reviewed   NA = Not applicable

---

Title: Same or Different
Company: Learning Technologies, Inc.
Date: 1985
Price: $24.95
Age: 4-8
Computer: Apple*, C64
Conceptual Area: CL/1,2
- Visual discrimination, matching

Final Rating: 55 ******
User Friendliness: 45 *****
Educational Value: 68 *******
Instructional Design: 54 *****

Comments: Child presses a number key to select which of four numbered objects is different from the others in some way or which of four objects matches one shown. Menus require reading. Offers a narrow range in content. Keeps score.

Title: Sesame Street Print Kit
Company: Hi Tech Expressions
Date: 1988
Price: $14.95
Age: 3-up
Computer: Apple*, IBM, C64, Atari
Conceptual Area: CP/4 LA/9
- Creating printed materials

Final Rating: 46 *****
User Friendliness: 32 ***
Educational Value: 60 ******
Instructional Design: 50 *****

Comments: A printing program featuring 60 Sesame Street characters, 20 borders, and 7 type faces in 3 sizes. Can make cards, banners, signs, stationery, or storybook. Design makes it difficult to use. Reading required. Young children will require assistance.

Title: Shape & Color Rodeo
Company: DLM
Date: 1984
Price: $32.95
Age: 4-8
Computer: Apple*, IBM, C64
Conceptual Area: CL/1
- Recognizing shapes and colors

Final Rating: 73 *******
User Friendliness: 62 ******
Educational Value: 92 *********
Instructional Design: 72 *******

Comments: Six activities. Child uses spacebar and RETURN to select matching shapes or colors or to find hidden shapes in a rodeo picture. Lively graphics and sounds. Menu requires reading. For one or two players.

LA = Language   CP = Creative projects   OT = Other topics   CL = Classification   SP = Spatial
relations   TI = Time   NB = Number   SE = Seriation   * = Version reviewed   NA = Not applicable

Title: Shape Games
Company: BeCi Software
Date: 1983
Price: $19.95
Age: 3-6
Computer: C64*, VIC 20
Conceptual Area: SE/4 CL/2
- Pattern recognition

Final Rating: 44 ****
User Friendliness: 39 ****
Educational Value: 69 *******
Instructional Design: 34 ***

Comments: Two activities on one disk: One Is Different — child enters number of shape that is different from four others. String a Bead — shows pattern of six beads of different shapes or colors. Child selects seventh from four choices. Blocky graphics. Adult help needed.

Title: Shapes & Patterns
Company: Mindscape, Inc.
Date: 1984
Price: $49.95
Age: 3-6
Computer: Apple
Conceptual Area: CL/1,2 SE/2
- Visual disc., cognitive skills

Final Rating: 66 *******
User Friendliness: 80 ********
Educational Value: 72 *******
Instructional Design: 52 *****

Comments: Child uses nodding heads to decide (1) if shapes shown are the same, (2) if there is a common shape among several objects, or (3) if pattern is correct. Easy-to-use format. Utilities provide feedback on last-played round and some selection of difficulty level.

Title: Shutterbug's Patterns
Company: Learning Technologies, Inc.
Date: 1985
Price: $24.95
Age: 4-8
Computer: Apple*, C64
Conceptual Area: CL/2
- Sequencing, pattern recognition

Final Rating: 36 ****
User Friendliness: 56 ******
Educational Value: 32 ***
Instructional Design: 36 ****

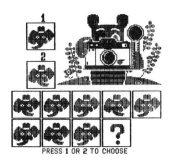

Comments: Child sees a series of eight pictures and must select the ninth and tenth of the series. Graphics are distracting. Content is limited.

LA = Language CP = Creative projects OT = Other topics CL = Classification SP = Spatial relations TI = Time NB = Number SE = Seriation * = Version reviewed NA = Not applicable

Title: Shutterbug's Pictures
Company: Learning Technologies, Inc.
Date: 1985
Price: $24.95
Age: 4-8
Computer: Apple*, C64
Conceptual Area: OT/1
■ Memory skills, reading readiness

Comments: One game in which child sees picture, then is flashed the same picture with one element missing. Child uses the number keys to select the missing object. No branching.

Final Rating: 61 ******
User Friendliness: 69 *******
Educational Value: 72 *******
Instructional Design: 51 *****

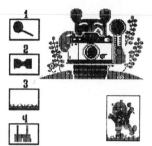

Title: Sight Word Spelling
Company: E.C.S.
Date: 1987
Price: $39.95
Age: 6-7
Computer: Apple
Conceptual Area: LA/4,5 NB/4 OT/1
■ Letter, word, and numeral recognition

Comments: Designed for first- and second-grade special education students, this program presents 10 words or numbers on the screen, one at a time, and pronounces them (Echo speech synthesizer required). The child must type what is shown. Poor design. Keeps records. Custom word lists can be created and stored.

Final Rating: 39 ****
User Friendliness: 30 ***
Educational Value: 55 ******
Instructional Design: 36 ****

Title: Simon Says
Company: Sunburst Communications, Inc.
Date: 1987
Price: $65.00
Age: 6-11
Computer: Apple*, C64
Conceptual Area: OT/1 SE/4
■ Chaining memory exercise

Comments: Child must re-create sequences of colors, numbers, or letters, which get longer with each correct answer. Options allow child to create the original sequence, select the speed with which it is flashed, or select the letters used. Uses regular keyboard, Muppet keyboard, or Touch Window. Can be played by one to four players.

Final Rating: 80 ********
User Friendliness: 83 ********
Educational Value: 91 *********
Instructional Design: 72 *******

Watch this, Warren.

LA = Language   CP = Creative projects   OT = Other topics   CL = Classification   SP = Spatial relations   TI = Time   NB = Number   SE = Seriation   * = Version reviewed   NA = Not applicable

Title: Size and Logic
Company: Hartley Courseware, Inc.
Date: 1984
Price: $35.95
Age: 3-6
Computer: Apple
Conceptual Area: SE/1,2,4 CL/1
■ Size discrimination, patterns

Final Rating: 77 ********
User Friendliness: 69 *******
Educational Value: 91 *********
Instructional Design: 75 ********

Comments: Four games in which child uses spacebar and RETURN to match objects by size, select the object that comes next in a series, or create a matching set. Three levels to each game. Child can use picture menu to select own difficulty level. Clear graphics.

Title: Sleepy Brown Cow, The
Company: D.C. Heath & Company
Date: 1988
Price: $75.00
Age: 5-10
Computer: Apple
Conceptual Area: LA/2,3,5,9 CP/4 SP/4,7
■ Language experience

Final Rating: 89 *********
User Friendliness: 85 *********
Educational Value: 94 *********
Instructional Design: 91 *********

Comments: Children use mouse, Koala Pad, joystick, or arrow keys to select or move objects, backgrounds, words or characters of a story. They can also add their own words. Resulting stories can be saved and printed in color. Good design. Fun to use.

Title: SocPix
Company: American Guidance Service
Date: 1985
Price: $49.95
Age: 3-7
Computer: Apple
Conceptual Area: CL/2,4
■ Classification (class membership)

Final Rating: 61 ******
User Friendliness: 80 ********
Educational Value: 57 ******
Instructional Design: 47 *****

Comments: Three activities on one disk. Child uses arrow keys and spacebar to decide whether pictures belong to a given category. Includes 175 pictures in 7 categories. A separate recordkeeping program ($19.95) keeps records for 40 children.

LA = Language   CP = Creative projects   OT = Other topics   CL = Classification   SP = Spatial
relations   TI = Time   NB = Number   SE = Seriation   * = Version reviewed   NA = Not applicable

Title: Sound Ideas: Consonants
Company: Houghton Mifflin Co.
Date: 1986
Price: $165.00
Age: 5-6
Computer: Apple (64K)
Conceptual Area: LA/4,5,6
■ Consonant sounds

Final Rating: 80 ********
User Friendliness: 79 ********
Educational Value: 88 *********
Instructional Design: 76 ********

Comments: Seven disks present the "th," "sh," and "ch" and 17 consonants. There are four levels. Child matches a sound (said by synthesizer) with a picture, a letter, or a word by using spacebar and RETURN to select a box in a multiple-choice format. Includes workbook and other materials. Requires Echo speech synthesizer.

Title: Sound Ideas: Vowels
Company: Houghton Mifflin Co.
Date: 1986
Price: $165.00
Age: 5-6
Computer: Apple (64K)
Conceptual Area: LA/4,5,6
■ Five vowel sounds (long, short) and y

Final Rating: 80 ********
User Friendliness: 79 ********
Educational Value: 88 *********
Instructional Design: 76 ********

Comments: Five disks. Child uses spacebar and RETURN to select 1 of 3 objects with the same vowel sound as a picture. Uses spoken and pictorial examples to illustrate letter/sound correspondence. Includes workbook and other support materials. Requires Echo speech synthesizer.

Title: Sound Ideas: Word Attack
Company: Houghton Mifflin Co.
Date: 1987
Price: $174.00
Age: 5-6
Computer: Apple (64K)
Conceptual Area: LA/4,5,6
■ Consonant blends, clusters and digraphs

Final Rating: 72 *******
User Friendliness: 71 *******
Educational Value: 94 *********
Instructional Design: 62 ******

Comments: Six disks. Each disk has three parts: a tutorial, a practice session, and a story. Successful completion of each part is required to get to the next level. Practice session gives child a choice of three games to play. Story puts phonics in sentence context. Workbook and support materials included. Provides verbal feedback. Requires Echo speech synthesizer.

LA = Language   CP = Creative projects   OT = Other topics   CL = Classification   SP = Spatial relations   TI = Time   NB = Number   SE = Seriation   * = Version reviewed   NA = Not applicable

Title: Sound Tracks
Company: MECC
Date: 1984
Price: $59.00
Age: 5-11
Computer: Apple (64K)
Conceptual Area: CP/1,2 SE/1
■ Making pictures

Final Rating: 74 *******
User Friendliness: 62 ******
Educational Value: 75 ********
Instructional Design: 84 ********

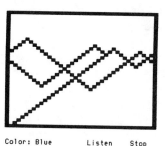

```
Color: Blue        Listen    Stop
Draw on    Erase   Music on   ? Help
```

Comments: Two activites on one disk: (1) Sound Doodles turns the keyboard into a piano. Pressing a key makes a randomly placed colored bar, line, or picture appear. (2) Sound Images lets child create pictures with blocks. Each block has a tone. Pictures can be saved on disk.

Title: Space Waste Race
Company: Sunburst Communications, Inc.
Date: 1984
Price: $65.00
Age: 3-7
Computer: Apple*, Atari, TRS 80
Conceptual Area: LA/8 NB/3,4 SP/4
■ Letter/numeral recognition

Final Rating: 49 *****
User Friendliness: 44 ****
Educational Value: 57 ******
Instructional Design: 47 *****

Comments: Consists of an animated musical storybook with theme-related drill-and-practice activities on counting, letter/numeral recognition, and spatial concepts. Reading required.

Title: Spaceship Lost
Company: Educational Activities, Inc.
Date: 1984
Price: $59.95
Age: 4-6
Computer: Apple
Conceptual Area: SP/3
■ Spatial relationships

Final Rating: 45 *****
User Friendliness: 28 ***
Educational Value: 63 ******
Instructional Design: 49 *****

Comments: Child moves captain through simple maze by typing first letter of direction term. Reading required. Two levels of difficulty: one with captain taking child's perspective each time, and one with child taking captain's perspective. Simple design of graphics limits the program.

LA = Language   CP = Creative projects   OT = Other topics   CL = Classification   SP = Spatial relations   TI = Time   NB = Number   SE = Seriation   * = Version reviewed   NA = Not applicable

Title: Spatial Relationships

Company: Aquarius People Materials

Date: 1982

Price: $29.95

Age: 3-6

Computer: Apple

Conceptual Area: SP/4

- Spatial relationships

Final Rating: 25 ***
User Friendliness: 33 ***
Educational Value: 30 ***
Instructional Design: 17 **

Comments: Child moves an animated spider in or around three boxes on screen, using U (up), L (left), R (right), and D (down) keys. Must read written prompt, e.g., "Put Spidy inside the medium-sized box." Some content not accurate. Not recommended. Discontinued.

Title: Spellicopter

Company: Designware, Inc.

Date: 1983

Price: $39.95

Age: 6-10

Computer: Apple*, IBM, C64 ($29.95)

Conceptual Area: LA/5 SP/4

- Spelling practice

Final Rating: 66 *******
User Friendliness: 59 ******
Educational Value: 77 ********
Instructional Design: 64 ******

Comments: Child pilots helicopter (using joystick or arrow keys) over obstacles to pick up scattered letters of a spelling word. A sentence is given for a clue. Up to 400 words are available (40 lists of 10 words).

Title: Spelling and Reading Primer

Company: EduWare

Date: 1982

Price: $39.95

Age: 4-8

Computer: Apple*, IBM, C64

Conceptual Area: LA/5

- Spelling and reading practice

Final Rating: 51 *****
User Friendliness: 46 *****
Educational Value: 65 *******
Instructional Design: 48 *****

Comments: Two activities: Reading Primer — child uses spacebar to move cursor to match word with 1 of 3 line drawings. Spelling Primer — child sees drawing and must type in word. Twenty-two word-lists with 350 words ranging from "pin" to "circle." Keeps a running record for one child.

LA = Language CP = Creative projects OT = Other topics CL = Classification SP = Spatial relations TI = Time NB = Number SE = Seriation * = Version reviewed NA = Not applicable

Title: Spelling Bee, The
Company: Troll Associates
Date: 1985
Price: $39.95
Age: 5-6
Computer: Apple
Conceptual Area: LA/5
■ Spelling skills

Final Rating: 32 ***
User Friendliness: 34 ***
Educational Value: 37 ****
Instructional Design: 24 *

Comments: Consists of a book, disk, and cassette tape. Three games: (1) Child sees three words, e.g., fan/me/mine, and selects one that is different; (2) child changes word to match picture; and (3) child matches picture to word. Reading required. Limited content. Cluttered graphics.

Title: Stepping Stones Level I
Company: Compu-Teach
Date: 1987
Price: $39.95
Age: 2-4
Computer: Apple, IBM*, Mac
Conceptual Area: LA/4,5,6 NB/2,3,4
■ Letters, numbers, and words

Final Rating: 59 ******
User Friendliness: 58 ******
Educational Value: 84 ********
Instructional Design: 47 *****

Comments: Three disks: Reading, Math, and Word Pieces. Five games that include pressing any letter to see a picture (e.g., a cat for C), counting, and typing simple words. Word Pieces is a clever game in which child sees incomplete word, e.g., __ IG and tries any letter to make a word. Variety of content.

Title: Stepping Stones Level II
Company: Compu-Teach
Date: 1987
Price: $39.95
Age: 5-7
Computer: Apple*, IBM, Mac
Conceptual Area: LA/4,5,6 NB/3,4
■ Vocabulary, counting, adding

Final Rating: 58 ******
User Friendliness: 60 ******
Educational Value: 76 ********
Instructional Design: 47 *****

The boy pushes the

Comments: Three activities on two disks. Language — Child uses spacebar to select pictures of elements of a sentence, which animates itself if correct. Reading — child matches pictures and words. Arithmetic — child counts up to 24 objects and enters answer. Menus require reading.

LA = Language   CP = Creative projects   OT = Other topics   CL = Classification   SP = Spatial
relations   TI = Time   NB = Number   SE = Seriation   * = Version reviewed   NA = Not applicable

Title: Stickers

Company: Springboard
Date: 1984
Price: $34.95
Age: 4-12
Computer: Apple, IBM*, C64
Conceptual Area: CP/1,4 SP/1,2,8
- Creative activity

Final Rating: 79 ********
User Friendliness: 77 ********
Educational Value: 74 *******
Instructional Design: 81 ********

Comments: Using arrow keys or joystick, child moves geometric shapes on screen to either match existing patterns or create own. Easy-to-use picture menu requires no reading. Keyboard or joystick can be used.

Title: Stickybear ABC

Company: Weekly Reader Software
Date: 1982
Price: $39.95
Age: 3-6
Computer: Apple*, Atari, C64
Conceptual Area: LA/4
- Letter recognition

Final Rating: 59 ******
User Friendliness: 76 ********
Educational Value: 53 *****
Instructional Design: 55 ******

Comments: Child presses any letter key to get 1 of 2 animated pictures related to letter. Easy-to-use program, but little challenge. Entertaining graphics. Talking version available for the Apple IIGS (see "New Talking Stickybear ABC's").

Title: Stickybear Math

Company: Weekly Reader Software
Date: 1984
Price: $39.95
Age: 6-9
Computer: Apple*, IBM, C64
Conceptual Area: NB/3,4,7
- Counting, addition and subtraction

Final Rating: 81 ********
User Friendliness: 70 *******
Educational Value: 90 *********
Instructional Design: 82 ********

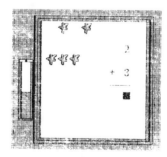

Comments: A 20-level math program that keeps names, levels, scores, and types of problems for up to 25 children. Automatically tracks and adjusts difficulty level. Content ranges from counting to three-place vertical-presentation subtraction with borrowing. Includes poster and stickers. Animated graphics illustrate problems.

LA = Language   CP = Creative projects   OT = Other topics   CL = Classification   SP = Spatial
relations   TI = Time   NB = Number   SE = Seriation   * = Version reviewed   NA = Not applicable

---

Title: Stickybear Numbers
Company: Weekly Reader Software
Date: 1982
Price: $39.95
Age: 3-6
Computer: Apple*, IBM, Atari, C64
Conceptual Area: NB/3,4,7
■ Counting

Final Rating: 64 ******
User Friendliness: 56 ******
Educational Value: 84 ********
Instructional Design: 59 ******

Comments: A continuous series of 25 counting activities controlled by the spacebar and number keys. Provides good number concept reinforcement, as there are 25 possible entertaining combinations. No CMI techniques used. Limited content.

Title: Stickybear Opposites
Company: Weekly Reader Software
Date: 1983
Price: $39.95
Age: 3-6
Computer: Apple*, Atari, C64
Conceptual Area: SP/4 SE/1
■ Opposites, e.g., "near/far"

Final Rating: 73 *******
User Friendliness: 75 ********
Educational Value: 79 ********
Instructional Design: 68 *******

Comments: Contains 21 antonym pairs that are changed using the arrow keys. Spacebar changes the scene. Colorful graphics and animation. Similar in design to "Inside Outside Opposites" and "City Country Opposites."

Title: Stickybear Printer
Company: Weekly Reader Software
Date: 1985
Price: $39.95
Age: 5-up
Computer: Apple
Conceptual Area: CP/4 OT/4
■ "Printing fun for everyone"

Final Rating: 43 ****
User Friendliness: 40 ****
Educational Value: 36 ****
Instructional Design: 49 *****

Comments: Allows creation of cards, stories, or posters. Multiple-menu design requires reading, limiting independent use by non-readers. Can utilize Imagewriter II color printer. A second package, "Stickybear Printer Picture Library" ($39.95), contains two disks of additional graphics.

LA = Language   CP = Creative projects   OT = Other topics   CL = Classification   SP = Spatial relations   TI = Time   NB = Number   SE = Seriation   * = Version reviewed   NA = Not applicable

Title: Stickybear Reading
Company: Weekly Reader Software
Date: 1984
Price: $39.95
Age: 5-8
Computer: Apple*, IBM, C64
Conceptual Area: LA/5,8,10
■ Word and sentence fun

Final Rating: 77 ********
User Friendliness: 68 *******
Educational Value: 89 *********
Instructional Design: 78 ********

Comments: Three activities: Child can use joystick, arrow keys, or mouse to match words with pictures, complete a sentence, or build a sentence by selecting its parts. Graphics animate each sentence or word used. Includes book and poster.

Title: Stickybear Shapes
Company: Weekly Reader Software
Date: 1983
Price: $39.95
Age: 3-6
Computer: Apple*, Atari, C64
Conceptual Area: SP/8
■ Shape Identification

Final Rating: 70 *******
User Friendliness: 56 ******
Educational Value: 80 ********
Instructional Design: 78 ********

Comments: The Stickybear series offers a book, a poster, and suggestions for extending concepts into noncomputer contexts. This program provides practice with five common shapes in three games: Pick It, Name It, and Find It. Paddles, arrow keys, or mouse can operate program.

Title: Stickybear Town Builder
Company: Weekly Reader Software
Date: 1984
Price: $39.95
Age: 6-9
Computer: Apple*, IBM, C64
Conceptual Area: SP/3,4,6,7 TI/5,6 CL/2
■ Map skills

Final Rating: 80 ********
User Friendliness: 68 *******
Educational Value: 97 **********
Instructional Design: 80 ********

Comments: Using joystick or arrow keys, child makes a town by placing 1 of 30 buildings on an empty map. The child can then drive car to find buildings in a matching game or to find hidden keys in the town. Towns can be saved. Joystick and color monitor recommended.

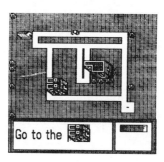

LA = Language   CP = Creative projects   OT = Other topics   CL = Classification   SP = Spatial
relations   TI = Time   NB = Number   SE = Seriation   * = Version reviewed   NA = Not applicable

Title: Stickybear Typing
Company: Weekly Reader Software
Date: 1985
Price: $39.95
Age: 5-8
Computer: Apple*, IBM, C64
Conceptual Area: LA/4
- Typing skills

Final Rating: 42 ****
User Friendliness: 49 *****
Educational Value: 41 ****
Instructional Design: 37 ****

Comments: Three activities give child practice with (1) finding letters with correct fingers, (2) building speed, and (3) typing stories. Includes 30 levels of difficulty, records scores, and gives WPM score. Slow key/screen response. Reading required.

Title: Story Machine
Company: Spinnaker Software Corp.
Date: 1982
Price: $29.95
Age: 5-9
Computer: Apple*, IBM, Atari, C64, TI
Conceptual Area: LA/4,8,9 CP/4
- Creative activity

Final Rating: 69 *******
User Friendliness: 39 ****
Educational Value: 80 ********
Instructional Design: 91 *********

Comments: Provides medium for child to animate written words. By typing "the cat walks to the store," a child can make a cat appear and walk to the store. Limited words are available, which reduces the usefulness of the program. Stories cannot be printed but can be saved on disk. Reading required. Discontinued in 1987.

Title: SuperPrint!
Company: Scholastic Software, Inc.
Date: 1987
Price: $59.95
Age: 5-up
Computer: Apple*, IBM
Conceptual Area: CP/1,4
- Printing utility

Final Rating: 62 ******
User Friendliness: 42 ****
Educational Value: 65 *******
Instructional Design: 78 ********

Comments: A program that prints signs, cards, banners, or posters that can be as large as 24 by 55 inches. All menus require reading. Four type styles and over 100 graphics. Prints in black and white or in color. Requires disk changing. See "Print Shop" for a better printing program.

LA = Language CP = Creative projects OT = Other topics CL = Classification SP = Spatial relations TI = Time NB = Number SE = Seriation * = Version reviewed NA = Not applicable

Title: Surrounding Patterns
Company: Strawberry Hill Software
Date: 1985
Price: $19.00
Age: 3-10
Computer: Apple*, C64
Conceptual Area: SP/1,2,3,4,8,9 CP/1,4
■ Visual imagery, symmetry

Final Rating: 77 ********
User Friendliness: 75 ********
Educational Value: 98 **********
Instructional Design: 65 *******

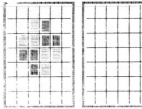

Comments: Child sees a pattern of colored shapes and uses joystick or arrow keys to copy it. Seven levels are available, or child can make own designs, which can be saved. Program design is easy to use and encourages experimentation.

Title: Sweet Shop, The
Company: D.C. Heath & Company
Date: 1983
Price: $45.00
Age: 3-8
Computer: Apple*, C64
Conceptual Area: NB/3
■ Number matching, basic facts

Final Rating: 54 *****
User Friendliness: 78 ********
Educational Value: 41 ****
Instructional Design: 43 ****

Comments: Child moves Mr. Jellybean with arrow keys to match numbers with jellybeans or select addition or subtraction answer. No tutorial steps or branching. All activities based on jellybeans, popcorn, or ice cream themes.

Title: Talk About a Walk
Company: Queue, Inc.
Date: 1984
Price: $39.95
Age: 4-6
Computer: Apple
Conceptual Area: LA/1,5 CL/2 SP/6
■ Classifying household objects

Final Rating: 56 ******
User Friendliness: 59 ******
Educational Value: 69 *******
Instructional Design: 46 *****

Comments: Two activites in which child sees 1 of 20 household items or words (spoon) and must place it in 1 of 4 rooms of a house. The second activity shows objects inside or outside a house. Child must press any key to indicate if the object is in the correct place.

LA = Language   CP = Creative projects   OT = Other topics   CL = Classification   SP = Spatial relations   TI = Time   NB = Number   SE = Seriation   * = Version reviewed   NA = Not applicable

Title: Talking ABC's
Company: Orange Cherry Software
Date: 1988
Price: $59.00
Age: 3-7
Computer: IIGS (512K)
Conceptual Area: LA/4 CL/2
- Letter recognition

Final Rating: 43 ****
User Friendliness: 41 ****
Educational Value: 50 *****
Instructional Design: 40 ****

Comments: Two 3.5-inch disks — one for the letters A – M, the other for N – Z. Contains three activities: (1) Child presses any letter to hear letter name and see letter-related picture. (2) Child sees picture, hears letter, and must press a key. (3) Child sees on-screen keyboard, hears letter name, and must press that key. Limited content.

Title: Talking Clock
Company: Orange Cherry Software
Date: 1988
Price: $59.00
Age: 5-8
Computer: IIGS (512K)
Conceptual Area: TI/9
- Clock-reading skills

Final Rating: 65 *******
User Friendliness: 63 ******
Educational Value: 69 *******
Instructional Design: 63 ******

Comments: Child sets the hour, minute, and second hands on a clock by clicking mouse on 1 of 2 arrows. Uses pull-down menus to access options. Limited content. Reads time from clock and provides feedback statements in digitized speech. Reading required.

Title: Talking Nouns I
Company: Laureate Learning Systems
Date: 1987
Price: $100.00
Age: 2.5-up
Computer: Apple (128K)
Conceptual Area: LA/5,8 CL/1,2
- Language development

Final Rating: 80 ********
User Friendliness: 95 **********
Educational Value: 87 *********
Instructional Design: 65 *******

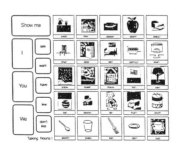

Comments: On an overlay for the Touch Window (required), child presses a picture to hear its name said in a clear voice (Echo speech synthesizer required). Other words allow creation of simple sentences, e.g., "You see the bus." Fifty nouns available. Recommended for nonverbal children. Adult setup required.

LA = Language   CP = Creative projects   OT = Other topics   CL = Classification   SP = Spatial relations   TI = Time   NB = Number   SE = Seriation   * = Version reviewed   NA = Not applicable

Title: Talking Nouns II
Company: Laureate Learning Systems
Date: 1987
Price: $100.00
Age: 2.5-up
Computer: Apple (128K)
Conceptual Area: LA/5,8 CL/1,2
■ Language development

Comments: Same as "Talking Nouns I."
Provides 50 additional nouns.

Final Rating: 80 ********
User Friendliness: 95 **********
Educational Value: 87 *********
Instructional Design: 65 *******

Title: Talking Numbers
Company: Orange Cherry Software
Date: 1988
Price: $59.00
Age: 5-7
Computer: IIGS
Conceptual Area: NB/4,8
■ Counting

Comments: Four activities on one disk: Child presses any number key to see and hear the number. Child hears a number and must press its key. Child hears and sees the computer count, or sees and hears number and must click mouse on the correct answer. Very limited content. Uses the internal IIGS speech capacity. Some reading required.

Final Rating: 41 ****
User Friendliness: 46 *****
Educational Value: 49 *****
Instructional Design: 33 ***

Title: Talking Teacher
Company: Firebird Licensees, Inc.
Date: 1985
Price: $39.95
Age: 2-8
Computer: C64
Conceptual Area: LA/4,5,6 CL/2
■ Letter identification

Comments: Three games on one disk "talk" in a deep voice. No special hardware is needed. Game 1 speaks and writes any letter typed. Game 2 asks child to find a letter on the keyboard, giving spoken clues if necessary. Game 3 asks child to identify the beginning letter of a word. Discontinued by publisher. May still be available in stores. Uses a two-sided disk.

Final Rating: 76 ********
User Friendliness: 56 ******
Educational Value: 87 *********
Instructional Design: 82 ********

LA = Language   CP = Creative projects   OT = Other topics   CL = Classification   SP = Spatial
relations   TI = Time   NB = Number   SE = Seriation   * = Version reviewed   NA = Not applicable

Title: Talking Textwriter
Company: Scholastic Software, Inc.
Date: 1986
Price: $187.45
Age: 3-9
Computer: Apple* (128K), Apple IIGS, IBM
Conceptual Area: LA/3,4,5,6,7,9 CP/4 OT/4
■ Exploration of written language

Final Rating: 75 ********
User Friendliness: 59 ******
Educational Value: 92 *********
Instructional Design: 78 ********

Comments: A large-print word processor that says letters, words, or sentences as they are typed. Requires Echo synthesizer ($50 extra). Stories can be saved and printed. Requires adult setup. Comes on two disks. Apple IIGS and IBM versions do not require the Echo.

Title: Talking Tiles
Company: Bright Star
Date: 1988
Price: $129.95
Age: 3-up
Computer: Mac (1 MB required)
Conceptual Area: LA/3,4,5,6,7,8,9
■ Letter and word sounds

Final Rating: 85 *********
User Friendliness: 72 *******
Educational Value: 98 **********
Instructional Design: 89 *********

Comments: Clicking the mouse on a letter produces an animated face that pronounces the letter. Letters can be "dragged" to the lower screen and combined with other letters to create any word, which is sounded out by the face. Children or adults can see, as well as hear the phonics through the Mac's speech synthesizer.

Title: Talking Verbs
Company: Laureate Learning Systems
Date: 1987
Price: $100.00
Age: 2.5-up
Computer: Apple (128K)
Conceptual Area: LA/5,8 CL/1,2
■ Language development

Final Rating: 80 ********
User Friendliness: 95 **********
Educational Value: 87 *********
Instructional Design: 65 *******

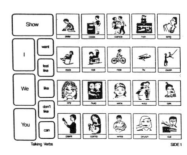

Comments: On an overlay for the Touch Window (required), child presses a verb picture (such as crying or talking). For picture pressed, word is said in a voice (Echo speech synthesizer required). Forty verbs and key-phrase words included. Adult setup required. Recommended for nonverbal children.

LA = Language   CP = Creative projects   OT = Other topics   CL = Classification   SP = Spatial relations   TI = Time   NB = Number   SE = Seriation   * = Version reviewed   NA = Not applicable

Title: Teddy and Iggy
Company: Sunburst Communications, Inc.
Date: 1987
Price: $65.00
Age: 6-8
Computer: Apple*, C64
Conceptual Area: CL/1 OT/1
■ Sequential memory practice

Final Rating: 78 ********
User Friendliness: 67 ******
Educational Value: 91 *********
Instructional Design: 79 ********

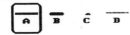

Comments: Three activities on one disk. Child must re-create order in which Teddy made his bed (recalling which color of sheet went on first), recall sequence in which several objects were flashed, or recall the order in which several boxes were opened. Uses keyboard, Muppet keyboard, or Touch Window. Requires reading, color monitor.

Title: Teddy Bear-rels of Fun
Company: DLM
Date: 1987
Price: $39.95
Age: 5-up
Computer: Apple*, C64
Conceptual Area: CP/1,4 LA/3 SP/2
■ Creating pictures, graphics, and stories

Final Rating: 56 ******
User Friendliness: 37 ****
Educational Value: 74 *******
Instructional Design: 62 ******

Comments: Child uses spacebar, RETURN, and arrow keys to create scenes with teddy bears. Includes over 200 pictures, backgrounds, and props that a child can arrange on the screen. Rather complex menus (a child must type CONTROL-C to go back) are better-suited to older children. Work can be saved or printed in color.

Title: Teddy Bears Counting Fun
Company: Micro-Learningware
Date: 1981
Price: $30.00
Age: 3-6
Computer: Apple
Conceptual Area: NB/3
■ Counting skills

Final Rating: 32 ***
User Friendliness: 45 *****
Educational Value: 30 ***
Instructional Design: 27 ***

Comments: Presents nine scenes in which child counts bears (a random number between 1-9 appears), "reads" poem, and inputs number. No CMI techniques. Very limited content. Not recommended.

LA = Language   CP = Creative projects   OT = Other topics   CL = Classification   SP = Spatial
relations   TI = Time   NB = Number   SE = Seriation   * = Version reviewed   NA = Not applicable

Title: Teddy's Playground
Company: Sunburst Communications, Inc.
Date: 1985
Price: $65.00
Age: 5-9
Computer: Apple
Conceptual Area: CL/2
■ Practice with color and shape attributes

Final Rating: 80 ********
User Friendliness: 81 ********
Educational Value: 88 *********
Instructional Design: 75 ********

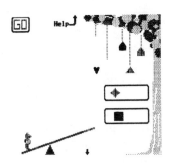

Comments: Child uses joystick, mouse or arrow keys to move freely around three main areas of Teddy's playground to arrange pieces by shape, color, or shading. Includes supplementary materials. Similar in design to "Gertrude's Secrets." Color monitor required.

Title: Telling Time
Company: Orange Cherry Software
Date: 1984
Price: $39.00
Age: 5-9
Computer: Apple*, C64, TRS 80, IBM, Atari, Pet
Conceptual Area: TI/9
■ Clock practice

Final Rating: 34 ***
User Friendliness: 31 ***
Educational Value: 31 ***
Instructional Design: 37 ****

Comments: Provides practice with clock-reading skills. Multiple-choice questions are presented concerning the time shown on a rough clock. Child enters answer by typing letter. Reading required. A better clock-reading program is in "Learning About Numbers" by C&C Software.

Title: This Land Is Your Land
Company: Polarware, Inc.
Date: 1986
Price: $14.95
Age: 3-up
Computer: Apple* (128K), IBM, C64
Conceptual Area: CP/1,4 SP/4
■ Coloring pictures

Final Rating: 80 ********
User Friendliness: 79 ********
Educational Value: 73 *******
Instructional Design: 84 ********

Comments: A coloring program with 30 blank scenes of the USA on one disk. Child moves cursor with mouse, joystick, or arrow keys to fill in sections of a picture with 1 of 16 available colors. Prints in color. Mouse and color monitor recommended. Very easy to use. Prints picture with calendar.

LA = Language   CP = Creative projects   OT = Other topics   CL = Classification   SP = Spatial relations   TI = Time   NB = Number   SE = Seriation   * = Version reviewed   NA = Not applicable

---

Title: Tiger's Tales

Company: Sunburst Communications, Inc.

Date: 1986

Price: $65.00

Age: 5-7

Computer: Apple*, C64

Conceptual Area: LA/5,8

■ Reading vocabulary & comprehension

Final Rating: 80 ********
User Friendliness: 66 *******
Educational Value: 94 *********
Instructional Design: 83 ********

Comments: Five interactive stories in which child selects pictures related to the story. Includes a picture/word matching activity. Large, easy-to-read letters. Supplementary worksheets and activities are included. Can be used with Muppet Learning Keys. Reading required.

Title: Time Master

Company: Micro Power & Light Company

Date: 1980

Price: $29.95

Age: 5-7

Computer: Apple

Conceptual Area: TI/9

■ Clock practice

Final Rating: 25 ***
User Friendliness: 28 ***
Educational Value: 38 ****
Instructional Design: 16 **

Comments: Child must be able to read "set hand to half past seven" to use this program. Hands are moved with arrow keys. Choices are hours, half hours, quarter hours, minutes, or start and set the clock. Poor design. Not recommended.

Title: Tink's Adventure

Company: Mindscape, Inc.

Date: 1984

Price: $19.95

Age: 4-8

Computer: Apple*, C64, IBM, Atari

Conceptual Area: LA/4 SP/4,7

■ Key location, alphabetical order

Final Rating: 41 ****
User Friendliness: 48 *****
Educational Value: 54 *****
Instructional Design: 28 ***

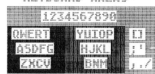

Comments: Five games on one disk, designed to give practice with alphabet order (e.g., F,G,___,I) and key location. Games are played by using joystick or arrow keys to steer Tink's boat or helicopter to various islands. Most games are not at a preschool level. Color monitor recommended.

LA = Language   CP = Creative projects   OT = Other topics   CL = Classification   SP = Spatial relations   TI = Time   NB = Number   SE = Seriation   * = Version reviewed   NA = Not applicable

Title: Tonk in the Land of Buddy-Bots

Company: Mindscape, Inc.

Date: 1984

Price: $19.95

Age: 4-8

Computer: Apple*, C64, IBM, Atari

Conceptual Area: SP/1,5,7 OT/1

- Problem solving

Final Rating: 56 ******
User Friendliness: 54 *****
Educational Value: 66 *******
Instructional Design: 49 *****

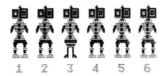

Comments: Child uses joystick or arrow keys to move "Tonk" through a 65-screen landscape filled with robot parts, sky holes, and enemy soldiers. Along the way, Tonk can stop to play 1 of 6 games on memory, matching, and spatial relations. Joystick use is optional.

Title: Touch & Write

Company: Sunburst Communications, Inc.

Date: 1986

Price: $75.00

Age: 5-7

Computer: Apple

Conceptual Area: LA/4,5

- Printing practice

Final Rating: 81 ********
User Friendliness: 89 *********
Educational Value: 87 *********
Instructional Design: 72 *******

Comments: Child touches screen (Touch Window required) to make letters. Contains 4 stroke lessons and 19 letter lessons, based on the Palmer Manuscript style. Allows flexibility in design. Child can practice strokes, letters, or words. Work can be printed.

Title: Touch and Match

Company: E.C.S.

Date: 1986

Price: $29.95

Age: 3-6

Computer: Apple

Conceptual Area: CL/2,4

- Classification

Final Rating: 65 *******
User Friendliness: 62 ******
Educational Value: 78 ********
Instructional Design: 59 ******

Comments: Child needs only touch the screen (Touch Window required) to identify identical, associated, or different pictures among four that are shown. Menu requires reading. Some setup required by adult. Clear but limited graphics. Easy for a child to use.

LA = Language   CP = Creative projects   OT = Other topics   CL = Classification   SP = Spatial relations   TI = Time   NB = Number   SE = Seriation   * = Version reviewed   NA = Not applicable

Title: Touch and See
Company: E.C.S.
Date: 1986
Price: $39.95
Age: 4-7
Computer: Apple
Conceptual Area: OT/1 CL/2
■ Memory skills

Final Rating: **61** ******
User Friendliness: **59** ******
Educational Value: **80** ********
Instructional Design: **49** *****

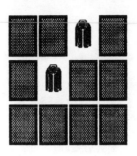

Comments: A memory game in which children match 6 pairs of shapes, letters, pictures, or words hidden in 12 boxes. Timer shows time limit. Child touches screen to make matches. Touch Window required. Written menus.

Title: Toybox
Company: S.D.L.
Date: 1986
Price: $10.00
Age: 1/2-up
Computer: C64*, Apple (128), IBM
Conceptual Area: TI/1 CP/1,2,4
■ Exploration of the computer

Final Rating: **56** ******
User Friendliness: **56** ******
Educational Value: **72** *******
Instructional Design: **64** ******

Comments: Each keystroke puts a different shape, color, or special effect on the screen in a random position. Effects accumulate on the screen, creating a composition that can be saved on the disk. Extremely easy to use.

Title: Tuk Goes to Town
Company: Mindscape, Inc.
Date: 1984
Price: $19.95
Age: 4-8
Computer: Apple*, C64, IBM, Atari
Conceptual Area: LA/4,5,11 SP/4
■ Develops spelling and vocabulary

Final Rating: **41** ****
User Friendliness: **44** ****
Educational Value: **59** ******
Instructional Design: **29** ***

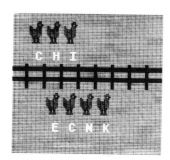

Comments: Seven games on one disk designed to give practice unscrambling or matching shapes or letters. Games take place in an interactive story that feature "Tuk" on his way to town. Some instructions are confusing. Games are not appropriate for the early childhood level. Discontinued in 1988.

LA = Language   CP = Creative projects   OT = Other topics   CL = Classification   SP = Spatial relations   TI = Time   NB = Number   SE = Seriation   * = Version reviewed   NA = Not applicable

Title: Up & Add 'Em
Company: Spinnaker Software Corp.
Date: 1984
Price: $9.95
Age: 3-7
Computer: Apple*, IBM, C64
Conceptual Area: NB/1,3,4,7
■ Matching numbers

Final Rating: 75 ******
User Friendliness: 82 ********
Educational Value: 86 *********
Instructional Design: 61 ******

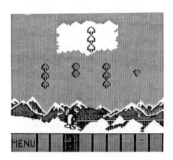

Comments: Child completes a rainbow by using joystick or arrow keys to match numbers to sets, match sets, or do simple addition or subtraction problems. Four levels (9 − 4 = 5 most difficult). Allows high level of child-control. IBM version comes on the back of the Apple disk.

Title: Video Smarts
Company: Connor Toy Corporation
Date: 1986
Price: $45.00
Age: 3-7
Computer: VHS videotape recorder
Conceptual Area: CL/2,5 NB/3 LA/4,6 and others
■ Matching, counting, letters, colors

Final Rating: 52 ***
User Friendliness: 74 *******
Educational Value: 56 ******
Instructional Design: 38 ****

2. **Question.** The cassette asks questions about the lesson and displays 2–4 possible solutions. A child then answers by pressing one of the computer buttons.

Comments: A 30-minute video cassette and 4-button keyboard that plugs into the audio output of a VHS videotape player. Throughout tape, child is asked 31 multiple-choice questions, presses button, and gets feedback. Tapes cover topics such as numbers 1-10, comparisons, letters, all about me, and nutrition. Twelve tapes now available, purchased separately. Four "C" batteries required.

Title: Webster's Numbers
Company: EduWare
Date: 1983
Price: $39.95
Age: 4-8
Computer: Apple*, C64
Conceptual Area: NB/3,4 SP/1,2,4
■ Basic math concepts

Final Rating: 67 *****
User Friendliness: 56 ******
Educational Value: 86 *********
Instructional Design: 65 *******

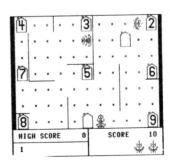

Comments: Four games: Ribbet — child moves through maze to catch numerals 1-9 in order. Balloon Race — child steers balloons to numerals to match a set. Shape Up — child moves shapes to match a model. Pushover — child unscrambles number blocks. Joystick or paddles required.

LA = Language   CP = Creative projects   OT = Other topics   CL = Classification   SP = Spatial
relations   TI = Time   NB = Number   SE = Seriation   * = Version reviewed   NA = Not applicable

Title: What Makes a Dinosaur Sore?
Company: D.C. Heath & Company
Date: 1988
Price: $75.00
Age: 5-10
Computer: Apple
Conceptual Area: LA/2,3,5,9 CP/4 SP/4,7
■ Language experience

Final Rating: 89 *********
User Friendliness: 85 *********
Educational Value: 94 *********
Instructional Design: 91 *********

Comments: Children use mouse, Koala Pad, joystick, or arrow keys to select or move objects, backgrounds, words, or characters of a story. They can also add their own words. Resulting stories can be saved and printed in color. Includes four copies of the storybook. Good design. Fun to use. Part of the Explore-a-Story Series.

Title: What's in a Frame?
Company: Sunburst Communications, Inc.
Date: 1987
Price: $65.00
Age: 5-11
Computer: Apple
Conceptual Area: OT/1 CL/1,4
■ Memory practice by context clues

Final Rating: 81 ********
User Friendliness: 67 *******
Educational Value: 91 *********
Instructional Design: 88 *********

Comments: Two activities. Did You See This? — frame shows several objects for a timed period. Then one object at a time is shown, and child must decide if it was in the original frame. What's in a Frame? — from given objects, child marks ones that were in an original frame. Keeps records. Touch Window optional.

Title: What's Next
Company: Strawberry Hill Software
Date: 1985
Price: $55.00
Age: 3-14
Computer: Apple*, C64
Conceptual Area: SE/1,2 CL/1,2 NB/1
■ Sequencing skills

Final Rating: 74 *******
User Friendliness: 69 *******
Educational Value: 94 *********
Instructional Design: 65 *******

Comments: Child sees a series of shapes or objects and must select which piece comes next in the series. There are eight levels of difficulty. Includes a "U-Design-It" feature that allows the design of custom patterns that can be saved. Offers a variety of sequences and objects.

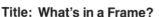

LA = Language   CP = Creative projects   OT = Other topics   CL = Classification   SP = Spatial
relations   TI = Time   NB = Number   SE = Seriation   * = Version reviewed   NA = Not applicable

Title: Where Did My Toothbrush Go?
Company: D.C. Heath & Company
Date: 1988
Price: $75.00
Age: 5-10
Computer: Apple
Conceptual Area: LA/2,3,5,9 CP/4 SP/4,7
■ Language experience

Final Rating: 89 *********
User Friendliness: 85 *********
Educational Value: 94 *********
Instructional Design: 91 *********

Comments: Children use mouse, Koala Pad, joystick, or arrow keys to select or move objects, backgrounds, words, or characters of a story. Children can also add their own words. Resulting stories can be saved and printed in color. Includes four copies of the storybook. Good design. Fun to use.

Title: Word Factory
Company: Island Software
Date: 1983
Price: $25.00
Age: 3-6
Computer: Apple
Conceptual Area: CL/2
■ Word discrimination

Final Rating: 22 **
User Friendliness: 25 ***
Educational Value: 26 ***
Instructional Design: 12 *

Comments: Child uses < or > key to discriminate between matching words. Leaves child with little control. Limited in content. Poor design. Not recommended.

Title: Words
Company: Lawrence Hall of Science
Date: 1984
Price: $34.95
Age: 4-6
Computer: Apple
Conceptual Area: LA/4,5,8
■ Letter disc., word experiences

Final Rating: 61 ******
User Friendliness: 49 *****
Educational Value: 88 *********
Instructional Design: 57 ******

FIRST PRESS ARROW KEYS TO PEEK
THEN PRESS ▮▮▮▮ TO GUESS.

Comments: Presents three games, two on letter recognition and one on simple sentence structure. Kindergarten children were able to use the Funny Letters and Words activity. Activities effectively focus on the attributes of letters. Best for 5-year-olds. Some reading used, e.g., "Press RETURN."

LA = Language   CP = Creative projects   OT = Other topics   CL = Classification   SP = Spatial relations   TI = Time   NB = Number   SE = Seriation   * = Version reviewed   NA = Not applicable

Title: Words & Concepts
Company: Laureate Learning Systems
Date: 1987
Price: $185.00
Age: 3-adult
Computer: Apple
Conceptual Area: LA/5,8 CL/1,2,4
■ Vocabulary training

Final Rating: 80 ********
User Friendliness: 97 **********
Educational Value: 86 *********
Instructional Design: 69 *******

Comments: Shows three objects — using a Touch Window, single switch, or number keys, a child responds to questions asked through an Echo speech synthesizer. Provides practice identifying, categorizing, associating, and discriminating 40 common nouns. Designed for children or adults who need training in vocabulary. Teacher setup allows much control over presentation. Keeps records.

Title: Words & Concepts II
Company: Laureate Learning Systems
Date: 1988
Price: $185.00
Age: 3-adult
Computer: Apple
Conceptual Area: LA/5,8 CL/1,2,4
■ Vocabulary training

Final Rating: 80 ********
User Friendliness: 97 **********
Educational Value: 86 *********
Instructional Design: 69 *******

Comments: Same as "Words & Concepts". Provides 40 additional nouns.

Title: Words & Concepts III
Company: Laureate Learning Systems
Date: 1988
Price: $185.00
Age: 3-adult
Computer: Apple
Conceptual Area: LA/5,8 CL/1,2,4
■ Vocabulary training

Final Rating: 80 ********
User Friendliness: 97 **********
Educational Value: 86 *********
Instructional Design: 69 *******

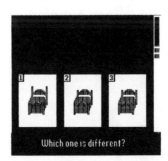

Comments: Same as "Words & Concepts" and "Words & Concepts II".Provides 40 additional nouns.

LA = Language   CP = Creative projects   OT = Other topics   CL = Classification   SP = Spatial
relations   TI = Time   NB = Number   SE = Seriation   * = Version reviewed   NA = Not applicable

Title: Writing to Read 2.0
Company: IBM Educational Systems
Date: 1982
Price: $716.00
Age: 5-6
Computer: IBM
Conceptual Area: LA/4,5,6
■ Reading skills

Final Rating: 45 *****
User Friendliness: 32 ***
Educational Value: 74 *******
Instructional Design: 41 ****

Comments: A 14-disk computer-based curriculum designed to teach reading skills through writing, using phonetic spelling. Computers are only one component. Each disk covers three words. Child hears letter or word and must type. Speech synthesizer required. Available in Spanish. Ratings apply only to software.

LA = Language   CP = Creative projects   OT = Other topics   CL = Classification   SP = Spatial relations   TI = Time   NB = Number   SE = Seriation   * = Version reviewed   NA = Not applicable

3

EVALUATION PROCESS

This chapter contains the Early Childhood Software Evaluation Instrument that was developed to

1. Focus specifically on the early childhood category of software, covering issues important when working with three- to six-year-old children

2. Generate numerical values in both specific and general categories to provide quick comparison of software packages

3. Record descriptive information about specific programs for purposes of recommendation, prescription, and documentation

Thirteen separate percentage scores ranging from 1 to 100 are generated by the Instrument and are defined in Calculation of a Component Score, found in this chapter, and Guide to the Software Descriptions, found in Chapter 1.

Terms used in the Instrument that may be unfamiliar to the reader have been included in the Glossary (Appendix 6).

EARLY CHILDHOOD SOFTWARE EVALUATION INSTRUMENT

© 1985 High/Scope Educational Research Foundation

Title _____

Company _____

Author(s) _____

Address _____

_____

_____

Phone 1 (_____) _____/_____

Phone 2 (_____) _____/_____

Date _____

Age-range _____

Price _____

Notes:

SUMMARY OF RATINGS

Minimum User Competency ____ %

Menu Design ____ %

Technical Features ____ %

Content Presentation ____ %

Content Strength ____ %

Ease of Use ____ %

Feedback ____ %

Embedded Reinforcements ____ %

CMI Techniques ____ %

User Friendliness ____ %

Educational Value ____ %

Instructional Design ____ %

OVERALL RATING ____ %

Computer

_____ Apple II	_____ IBM PC	_____ C64	_____ Atari 400	_____ TRS 80
_____ Apple II +	_____ IBM PC jr	_____ C128	_____ Atari 800	_____ MacIntosh
_____ Apple IIe	_____ Acorn	_____ PET	_____ Atari ST	_____ Apple IIGS
_____ Apple IIc	_____ Adam	_____ Amiga	_____ Other	

Components

____ 5¼" disk

____ 3½" disk

____ ROM cartridge

____ Classroom applications

____ User's guide

____ Warranty (list terms)

Peripherals

Req.		Opt.
____	Keyboard	____
____	Color monitor	____
____	Joystick(s)	____
____	Paddle(s)	____
____	Mouse	____
____	Muppet keyboard	____
____	Koala Pad	____
____	Touch Window	____
____	Voice synthesis	____
____	Printer	____
____	Other (specify):	

Intentions

____ Specified by developer

____ Inferred by analyst

"This program is designed to provide experience with

____ counting skills.

____ letter recognition skills.

____ matching or discrimination skills.

____ computer skills.

____ a medium for creative activity.

List the specific objectives of the program:

Mode of Interaction

____ Drill and practice

____ Tutorial

____ Gaming

____ Simulation

____ Problem solving

____ Open-ended/ divergent

Summary of program: Provide a concise summary of the program's main points, content features, strengths, and weaknesses.

Classroom Observations

Conceptual Areas

Check the item(s) present in the program.

LANGUAGE (LA)

1 ____ Describing objects, events, and relations
2 ____ Describing feelings, one's own and others'
3 ____ Having one's own spoken language written and read aloud
4 ____ Recognizing letters
5 ____ Recognizing words — matching written words
6 ____ Matching sounds and symbols
7 ____ Matching rhyming words
8 ____ Using language to specify actions: sit, run fast, slow, into, toward, etc.
9 ____ Writing stories
10 ____ Following a simple (2- or 3-step) sequence of oral or written directions

NUMBER (NB)

1 ____ Comparing amounts: more, less, same
2 ____ Arranging two sets of symbols in one-to-one correspondence
3 ____ Counting objects; counting by 2s
4 ____ Recognizing numerals
5 ____ Estimating the number of objects
6 ____ Measuring (length) using units
7 ____ Combining groups of objects; taking objects away
8 ____ Recognizing and naming the numerals 1, 2, 3, etc.

CLASSIFICATION (CL)

1 ____ Identifying attributes of things: color, shape, size, function
2 ____ Identifying how things are the same or different; sorting and matching
3 ____ Describing objects in different ways; sorting and re-sorting
4 ____ Identifying attributes an object does not possess; finding the object that does not belong to a set
5 ____ Holding more than one attribute in mind at a time
6 ____ Distinguishing between "all" and "some"

TIME (TI)

1 ____ Stopping and starting an action on signal
2 ____ Observing and describing changes
3 ____ Experiencing and describing different rates of speed
4 ____ Experiencing and describing time intervals — long, short, comparative terms
5 ____ Anticipating future events and making appropriate preparations
6 ____ Identifying the order of a sequence of events; reversing the order of events — before, after, at the same time
7 ____ Comparing the duration of events occurring at the same time — longer, shorter, etc.
8 ____ Using a timer to measure the duration of events
9 ____ Reading time from clocks and watches

SPATIAL RELATIONS (SP)

1 ____ Fitting things together and taking them apart
2 ____ Rearranging and reshaping objects
3 ____ Identifying things from different points of view
4 ____ Experiencing and describing the relative positions, directions, and distances of things — inside, outside, above, below, before, behind, on, under, toward, away
5 ____ Identifying and naming body parts: head, legs, arms, etc.
6 ____ Locating things in the classroom or school on simple maps
7 ____ Interpreting representations of spatial relations in drawings and pictures
8 ____ Distinguishing and describing shapes — circle, square, triangle, doughnut (open & closed shapes)
9 ____ Identifying and reversing spatial order
10 ____ Identifying shapes produced by cuts and folds

SERIATION (SE)

1 ____ Making comparisons — shape, shades of color, pitch, and/or speed
2 ____ Arranging several things in order and describing their relations by size, color, etc.
3 ____ Fitting one ordered set of objects to another through trial and error
4 ____ Inserting objects into an ordered sequence

CREATIVE PROJECTS (CP)

1 ____ Drawing pictures
2 ____ Creating sounds or music
3 ____ Programming
4 ____ Designing, changing, and printing a plan or product

OTHER TOPICS (OT)

1 ____ Practicing memory skills
2 ____ Recognizing and naming the parts of the computer
3 ____ Typing or practicing keyboard skills
4 ____ Making signs, word processing, or keeping records. (Of potential use to preschool and kindergarten teachers.)
5 ____ Nutrition, health, and safety

User Friendliness

Minimum User Competency

When considering the portions of the program designed or intended for the child's use, rate the method in which the child's answers are entered into the computer. (Numbers indicate the method's point-value.)

9 ___ Touch screen or use voice.
8 ___ Touch any key or one key.
7 ___ Move the cursor to a visual representation (icon) using a joystick, graphics tablet, light pen, or mouse.
6 ___ Use only 1-4 keys on the keyboard consistently, e.g, spacebar and RETURN.
5 ___ Move the cursor with the arrow keys.
4 ___ Find and press one of the number keys and/or RETURN.
3 ___ Find and press one of the letter keys and/or RETURN.
2 ___ Type in a word/RETURN.
1 ___ Press more than one key simultaneously, e.g., CONTROL-C.

Menu Design

6 ___ Picture or talking menu, touch screen to make the selection.
5 ___ Picture or talking menu, move cursor to selection with peripheral device, such as a joystick or a mouse.
4 ___ Picture or talking menu, move cursor to selection with arrow keys/RETURN to make the selection.
3 ___ Picture or talking menu, press specific key to make choice (e.g., a number key).
2 ___ Simple written menu, with less than six choices, using large letters.
1 ___ Written menu with more than six choices or small letters.

Technical Features

	always	some extent	never	N/A
• Program instructions can be reviewed on the screen	___	___	___	___
• When a child holds a key down, only one input is sent to the computer, except where intended, such as in a drawing program	___	___	___	___
• Getting to the part of the program to be used by the child requires only inserting a disk and starting the computer	___	___	___	___
• If there are data files. e.g., vocabulary words, that can be changed, doing so is easy	___	___	___	___
• Random generation is a part of the program's design	___	___	___	___
• Packaging of the program is well designed, providing storage capacity for the program materials	___	___	___	___
• Program package comes complete and ready-to-use	___	___	___	___
• Program design allows for quick loading time and minimal disk-reading time	___	___	___	___
• Program provides quick, obvious movement to and from the menu	___	___	___	___
• The title screen sequence is not long or can be bypassed	___	___	___	___
• Color is used	___	___	___	___
• Animated graphics are used	___	___	___	___
• Sound can be turned off or on from the program	___	___	___	___
total (13 possible)	___	___	___	___

Educational Value

Content Presentation

	always	some extent	never	N/A
• The concept, rather than the game, is the central learning outcome	___	___	___	___
• The program is enjoyable to use	___	___	___	___
• Content is arranged in a challenging way	___	___	___	___
• Elements of the program are motivating to the child	___	___	___	___
• This program could be of interest to users other than the program's target audience, e.g., parents, older siblings, etc	___	___	___	___
• Content is applicable for early childhood age-range	___	___	___	___
• The child can control own sequence throughout the program	___	___	___	___
• Child can exit the activity at any point	___	___	___	___
• Language, text, or print is appropriate for the early childhood age-range	___	___	___	___
• The program includes data files (e.g., words, numbers) that can be changed	___	___	___	___
• The program provides demonstrations	___	___	___	___
• Practice is meaningful to the child (e.g., geographic location, home environment)	___	___	___	___
• The graphics				
— are not overly "cute"	___	___	___	___
— do not detract from the program's overall intentions	___	___	___	___
• Graphics do not promote unnecessary stimulation	___	___	___	___
• Music/sound does not promote unnecessary stimulation	___	___	___	___
• Content is free from racial bias	___	___	___	___
• Content is free from ethnic bias	___	___	___	___
• Content is free from sexual bias	___	___	___	___
total (19 possible)	___	___	___	___

Content Strength

	always	some extent	never	N/A
• This program provides a good presentation of one or more conceptual areas	___	___	___	___
• The program presents a clear focus on one or more conceptual areas	___	___	___	___
• The concept, rather than the game, is the central learning outcome	___	___	___	___
• The program provides practice with the concept in differing contexts	___	___	___	___
• Elements of the program match direct experiences	___	___	___	___
• The program is enjoyable to use	___	___	___	___
total (6 possible)	___	___	___	___

Instructional Design

Ease of Use

	always	some extent	never	N/A
• Can the child do the program the first time without help				
• Can the child do the program after the first few times without help				
• Does the child have control over:				
— time allowed for problems				
— rate of display				
— order of display				
— exiting at any time				
• The written instructions:				
— provide technical details for the program where needed				
— provide stategies for extending the concepts into noncomputer contexts				
— are well organized				
total (9 possible)				

Feedback

	always	some extent	never	N/A
• The child is aware of when he/she makes an incorrect response				
• The child is aware of when he/she makes a correct response				
• Feedback explains/shows why responses are not correct				
• Feedback responses are varied				
• Feedback is directly correlated to keystroke				
• Feedback is appropriate because it				
— is nonthreatening				
— reinforces content				
— is understood by the child				
• Feedback effectively makes use of sound and graphic capacities of the computer				
• A record of the child's work				
— can be stored on disk				
— can be printed				
— is informative				
total (12 possible)				

Embedded Reinforcements

	always	some extent	never	N/A
• Graphic reinforcements are in support of, or reinforce, the content or concepts presented				
• Sound reinforcements are in support of, or reinforce, the content or concepts presented				
total (4 possible)				

CMI Techniques

Techniques of Computer Managed Instruction
____ are not used in this convergent-style program (0 points)
____ are not appliable to this divergent-style program (NA)
____ are not applicable because the user or adult selects difficulty level (NA)
____ are used (check those that apply — 1 point each)
    ____ feedback is individualized to the child's response
    ____ program helps a child understand his or her progress, e.g., how many problems remaining
    ____ a record of the child's work is recorded
    ____ program is designed so that it can automatically adapt to an appropriate difficulty level

____ total (4 possible)

Comments of Reviewer
to Software Producer

CALCULATION OF A COMPONENT SCORE

The following formula is used to compute the specific scores for each component of the program:

$$\frac{(X + Y/2) \times 100}{n - Z} = S$$

Where

X = Total of checks in "always" column
Y = Total of checks in "some extent" column
Z = Total of checks in the "N/A" column
n = Number of items in a category (such as Feedback)
S = Score for a component of the program (as a percent)

For example:

Feedback

	always	some extent	never	N/A
• The child is aware of when he/she makes an incorrect response	✓			
• The child is aware of when he/she makes a correct response	✓			
• Feedback explains/shows why responses are not correct			✓	
• Feedback responses are varied	✓			
• Feedback is directly correlated to keystroke	✓			
• Feedback is appropriate because it				
— is nonthreatening	✓			
— reinforces content		✓		
— is understood by the user		✓		
• Feedback effectively makes use of sound and graphic capacities of the computer	✓			
• A record of the child's work				
— can be stored on disk			✓	
— can be printed				✓
— is informative				✓
Total (12 possible)	6	2	2	2

In this example

X = 6 (Total of checks under "always")
Y = 2 (Total of checks under "some extent")
Z = 2 (Total of checks under "N/A")
n = 12 (Number of items under the heading "Feedback")

So, when applying the formula above,

$$\frac{6 + 2/2 \times 100}{12 - 2} = 70$$

The component score (S) for Feedback is 70%.

APPENDIXES

APPENDIX 1: EARLY CHILDHOOD SOFTWARE PRODUCERS

Alphaphonics
P.O. Box 2024
San Mateo, CA 94401
415/588-8082
  Alphaget
  Astro's ABCs

Advanced Ideas, Inc.
2550 Ninth Street
Berkeley, CA 94710
415/526-9100
  Dinosaurs

American Guidance Service
Publishers Building
Circle Pines, MN 55014
800/328-2560
  SocPix

Apple Computer Company
20525 Mariani Avenue
Cupertino, CA 95014
408/973-3708
  Makers of Apple computers

Apple Support Center
5130 Plaza Boulevard Parkway
Charlotte, NC 28210
704/525-8120
  A regional office to support
  Apple users

Apple Support Center
904 Caribbean Drive
Sunnyvale, CA 94089
408/734-9790
  A regional office to support
  Apple users

Apple Support Center
5655 Meadowbrook Court
Rolling Meadows, IL 60008
312/577-3600
  A regional office to support
  Apple users

Aquarius People Materials
P.O. Box 128
Indian Rocks Beach, FL 33535
800/338-2644
In FL, 813/595-7890
  Alpha Teach
  Counting Skills
  Critter Count
  Jr. Typer
  Language
  Ordering/Sequencing
  Spatial Relationships

Artworx
150 North Main Street
Fairport, NY 14450
800/828-6573
  Hodge Podge
  Monkey Math

Baudville
5380 52nd Street S.E.
Grand Rapids, MI 49508
616/698-0888
  Rainy Day Games

BeCi Software
78 Dartmouth Street
Boston, MA 02116
617/531-5116
  Fruit Tree/Gumball
  My Book
  Number BeCi
  Shape Games

Bright Star Technology
14450 N.E. 29th Place
Bellevue, WA 98007
206/885-5446
  Talking Tiles

Broderbund Software
17 Paul Drive
San Rafael, CA 94903
415/492-3200
  Print Shop, The

CBS Software
CBS Inc., One Fawcett Place
Greenwich, CT 06836
  Dr. Seuss Fix-Up the
    Mix-Up Puzzler
  Pals Around Town
Note: In 1987, CBS Software was
dissolved. See Mindscape, Hi Tech
Expressions, or Joyce Hakansson
Associates, Inc. for information on
old CBS titles.

C&C Software
5713 Kentford Circle
Wichita, KS 67220
316/683-6056
  Learning About Numbers
  Letters and First Words
  Magic Crayon
  Telling Time

Compu-Tations
P.O. Box 502
Troy, MI 48099
313/689-5059
  Early Elementary I
  Early Elementary II

Compu-Teach
78 Olive Street
New Haven, CT 06511
800/448-3224
In CT, 203/777-7738
  Once Upon a Time . . .
  Stepping Stones Level I
  Stepping Stones Level II

Connor Toy Corporation
833 South 60th Avenue
Wausau, WI 54401
800/345-7817
  Video Smarts

Data Command
P.O. Box 548
Kankakee, IL 60901
815/933-7735
  Alphabet Sounds
  One Banana More

Davidson and Associates, Inc.
6069 Groveoak Place #12
Rancho Palos Verdes, CA 90272
213/378-7826
  Math and Me
  Reading and Me

D.C. Heath & Company
125 Spring Street
Lexington, MA 02173
800/334-3284
  Alphabots
  Bald Headed Chicken, The
  Brand New View, A
  Grabbit Factory, The
  Great Leap, A
  Just Around the Block
  Learning Line, The
  Math Maze
  Maze-o
  Not Too Messy, Not Too Neat
  Picture Dictionary
  Read, Write, & Publish
  Rosie the Counting Rabbit
  Sleepy Brown Cow, The
  Sweet Shop, The
  What Makes a Dinosaur Sore
  Where Did My Toothbrush Go?

Designware, Inc.
185 Berry Street
San Francisco, CA 94107
415/546-1866
    Creature Creator
    Notable Phantom, The
    Spellicopter

Developmental Equipment, Inc.
Building 115
1000 North Rand Road
Wauconda, IL 60084
312/526-2682
    Makers of the single switch

DIL International
Suite 180
2025 Lavoisier Street
Sainte-Foy (Quebec)
    CANADA G1V 1N6
800/463-5581
    Extrateletactograph, The
    Mary Marvel and Willy Wiz at the
        Costume Ball
    Mary Marvel and Willy Wiz in the
        Garden
    WonderWorker, The ($99.95)

DLM
One DLM Park
Allen, TX 75002
800/527-4747
    Alphabet Circus
    Animal Photo Fun
    Comparison Kitchen
    Curious George in Outer Space
    Fish Scales
    Number Farm
    Shape & Color Rodeo
    Teddy Bear-rels of Fun

Dunamis, Inc.
3620 Highway 317
Suwanee, GA 30174
404/932-0485
    Distributors for the
    PowerPad ($99.95)

E.C.S.
Exceptional Children's Software, Inc.
P.O. Box 487
Hays, KS 67601
913/625-9281
    Adventures of Jimmy Jumper, The
    Color Find
    Rabbit Scanner, The
    Run Rabbit Run
    Sight Word Spelling
    Touch and Match
    Touch and See

Edmark Corporation
P.O. Box 3903
Bellevue, WA 98009
800/426-0856
In WA, 800/422-3118
    Producers of the Touch Window

Education Systems Corporation
6170 Cornerstone Court East
San Diego, CA 93121-3710
800/548-8372
In CA, 619/587-0087
    Integrated Learning System

Educational Activities, Inc.
P.O. Box 392
Freeport, NY 11520
800/645-3739
    Adventures of Dobot, The
    Copycats: ABC for Micro and Me!
    Early Childhood Learning Program
    First Encounters
    First Numbers: First Words
    It's No Game
    Spaceship Lost

Edusoft
P.O Box 2560
Berkeley, CA 94702
800/227-2778
In CA, 415/548-2304
    Alphabet Song and Count

EduWare
185 Berry Street
San Francisco, CA 94107
800/572-2272
In CA, 415/546-1937
    Introduction to Counting
    Spelling and Reading Primer
    Webster's Numbers

Firebird Licensees, Inc.
71 Franklin Turnpike
Waldwick, NJ 07463
    Fantastic Animals
    Talking Teacher

First Byte, Inc.
Suite 302
333 East Spring Street
Long Beach, CA 90806
213/595-7006
800/523-8070
In CA, 800/624-2692
    First Letters and Words
    First Shapes
    Kid Talk

First Star Software
18 East 41st Street
New York, NY 10017
800/223-1545
    I Love My Alphabet

47th Street Photo
36 East 19th Street
New York, NY 10003
800/221-7774
    A discount mail order computer
    dealer. A good place to call
    to check hardware prices.

Great Wave Software
5353 Scotts Valley Drive
Scotts Valley, CA 95066
408/438-1990
    KidsTime

Grolier Electronic Publishing
Sherman Turnpike
Danbury, CT 06816
800/658-8858
    Exploring Your World: The Weather
    First Steps to Reading
    Play Together Learn Together
    Rhyming to Read

Hartley Courseware, Inc.
Box 419
Dimondale, MI 48821
800/247-1380
In MI, 517/646-6458
    Bird's Eye View
    Colors and Shapes
    Conservation and Counting
    Dr. Peet's Talk/Writer
    Early Skills
    Letter Recognition
    My Words
    Observation and Classification
    Ollie and Seymour
    Patterns and Sequences
    Pictures, Letters, and Sounds
    Size and Logic

Hi Tech Expressions
Suite 9
1700 N.W. 65th Avenue
Plantation, FL 33313
800/848-9273
In FL, 305/584-6386
    Astro-Grover
    Big Bird's Funhouse
    Big Bird's Special Delivery
    Ernie's Big Splash
    Ernie's Magic Shapes
    Grover's Animal Adventures
    Letter-Go-Round
    Sesame Street Print Kit

Houghton Mifflin Co.
Educational Software Division
P.O. Box 683
Hanover, NH 03755
800/258-3545
In NH, 312/980-9710
　　Kindermath II
　　Reading Comprehension: Level 1
　　Reading Helpers
　　Reading Starters
　　Sound Ideas: Consonants
　　Sound Ideas: Vowels
　　Sound Ideas: Word Attack

HRM Software
Has been acquired by Queue, Inc.
　　Alice in Wonderland
　　Jack and the Beanstalk

Human Touch, Inc.
CD-I Software Production Division
2381 Blue Haven Drive
Rowland Heights, CA 91748-3204
714/595-1355
　　Magic Melody Box

IBM Educational Systems
P.O. Box 1328-W
Boca Raton, FL 33429
407/443-1929
　　Bouncy Bee Learns Letters 1.0
　　Bouncy Bee Learns Words 1.0
　　Primary Editor Plus
　　Writing to Read 2.0

Island Software
Box 300
Lake Grove, NY 11755
516/585-3755
　　Letter Games
　　Milk Bottles
　　Puss in Boot
　　Word Factory

Jostens Learning Systems, Inc.
600 West University Drive
Arlington Heights, IL 60004
　　Distributors of the Ufonic
　　speech synthesizer

Joyce Hakansson Associates, Inc.
2029 Durant
Berkeley, CA 94704
415/540-5963
　　Ducks Ahoy
　　Kermit's Electronic Story Maker
　　The Great Gonzo in WordRider

Kidsview Software, Inc.
P.O. Box 98
Warner, NH 03278
603/927-4428
　　Mount Murdoch

Laureate Learning Systems
110 East Spring Street
Winooski, VT 05404
802/655-4755
　　Concentrate
　　Micro-LADS
　　Talking Nouns I
　　Talking Nouns II
　　Talking Verbs
　　Words & Concepts
　　Words & Concepts II
　　Words & Concepts III

Lawrence Hall of Science
University of California
Berkeley, CA 94720
415/642-3167
　　Estimation
　　Music
　　Numbers
　　Words

Learning Company, The
6493 Kaiser Drive
Fremont, CA 94555
800/852-2255
　　Bumble Games
　　Gertrude's Secrets
　　Juggle's Rainbow
　　Math Rabbit
　　Moptown Parade
　　Reader Rabbit

Learning Lab Software
8833 Receda Boulevard
Northridge, CA 91324
800/247-4641
　　Monsters and Make Believe

Learning Technologies, Inc.
Suite 131
4255 LBJ Freeway
Dallas, TX 75244
800/238-4277
In TX, 214/991-4958
　　Animal Hotel
　　Bike Hike
　　Flying Carpet, The
　　How to Weigh an Elephant
　　Let's Go Fishing
　　Lion's Workshop
　　Same or Different
　　Shutterbug's Patterns
　　Shutterbug's Pictures

MECC
Minnesota Educational Computing
　　Consortium
3490 Lexington Avenue North
St. Paul, MN 55126-8097
800/228-3504 or 612/481-3500
In MN, 800/782-0032
　　Arithmetic Critters
　　Counting
　　Counting Critters 1.0
　　EZ Logo
　　First Letter Fun
　　Fun From A to Z
　　Money Works
　　Paint With Words
　　Path-Tactics
　　Patterns
　　Sound Tracks

Micro-Learningware
P.O. Box 307
Richmond, VA 23220
507/625-2205
　　Teddy Bears Counting Fun

Micro Power & Light Company
Suite 219
12820 Hillcrest Road
Dallas, TX 75230
214/239-6620
　　Alphabet Recognition
　　Country Combo
　　Counting and Ordering
　　Time Master

MicroED, Inc.
P.O. Box 24750
Edina, MN 55424
612/929-2242
　　Beginning Counting
　　Beginning Reading Skills
　　Counting
　　Early Math
　　Learning the Alphabet

Milliken Publishing Co.
1100 Research Boulevard
St. Louis, MO 63132
314/991-4220
　　Alphabetization Sequence
　　Math Sequences
　　The First "R"

MindPlay
100 Conifer Hill Drive
Danvers, MA 01923
800/221-7911
   Cat 'n Mouse
   Cotton's First Files
   Cotton Tales
   Easy Street
   Math Magic
   Picture Perfect
   Race the Clock

Mindscape, Inc.
3444 Dundee Road
Northbrook, IL 60062
800/221-9884
In IL, 312/480-7667
   Best Electronic Word Book Ever
   Body Awareness
   Castle Clobber
   Color Me
   Counting Critters
   Fun With Directions
   Grownup and Small
   Knowing Numbers
   Letters and Words
   LOGO Power
   Many Ways to Say I Love You
   Shapes & Patterns
   Tink's Adventure
   Tonk in the Land of Buddy-Bots
   Tuk Goes to Town

Nordic Software, Inc.
3939 North 48th Street
Lincoln, NE 68504
800/228-0417
   Clock Works
   Coin Works
   Preschool Disk 1
   Preschool Disk 2

Ohm Software Company
163 Richard Drive
Tiverton, RI 02878
401/253-9354
   Kieran

Orange Cherry Software
P.O. Box 390
Pound Ridge, NY 10576
800/672-6002
   Talking ABC's
   Talking Clock
   Talking Numbers
   Telling Time

Paperback Software
2612 Eighth Street
Berkeley, CA 94710
415/644-2116
   My ABC's

PDI Software
95 East Putnum Avenue
Greenwich, CT 06830
203/661-8799
   Alphabet Arcade, The
   Preschool IQ Builder
   Preschool IQ Builder II

P.E.A.L. Software
5000 North Parkway
Calabasas Suite 105
Calabasas, CA 91302
818/883-7849
   Exploratory Play
   Keytalk
   Representational Play

Personal Touch Corporation
   See Edmark Corporation

Polarware, Inc.
P.O. Box 311
2600 Keslinger Road
Geneva, IL 60134
312/232-1984
   ABC's
   Dinosaurs Are Forever
   Fun on the Farm
   Holidays & Seasons
   Letters For You
   Numbers Count
   This Land Is Your Land

PTI/Koala Industries
269 Mount Herman Road
Scotts Valley, CA 95066
800/223-3022
   Koala Pad Graphics Exhibitor

Queue, Inc.
562 Boston Avenue
Bridgeport, CT 06610
800/232-2224
   Developing Language Skills
   Diskovery Adding Machine
   Diskovery Take Away Zoo
   Kinder Koncepts Math
   Kinder Koncepts Reading
   Talk About a Walk

Random House Software
400 Hahn Road
Westminster, MD 21157
800/638-6460
In MD, 800/492-0782
In CD, AL or HI, 301/848-1900
   Animal Alphabet and Other Things
   Boars Tell Time, The
   Charlie Brown's 1-2-3's
   Charlie Brown's ABC's
   City Country Opposites
   Inside Outside Opposites
   Inside Outside Shapes
   Mr. and Mrs. Potato Head
   Peanuts Maze Marathon
   Peanuts Picture Puzzlers

RC Systems, Inc.
121 West Winesap Road
Bothell, WA 98012
206/672-6909
   Makers of the Slotbuster II

R.J. Cooper & Associates
Suite 283
24843 Del Prado
Dana Point, CA 92629
714/240-1912
   Early & Advanced Switch Games
   R.J.'s Switch Progressions

Scandura Training Systems
798 North Avenue Drive
Bridgeport, CT 06606
203/335-0960
   Adventures in Space
   Beginner Reader

Scarborough Systems, Inc.
55 South Broadway
Tarrytown, NY 10591
914/332-4545
   Build a Book About You

Scholastic Software
730 Broadway
New York, NY 10003
800/325-6149
   Bank Street Writer III, The
   Computergarten
   Microzine Jr. (Sept/Oct '88)
   SuperPrint!
   Talking Textwriter

S.D.L.
Dale Moss
2715 Cabrillo #105
San Francisco, CA 94121
415/221-2479
   Toybox

Sierra On-Line
Sierra On-Line Bldg.
Coarsegold, CA 93614
209/683-6858
   Learning With Fuzzywump
   Learning With Leeper

Silicon Express
Box 850
East Mill Street
Pataskala, OH 43062
800/999-6868
  A good place to call for
  discounted mail order software

SouthWest EdPsych Services
P.O. Box 1870
Phoenix, AZ 85001
602/253-6528
  Reading Machine, The

Spinnaker Software Corp.
One Kendall Square
Cambridge, MA 02139
800/826-0706
  Alpha Build
  Alphabet Zoo
  Delta Drawing
  Early Learning Friends
  Facemaker
  Facemaker Golden Edition 1.0
  Grandma's House
  Hey Diddle Diddle
  Kids on Keys
  Kidwriter
  Kindercomp
  Kindercomp Golden Edition
  Learn The Alphabet
  Peter and the Wolf Music
  Peter Rabbit Reading
  Story Machine
  Up & Add 'Em

Springboard
7808 Creekridge Circle
Minneapolis, MN 55435
800/445-4780 ext. 1000
  Early Games
  Easy as ABC
  Make a Match
  Mask Parade
  Music Maestro
  Puzzle Master
  Rainbow Painter
  Stickers

S.R.A.
P.O. Box 5380
Chicago, IL 60680-5380
312/984-7000
  Ollie Finds It
  Ollie Hears and Sequences
  Ollie Remembers It

Stone & Associates
Suite 319
7910 Ivanhoe Avenue
La Jolla, CA 92037
800/621-0852 ext. 520
  1st Math
  Kid's Stuff
  Memory Master
  My Letters, Numbers, and Words

Strawberry Hill Software
202-11961-88th Avenue
Delta, British Columbia
Canada V4C 3C9
604/594-5947
  Hobo's Luck
  Peter's Growning Patterns
  Surrounding Patterns
  What's Next

Street Electronics
6420 Via Real
Carpenteria, CA 93013
805/684-4593
  Makers of the Echo
  and Cricket speech
  synthesizers

Sunburst Communications, Inc.
39 Washington Avenue
Pleasantville, NY 10570
800/431-1934
In Canada, 800/247-6756
  1-2-3 Sequence Me
  Balancing Bear
  Counters
  Getting Ready to Read and Add
  Magic Slate
  Memory Building Blocks
  Muppet Slate
  Muppet Word Book
  Muppets On Stage
  Muppetville
  Now You See It, Now You Don't
  Odd One Out
  Simon Says
  Space Waste Race
  Teddy's and Iggy
  Teddy's Playground
  Tiger's Tales
  Touch & Write
  What's in a Frame

Teacher Support Software
P.O. Box 7130
Gainesville, FL 32605-7130
800/228-2871
In FL, 904/371-3802
  Language Experience Recorder
  Plus

THESIS
P.O. Box 147-CC
Garden City, MI 48135
800/354-0550
  Math Facts Level I
  Preschool Fun

Tom Snyder Productions, Inc.
90 Sherman Street
Cambridge, MA 02140
800/342-0236
617/876-4433
  Flodd, the Bad Guy
  Jack and the Beanstalk

Troll Associates
100 Corporate Drive
Mahwah, NJ 07430
800/526-5289
  Bremen Town Musicians
  I Can Count
  Magic String, The
  Reading Fun: Beg. Consonants
  Rumpelstiltskin
  Spelling Bee, The

T.Y.C. Software, Inc.
Teach Yourself by Computer
  Software, Inc.
2128 West Jefferson Road
Pittsford, NY 14534
716/427-7065
  Match-On-A-Mac

Weekly Reader Software and
  Optimum Resource, Inc.
10 Station Place
Norfolk, CT 06058
800/327-1473
  New Talking Stickybear ABC, The
  Stickybear ABC
  Stickybear Math
  Stickybear Numbers
  Stickybear Opposites
  Stickybear Printer
  Stickybear Reading
  Stickybear Shapes
  Stickybear Town Builder
  Stickybear Typing

Wescott Software
2316 Park Place
Evanston, IL 60201
312/328-1367
  Fun With Letters and Words
  Fun With Memory
  Fun With Numbers

World Book, Inc.
Merchandise Mart Plaza
Chicago, IL 60654
312/245-3456
  Come Play With Pockets
  Happy Birthday, Pockets
  Pockets and Her New Sneakers
  Pockets Goes on a Picnic
  Pockets Goes on Vacation
  Pockets Goes to the Carnival
  Pockets Leads the Parade

APPENDIX 2: SOFTWARE LISTING BY CONTENT AREA

LANGUAGE

Title	Concept	Final Rating
Bald-Headed Chicken, The	■ Language experience	89
Brand New View, A	■ Language experience	89
Great Leap, A	■ Language experience	89
Just Around the Block	■ Language experience	89
Kid Talk	■ Language experience	89
Not Too Messy, Not Too Neat	■ Language experience	89
Rosie the Counting Rabbit	■ Language experience	89
Sleepy Brown Cow, The	■ Language experience	89
What Makes a Dinosaur Sore?	■ Language experience	89
Where Did My Toothbrush Go?	■ Language experience	89
Muppet Slate	■ Language experiences	88
Talking Tiles	■ Letter and word sounds	85
First Letter Fun	■ Letter recognition	82
KidsTime	■ Letters, numbers, matching, writing, music	82
Muppet Word Book	■ Letters and words	82
Reading Comprehension: Lev. 1	■ Reading comprehension skills	82
Animal Alph. and Other Things	■ Letter recognition, alphabetical order	81
Fun From A to Z	■ Alphabet skills practice	81
Magic Slate	■ Word processing	81
Read, Write, & Publish 1	■ Word processing and story illustrating	81
Touch & Write	■ Printing practice	81
Easy as ABC	■ Letter recognition, alphabet order	80
Sound Ideas: Consonants	■ Consonant sounds	80
Sound Ideas: Vowels	■ Five vowel sounds (long, short) and y	80
Talking Nouns I	■ Language development	80
Talking Nouns II	■ Language development	80
Talking Verbs	■ Language development	80
Tiger's Tales	■ Reading vocabulary & comprehension	80
Words & Concepts	■ Vocabulary training	80
Words & Concepts II	■ Vocabulary training	80
Words & Concepts III	■ Vocabulary training	80
Dr. Peet's Talk/Writer	■ Language exploration and skills	79
Integrated Learning System	■ Math and reading K-9	79
Peter Rabbit Reading	■ Letters, letter sounds, and words	79
Cotton Tales	■ Word processing, language development	78
My Words	■ Language experience	78
Pictures, Letters, and Sounds	■ Letter recognition	78
Kermit's Electronic Storymaker	■ Words and their meaning	77
Stickybear Reading	■ Word and sentence fun	77
FirstWriter	■ Creative writing	76
Fun With Letters and Words	■ Letter recognition	76
Keytalk	■ A beginning literacy activity	76
Kid's Stuff	■ Counting skills, letter recognition	76

Title	Concept	Final Rating
Talking Teacher	Letter identification	76
Micro-LADS	Syntactic comprehension	75
Talking Textwriter	Exploration of written language	75
First "R": Kindergarten, The	Letter recognition; initial, ending sounds	74
First Letters and Words	Letters & words, dinosaurs	74
Primary Editor Plus	Word processing, drawing, making banners	74
Kidwriter	Creating computer storybooks	73
Muppets On Stage	Counting skills, letter recognition	73
Paint With Words	Word recognition	73
Bouncy Bee Learns Letters 1.0	Letter recognition	72
Sound Ideas: Word Attack	Consonant blends, clusters and digraphs	72
Bank Street Writer III, The	Word processing	71
Exploratory Play	Early language acquisition	71
Reader Rabbit	Basic reading skills/comprehension	71
Representational Play	Early language acquisition	71
Best Electronic Word Book Ever	Reading readiness skills	70
Flodd, the Bad Guy	Letter and word recognition, stories	70
Jack and the Beanstalk	Letter and word recognition, stories	70
Kieran	Letters, numbers, clocks, upper/lower case	70
Adventures of Jimmy Jumper	Prepositional concepts	69
Alice in Wonderland	Remembering a sequence of events	69
Jack and the Beanstalk	Word recognition, event sequence	69
Race the Clock	Memory	69
Reading Helpers	Reading skills	69
Story Machine	Creative activity	69
Alphabet Circus	Letter recognition, alphabet order	68
Build a Book About You	Creating a book	68
Letters and First Words	Letters, initial consonants	68
Letters and Words	Letter recognition, alphabet order	68
Alphabetization Sequence	Alphabetizing, letter discrimination	67
Spellicopter	Spelling practice	66
Cat 'n Mouse	Relational concepts	65
Reading Machine, The	Various language skills	65
Charlie Brown's ABC's	Letter recognition & association	64
New Talking Stickybear ABC's, The	Letter recognition	64
Getting Ready to Read and Add	Numerals, U/L-case letters	63
My ABC's	Letter and numeral recognition	63
Reading Starters	Reading skills	63
Astro's ABCs	Letter recognition skills	62
Bouncy Bee Learns Words 1.0	Word knowledge	62
It's No Game	Personal safety skills	62
Kids on Keys	Letter recognition	62
Preschool Disk 1	Letters, counting, alphabetical order	62
Words	Letter disc., word experiences	61
I Love My Alphabet	Letters, alphabetical order	59
Once Upon a Time . . .	Language experience, bookmaking	59
Stepping Stones Level I	Letters, numbers, and words	59
Stickybear ABC	Letter recognition	59
Stepping Stones Level II	Vocabulary, counting, adding	58
Beginning Reading Skills	Beginning reading skills	57
Alpha Build	Upper/lower-case, alphabetical order	56
Learn the Alphabet	Upper/lower case, alphabetical order	56
Letter-Go-Round	Letter matching	56
Memory Master	Memory skills	56

Title	Concept	Final Rating
Reading Fun: Beg. Consonants	■ Beginning consonants	56
Talk About a Walk	■ Classifying household objects	56
Language Experience Recorder Plus	■ Word processing	55
Maze-o	■ Spelling words	55
Alphabots	■ Letter recognition	54
Picture Dictionary	■ Word recall and memory	53
Alphabet Song and Count	■ Alphabet order, counting skills	51
Alphabet Zoo	■ Letter recognition	51
Alphaget	■ Letter recognition practice	51
Expl. Your World: The Weather	■ Body parts, weather words	51
Hodge Podge	■ Letter recognition	51
Spelling and Reading Primer	■ Spelling and reading practice	51
Learning the Alphabet	■ Matching letters, alphabetical order	50
Space Waste Race	■ Letter/numeral recognition	49
Copycats: ABC for Micro & Me!	■ Matching, alphabet order	48
Letter Recognition	■ Location of letters on keyboard	48
Hey Diddle Diddle	■ Rhyming words and phrases	47
Alphabet Recognition	■ Letter recognition, upper/lower-case	46
Magic String, The	■ Reading skills	46
My Letters, Numbers, and Words	■ Letter recognition	46
Bremen Town Musicians	■ Homonyms, context clues, comprehension	45
Developing Language Skills	■ Knowledge of words	45
Mount Murdoch	■ Adventure game and word processor	45
Writing To Read 2.0	■ Reading skills	45
Kinder Koncepts Reading	■ Reading readiness	44
Preschool Fun	■ Counting, letters, & matching	44
First Steps to Reading	■ Initial consonants	43
Rumpelstiltskin	■ Reading comprehension	43
Talking ABC's	■ Letter recognition	43
Alphabet Arcade, The	■ Alphabetizing, dictionary skills	42
Stickybear Typing	■ Typing skills	42
First Numbers: First Words	■ 1-to-1 correspondence, visual memory	41
Jr. Typer	■ Touch typing	41
Tink's Adventure	■ Key location, alphabetical order	41
Tuk Goes to Town	■ Develops spelling and vocabulary	41
Alpha Teach	■ Alphabet, initial consonants	39
Beginner Reader	■ Rhyming words	39
Sight Word Spelling	■ Letter, word, and numeral recognition	39
My Book	■ Writing stories	38
Language	■ Language recognition	37
Rhyming to Read	■ Rhyming words	37
Letter Games	■ Letter recognition	34
Spelling Bee, The	■ Spelling skills	32
Alphabet Sounds	■ Letter sounds, initial consonants	29
Early Elementary II	■ Letter recognition, counting	28

NUMBER

Title	Concept	Final Rating
Counting Critters 1.0	■ Counting and early math concepts	81
Stickybear Math	■ Counting, addition and subtraction	81
Arithmetic Critters	■ Counting, addition, and subtraction	78
Fish Scales	■ Measurement	78
Learning About Numbers	■ Counting, clocks, basic math facts	78
Math and Me	■ Shapes, patterns, numbers, and addition	78
Math Rabbit	■ Counting, matching sets, basic math facts	78
Number Farm	■ Counting skills	78
Balancing Bear	■ Comparing amounts, addition, logic	77
Money Works	■ Money skills	76
1st Math	■ Addition & subtraction equations, patterns	75
Up & Add 'Em	■ Matching numbers	75
Learning With Fuzzywomp	■ Counting, matching, numerical order	73
Math Concepts Level P	■ Math concepts and symbols	73
Coin Works	■ Value of coins	71
Conservation and Counting	■ Counting skills	71
Kindercomp Golden Edition	■ Counting, letters, matching, and drawing	70
Counters	■ Counting experiences	69
Diskovery Adding Machine	■ Counting, addition skills	69
Math Sequences	■ Number readiness	69
Path-Tactics	■ Counting, basic math facts	69
Diskovery Take Away Zoo	■ Counting, subtraction practice	68
Pockets Goes to the Carnival	■ Counting, 1-1 correspondence	68
Charlie Brown's 1-2-3's	■ Numeral recognition, counting	67
Knowing Numbers	■ Fundamental math skill practice	67
Webster's Numbers	■ Basic math concepts	67
Introduction to Counting	■ Counting	66
Stickybear Numbers	■ Counting	64
Counting Critters	■ Counting, addition, and subtraction	62
Counting	■ Primary arithmetic skills	60
Fun With Numbers	■ Numeral recognition, adding and sub.	59
Numbers	■ Numeral disc., counting	58
Kinder Koncepts MATH	■ Number and math skills	57
Kindermath II	■ Math fundamentals	57
Counting and Ordering	■ 1-9 counting, numeral recognition	56
Hobo's Luck	■ Counting and probability	54
Sweet Shop, The	■ Number matching, basic facts	54
Counting	■ Counting skills, basic facts	53
Math Magic	■ Math facts (add, sub., mult., div.)	53
Grabbit Factory, The	■ Numerals, basic math facts	52
Math Maze	■ Basic math facts	52
Bumble Games	■ Plotting (x,y) points on a grid.	49
Monkey Math	■ Basic math facts, numerical order	49
Beginning Counting	■ Counting from 1 to 9	43
Early Math	■ Counting, numerical order, basic skills	43
How to Weigh an Elephant	■ Estimation of weight.	42
Astro-Grover	■ Counting, adding, and subtracting	41
Talking Numbers	■ Counting	41
Counting Skills	■ Counting skills	40

Title	Concept	Final Rating
I Can Count	■ Counting up to 10	40
Milk Bottles	■ Comparing amounts	39
Math Facts Level 1	■ Counting, numeral recognition	38
Let's Go Fishing	■ Counting and addition skills	36
Critter Count	■ Basic math facts	34
Teddy Bears Counting Fun	■ Counting skills	32
Number BeCi	■ Grouping and counting	29
Fruit Tree/Gumball	■ Counting, adding, and subtracting	28

CLASSIFICATION

Title	Concept	Final Rating
Muppetville	■ Classifying, memory skills	87
Easy Street	■ Classification, matching, and counting	84
Gertrude's Secrets	■ Classifying and seriating	84
Observation and Classification	■ Classification skills	80
Teddy's Playground	■ Practice with color and shape attributes	80
Match-On-A-Mac	■ Matching letters, shapes, numbers, words	79
Patterns	■ Pattern recognition	79
Reading and Me	■ Matching, classifying, recognizing letters	79
Teddy and Iggy	■ Sequential memory practice	78
Cotton's First Files	■ Beginning database management, animals	77
Ollie and Seymour	■ Pedestrian safety, readiness skills	77
Peter and the Wolf Music	■ Music skills: pitch and melody	77
Colors and Shapes	■ Color ID, visual discrimination	76
Grover's Animal Adventures	■ Classifying animals	76
Early & Advanced Switch Games	■ Cause/effect, matching, counting, scanning	75
First Shapes	■ Five basic shapes	75
Make a Match	■ Matching	75
Pockets Leads the Parade	■ Pattern recognition	75
Preschool Disk 2	■ Matching, counting, adding, memory skills	75
Odd One Out	■ Matching/discrimination	74
Shape & Color Rodeo	■ Recognizing shapes and colors	73
Comparison Kitchen	■ Compare and categorize pictures	72
Patterns and Sequences	■ Matching/discrimination	72

Title	Concept	Final Rating
Happy Birthday, Pockets	■ Visual discrimination	71
Color Find	■ Matching colors	69
Come Play With Pockets	■ Visual memory, tracking skills	66
Shapes & Patterns	■ Visual disc., cognitive skills	66
Dinosaurs	■ Reading, math, and memory skills	65
Touch and Match	■ Classification	65
Ollie Finds It	■ Matching shapes, letters, and words	64
Ollie Hears and Sequences	■ Auditory memory skills	64
Learning Line, The	■ Matching	62
Mary Marvel . . . Costume Ball	■ Variety of basic skills	62
Mary Marvel . . . the Garden	■ Functional intelligence, social skills	62
Pockets and Her New Sneakers	■ Sorting and classification skills	62
Early Skills	■ Shape and word discrimination	61
Pockets Goes on a Picnic	■ Classification, part/whole rel.	61
SocPix	■ Classification (class membership)	61
Castle Clobber	■ Logical thinking skills	56
Moptown Parade	■ Classification and seriation	55
Same or Different	■ Visual discrimination, matching	55
Video Smarts	■ Matching, counting, letters, colors	52
Lion's Workshop	■ Visual discrimination	49
Ernie's Magic Shapes	■ Visual discrimination practice	45
Preschool IQ Builder II	■ Matching, shapes, numbers, letters	43
Preschool IQ Builder I	■ Concepts of same and different	38
Shutterbug's Patterns	■ Sequencing, pattern recognition	36
One Banana More	■ Reading readiness, counting	34
Big Bird's Special Delivery	■ Object recognition	31
Early Elementary I	■ Counting and matching	27
Country Combo	■ Creative experience	26
Word Factory	■ Word discrimination	22

SERIATION

Title	Concept	Final Rating
City Country Opposites	▪ Word meanings through context	78
Size and Logic	▪ Size discrimination, patterns	77
What's Next	▪ Sequencing skills	74
Peter's Growing Patterns	▪ Pattern recognition	73
Inside Outside Opposites	▪ Opposites	72
Grownup and Small	▪ Adult and baby names	68
Notable Phantom, The	▪ Musical notation, pitch recognition	66
Curious George in Outer Space	▪ Size comparisons	62
Shape Games	▪ Pattern recognition	44
Ordering/Sequencing	▪ Seriation concepts	38

SPATIAL RELATIONS

Title	Concept	Final Rating
Stickybear Town Builder	▪ Map skills	80
Puzzle Master	▪ Problem solving (puzzles)	79
Delta Drawing	▪ Drawing, programming concepts	78
Surrounding Patterns	▪ Visual imagery, symmetry	77
Inside Outside Shapes	▪ Six shapes and corresponding words	76
Bird's Eye View	▪ Perspective and positional relationships	73
Pals Around Town	▪ Community Exploration	73
Stickybear Opposites	▪ Opposites, e.g., "near/far"	73
Mr. and Mrs. Potato Head	▪ Creative projects, imagination, memory	71
Adventures of Dobot, The	▪ Problem solving, critical thinking	70
Dr. Seuss Fix-Up . . . Puzzler	▪ Problem solving	70
Fantastic Animals	▪ Part/whole relationships	70
Stickybear Shapes	▪ Shape Identification	70
Grandma's House	▪ Exploring and arranging	68
Body Awareness	▪ Location of body parts	64
Pockets Goes on Vacation	▪ Positional relationships	63

Title	Concept	Final Rating
Fun With Directions	▪ Perceptual and cognitive skills	62
Juggle's Rainbow	▪ Spatial relationships	62
Facemaker Golden Edition	▪ Creativity, memory, and concentration	61
Ernie's Big Splash	▪ Planning, predicting, problem solving	59
Peanuts Picture Puzzlers	▪ Problem solving (puzzles)	59
Tonk in the Land of Buddy-Bots	▪ Problem solving	56
Adventures in Space	▪ Spatial relationships	46
Spaceship Lost	▪ Spatial relationships	45
Flying Carpet, The	▪ Shape recognition	44
Puss in Boot	▪ Spatial concepts	34
Spatial Relationships	▪ Spatial relationships	25

TIME

Title	Concept	Final Rating
Estimation	▪ Est. of length, area, & time units	78
Ducks Ahoy	▪ Logical reasoning skills	78
1-2-3 Sequence Me	▪ Sequencing skills	75
Great Gonzo in WordRider, The	▪ Fun with words, timing, and strategy	73
Clock Works	▪ Clock-reading skills, units of time	72
Early Learning Friends	▪ Shapes, colors, sizes, and timing	71
Run Rabbit Run	▪ Scanning, directionality, and attention	70
Boars Tell Time, The	▪ Clock skills	68
Rabbit Scanner, The	▪ Eye tracking, matching	67
R.J.'s Switch Progressions	▪ Cause and effect, progressions	65
Talking Clock	▪ Clock reading skills	65
Creature Creator	▪ Pattern matching, programming	62
Toybox	▪ Exploration of the computer	56
Peanuts Maze Marathon	▪ Problem solving (mazes)	46
Telling Time	▪ Clock practice	34
Time Master	▪ Clock practice	25

CREATIVE PROJECTS

Title	Concept	Final Rating
Color Me	▪ Drawing, creating	89
Print Shop, The	▪ Creation of printed materials	85
Microzine Jr. (Sept/Oct.'88)	▪ Habitats, making masks, programming	81
ABC's	▪ Coloring pictures	80
Dinosaurs Are Forever	▪ Coloring pictures	80
Fun on the Farm	▪ Coloring pictures	80
Holidays & Seasons	▪ Coloring pictures	80
Letters for You	▪ Coloring pictures	80
Numbers Count	▪ Coloring pictures	80
Rainbow Painter	▪ Drawing	80
This Land Is Your Land	▪ Coloring pictures	80
Picture Perfect	▪ Draw, color, and write	79
Stickers	▪ Creative activity	79
Mask Parade	▪ Creative design	77
Koala Pad Graphics Exhibitor	▪ Drawing	76
Magic Crayon	▪ Drawing with arrow keys	75
EZ Logo	▪ Problem solving, directionality	74
Sound Tracks	▪ Making pictures	74
Extrateletactograph, The	▪ Drawing and writing stories	73
Music Maestro	▪ Practice with musical notation	73
Monsters and Make-Believe	▪ Creative writing, matching, space	71
Learning With Leeper	▪ Counting, matching, drawing	69
Many Ways to Say I Love You	▪ Creative design	69
Kindercomp	▪ Matching, U/L-case practice, drawing	68
SuperPrint!	▪ Printing utility	62
Early Games	▪ Counting, letters, and drawing	60
LOGO Power	▪ Teach 12 basic LOGO commands	59
Magic Melody Box	▪ Creating music	59
Music	▪ Seriation of pitch	59
Teddy Bear-rels of Fun	▪ Creating pictures, graphics, and stories	56
Facemaker	▪ Pattern matching, creative activity	54
Early Childhood . . . Program	▪ Conceptual skill development	53
Sesame Street Print Kit	▪ Creating printed materials	46
Stickybear Printer	▪ "Printing fun for everyone"	43

OTHER TOPICS

Title	Concept	Final Rating
Memory Building Blocks	▪ Visual and auditory memory skills	83
Rainy Day Games	▪ Memory practice	83
What's in a Frame?	▪ Memory practice by context clues	81
Concentrate	▪ Short-term memory skills	80
Simon Says	▪ Chaining memory exercise	80
Now You See It, Now You Don't	▪ Memory skills	79
Fun With Memory	▪ Memory	77
Animal Photo Fun	▪ Animals and their habitats	70
Ollie Remembers It	▪ Visual Memory	64
Shutterbug's Pictures	▪ Memory skills, reading readiness	61
Touch and See	▪ Memory skills	61
Big Bird's Funhouse	▪ Concentration and memory	49
Animal Hotel	▪ Memory skills	45
Play Together Learn Together	▪ Introduction to computer use	44
Bike Hike	▪ Memory, recall of objects	41
First Encounters	▪ Computer literacy skills	32
Computergarten	▪ Keyboard skills, computer terms	27

APPENDIX 3: TALLY OF SOFTWARE TITLES
BY CONCEPTUAL AREA

— LANGUAGE —

#	EXPERIENCE	PROGRAMS (X = 1 program)
LA/1	Describing objects, events, and relations	XXXXXXXXXXXXXXXXXX (18)
LA/2	Describing feelings, one's own and others'	XXXXXXXXXXXXX (13)
LA/3	Having one's own spoken language written and read aloud	XXXXXXXXXXXXXXXXXXXX XXXXXXXX (28)
LA/4	Recognizing letters	XXXXXXXXXXXXXXXXXXXX XXXXXXXXXXXXXXXXXXXX XXXXXXXXXXXXXXXXXXXX XXXXXXXXXXXXXXXXXXXX XXXXXXXXXXXXXXXXXX (98)
LA/5	Recognizing words — matching written words	XXXXXXXXXXXXXXXXXXXX XXXXXXXXXXXXXXXXXXXX XXXXXXXXXXXXXXXXXXXX XXXXXXXXXXXXXXXXXXXX X (81)
LA/6	Matching sounds and symbols	XXXXXXXXXXXXXXXXXXXX XXXXXXXXX (29)
LA/7	Matching rhyming words	XXXXXXXXX (9)
LA/8	Using language to specify actions: sit, run, fast, slow, into, toward, etc.	XXXXXXXXXXXXXXXXXXXX XXXXXXX (27)
LA/9	Writing stories	XXXXXXXXXXXXXXXXXXXX XXXXXXXXXXXXX (33)
LA/10	Following a simple (2- or 3-step) sequence of oral or written directions	XXXXX (5)

— SERIATION —

#	EXPERIENCE	PROGRAMS (X = 1 program)
SE/1	Making comparisons — shape, shades of color, pitch, and/or speed	XXXXXXXXXXX (11)
SE/2	Arranging several things in order and describing their relations by size, color, etc.	XXXXXXXXX (9)
SE/3	Fitting one ordered set of objects to another through trial and error	XX (2)
SE/4	Inserting objects into an ordered sequence	XXXXXXXXXX (10)

— NUMBER —

#	EXPERIENCE	PROGRAMS (X = 1 program)
NB/1	Comparing amounts: more, less, same	XXXXXXXXXXXXXXXXXXXX XXXX (24)
NB/2	Arranging two sets of symbols in one-to-one correspondence	XXXXXXXXXXXXXX (14)
NB/3	Counting objects; counting by 2s	XXXXXXXXXXXXXXXXXXXX XXXXXXXXXXXXXXXXXXXX XXXXXXXXXXXXXXXXXXXX XXXXXXXXXXX (71)
NB/4	Recognizing numerals	XXXXXXXXXXXXXXXXXXXX XXXXXXXXXXXXXXXXXXXX XXXXXXXXX (49)
NB/5	Estimating the number of objects	XXXXXXXXX (9)
NB/6	Measuring (length) using units	XXXXXXXXX (9)
NB/7	Combining groups of objects; taking objects away	XXXXXXXXXXXXXXXX (16)
NB/8	Recognizing and naming the numerals 1, 2, 3, etc.	XXXXXXXXXXXXXXXXXXXX (20)

— CLASSIFICATION —

#	EXPERIENCE	PROGRAMS (X = 1 program)
CL/1	Identifying attributes of things: color, shape, size, function	XXXXXXXXXXXXXXXXXXXX XXXXXXXXXXXXXXXXXXXX X (41)
CL/2	Identifying how things are the same or different; sorting and matching	XXXXXXXXXXXXXXXXXXXX XXXXXXXXXXXXXXXXXXXX XXXXXXXXXXXXXXXXXXXX XXXXXXXXXXXXXXXXXXXX XXXXXXXXXXXX (92)
CL/3	Describing objects in different ways; sorting and re-sorting	XXXXX (5)
CL/4	Identifying attributes an object does not possess; finding the object that does not belong to a set	XXXXXXXXXXXXXX (14)
CL/5	Holding more than one attribute in mind at a time	XXXXXX (6)
CL/6	Distinguishing between "all" and "some"	XXX (3)

— SPATIAL RELATIONS —

#	EXPERIENCE	PROGRAMS (X = 1 program)
SP/1	Fitting things together and taking them apart	XXXXXXXXXXXXXXXXXX (18)
SP/2	Rearranging and reshaping objects	XXXXXXXXXXXXXX (14)
SP/3	Identifying things from different points of view	XXXXXX (6)
SP/4	Experiencing and describing the relative positions, directions, and distances of things — inside, outside, above, below, before, behind, on, under, toward, away	XXXXXXXXXXXXXXXXXXXX XXXXXXXXXXXXXXXXXXXX XXXXXXXXXXXXXX (54)
SP/5	Identifying and naming body parts: head, legs, arms, etc.	XXXXXXXXXXXX (12)
SP/6	Locating things in the classroom or school on simple maps	XXXX (4)
SP/7	Interpreting representations of spatial relations in drawings and pictures	XXXXXXXXXXXXXXXXXXXX (20)
SP/8	Distinguishing and describing shapes — circle, square, triangle, doughnut (open and closed shapes)	XXXXXXXXXXXXXXXX (16)
SP/9	Identifying and reversing spatial order	XXX (3)
SP/10	Identifying shapes produced by cuts and folds	

— CREATIVE PROJECTS —

#	EXPERIENCE	PROGRAMS (X = 1 program)
CP/1	Drawing pictures	XXXXXXXXXXXXXXXXXXXX XXXXXXXXXXXXXXXX (36)
CP/2	Creating sounds or music	XXXXXXXXXX (10)
CP/3	Programming	XXXXXXXXXX (10)
CP/4	Designing, changing, and printing a plan or product	XXXXXXXXXXXXXXXXXXXX XXXXXXXXXXXXXXXXXXXX XXXXXXXXXXXXXXX (55)

— TIME —

#	EXPERIENCE	PROGRAMS (X = 1 program)
TI/1	Stopping and starting an action on signal	XXXXXXXXXXX (11)
TI/2	Observing and describing changes	X (1)
TI/3	Experiencing and describing different rates of speed	XXXXXXXXXX (10)
TI/4	Experiencing and describing time intervals — long, short, comparative terms	XXXX (4)
TI/5	Anticipating future events and making appropriate preparations	XXXXXXX (7)
TI/6	Identifying the order of a sequence of events; reversing the order of events — before, after, at the same time	XXXXXXXXX (9)
TI/7	Comparing the duration of events occurring at the same time — longer, shorter, etc.	
TI/8	Using a timer to measure the duration of events	
TI/9	Reading time from clocks and watches	XXXXXXX (7)

— OTHER TOPICS —

#	EXPERIENCE	PROGRAMS (X = 1 program)
OT/1	Practicing memory skills	XXXXXXXXXXXXXXXXXXXX XXXXXXXXXXXXXXXXXXXX XXX (43)
OT/2	Recognizing and naming the parts of the computer	XX (2)
OT/3	Typing or keyboarding practice	XXXX (4)
OT/4	Making signs, word processing, or keeping records. (Of potential use to preschool and kindergarten teachers.)	XXXXXXXX (8)

APPENDIX 4: SOFTWARE LISTING BY COMPUTER BRAND

APPLE (307 titles)

Title	Computer (* = version reviewed)	Final Rating
1-2-3 Sequence Me	Apple	75
ABC's	Apple* (128K), IBM, C64	80
Adventures in Space	Apple	46
Adventures of Dobot, The	Apple*, IBM, C64	70
Adventures of Jimmy Jumper	Apple	69
Alice in Wonderland	Apple	69
Alpha Build	Apple*, IBM, C64 (cartridge)	56
Alpha Teach	Apple	39
Alphabet Arcade, The	Apple*, C64, Atari	42
Alphabet Circus	Apple*, IBM, C64	68
Alphabet Recognition	Apple	46
Alphabet Song and Count	Apple	51
Alphabet Sounds	Apple	29
Alphabet Zoo	Apple*, IBM, C64 ($20.95)	51
Alphabetization Sequence	Apple	67
Alphabots	Apple	54
Alphaget	Apple	51
Animal Alph. and Other Things	Apple	81
Animal Hotel	Apple*, C64	45
Animal Photo Fun	Apple	70
Arithmetic Critters	Apple (64K)	78
Astro's ABCs	Apple	62
Astro-Grover	Apple, IBM, C64*	41
Balancing Bear	Apple	77
Bald-Headed Chicken, The	Apple	89
Bank Street Writer III, The	Apple*, IBM	71
Beginner Reader	Apple	39
Best Electronic Word Book Ever!	Apple*, C64	70
Big Bird's Special Delivery	C64* (cartridge), IBM, Apple	31
Bike Hike	Apple*, C64	41
Bird's Eye View	Apple*, IBM	73
Boars Tell Time, The	Apple	68
Body Awareness	Apple	64
Brand New View, A	Apple	89
Bremen Town Musicians	Apple	45
Build a Book About You	Apple	68
Bumble Games	Apple	49
Castle Clobber	Apple, IBM*, C64, Atari	56
Cat 'n Mouse	Apple*, IBM	65
Charlie Brown's 1-2-3's	Apple	67
Charlie Brown's ABC's	Apple*, C64, IBM	64
City Country Opposites	Apple	78
Color Find	Apple	69
Color Me	Apple*, IBM, C64 ($34.95)	89
Colors and Shapes	Apple	76
Comparison Kitchen	Apple*, IBM	72
Computergarten	Apple*, C64	27

Title	Computer (* = version reviewed)	Final Rating
Concentrate	Apple	80
Conservation and Counting	Apple	71
Copycats: ABC for Micro & Me!	Apple*, C64	48
Cotton Tales	Apple*, IBM, Mac	78
Cotton's First Files	Apple	77
Counters	Apple	69
Counting	Apple*, C64	53
Counting and Ordering	Apple	56
Counting Critters	Apple	62
Counting Critters 1.0	Apple (64K)	81
Counting Skills	Apple*, TRS 80	40
Country Combo	Apple	26
Creature Creator	Apple*, IBM	62
Critter Count	Apple	34
Curious George in Outer Space	Apple	62
Delta Drawing	Apple, IBM*, C64*	78
Developing Language Skills	Apple	45
Dinosaurs	Apple*, IBM, C64 ($34.95)	65
Dinosaurs Are Forever	Apple* (128K), IBM, C64	80
Diskovery Adding Machine	Apple	69
Diskovery Take Away Zoo	Apple	68
Dr. Peet's Talk/Writer	Apple	79
Dr. Seuss Fix-Up . . . Puzzler	Apple, C64*	70
Early & Advanced Switch Games	Apple	75
Early Childhood . . . Program	Apple*, C64	53
Early Elementary I	Apple*, Atari, IBM	27
Early Elementary II	Apple	28
Early Games	Apple*, IBM, C64, Atari	60
Early Skills	Apple	61
Easy as ABC	Apple*, Mac, IBM, C64	80
Easy Street	Apple*, IBM, Mac, IIGS	84
Ernie's Big Splash	C64*, IBM, Apple	59
Ernie's Magic Shapes	C64*, Atari, IBM, Apple	45
Estimation	Apple	78
Expl. Your World: The Weather	Apple*, C64	51
Exploratory Play	Apple (64K)	71
Extrateletactograph, The	Apple II + or IIe (not IIc)	73
EZ Logo	Apple (64K)	74
Facemaker	Apple, IBM*, C64, Atari	54
Facemaker Golden Edition	Apple*, Amiga ($49.95), IBM (3.5)	61
Fantastic Animals	Apple*, IBM, C64 ($7.99)	70
First "R": Kindergarten, The	Apple	74
First Encounters	Apple	32
First Letter Fun	Apple (64K)	82
First Letters and Words	Apple IIGS*, Mac, Amiga, Atari ST	74
First Numbers: First Words	Apple*, C64	41
First Shapes	Apple IIGS*, Mac, Amiga, Atari ST	75
First Steps to Reading	Apple*, C64	43
FirstWriter	Apple	76
Fish Scales	Apple	78
Flodd, the Bad Guy	Apple*, IBM, Mac	70
Flying Carpet, The	Apple*, C64	44
Fun From A to Z	Apple (64K)	81
Fun on the Farm	Apple* (128K), IBM, C64	80

Title	Computer (* = version reviewed)	Final Rating
Fun With Directions	Apple	62
Gertrude's Secrets	Apple*, IBM*, C64 ($29.95)	84
Getting Ready to Read and Add	Apple, IBM*, Atari, C64*	63
Grabbit Factory, The	Apple*, C64	52
Grandma's House	Apple*, C64, Atari	68
Great Gonzo in WordRider, The	Apple	73
Great Leap, A	Apple (128K)	89
Grover's Animal Adventures	C64*, IBM, Apple	76
Grownup and Small	Apple	68
Hey Diddle Diddle	Apple*, C64, Atari, IBM	47
Hobo's Luck	Apple*, C64	54
Hodge Podge	Apple*, C64, IBM, Atari	51
Holidays & Seasons	Apple* (128K), IBM, C64	80
How to Weigh an Elephant	Apple*, C64	42
I Can Count	Apple	40
I Love My Alphabet	Apple*, C64, Atari	59
Inside Outside Opposites	Apple	72
Inside Outside Shapes	Apple	76
Integrated Learning System	Apple IIGS, IBM*, Mac	79
Introduction to Counting	Apple*, IBM, Atari	66
It's No Game	Apple	62
Jack and the Beanstalk	Apple*, IBM, Mac	70
Jack and the Beanstalk	Apple	69
Jr. Typer	Apple*, TRS 80	41
Juggle's Rainbow	Apple, IBM*, C64	62
Just Around the Block	Apple	89
Keytalk	Apple (64K)	76
Kid's Stuff	IBM*, Apple, Atari ST	76
Kids on Keys	Apple*, IBM, C64 ($20.95), Atari	62
Kidwriter	Apple*, C64*, IBM (3.5)	73
Kinder Koncepts MATH	Apple*	57
Kinder Koncepts Reading	Apple	44
Kindercomp	Apple, IBM*, C64, Atari	68
Kindercomp Golden Edition	Apple*, IBM 3.5	70
Kindermath II	Apple (64K)	57
Knowing Numbers	Apple	67
Koala Pad Graphics Exhibitor	Apple IIe*, II+, IBM	76
Language	Apple*, TRS 80	37
Language Experience Recorder Plus	Apple	55
Learn the Alphabet	Apple*, IBM, C64 (cartridge)	56
Learning About Numbers	Apple	78
Learning Line, The	Apple	62
Learning With Fuzzywomp	Apple*, C64	73
Learning With Leeper	Apple*, C64, Atari	69
Let's Go Fishing	Apple*, C64	36
Letter Games	Apple	34
Letter Recognition	Apple	48
Letters and First Words	Apple	68
Letters and Words	Apple	68
Letters for You	Apple* (128K), IBM, C64	80
Lion's Workshop	Apple*, C64	49
LOGO Power	Apple	59
Magic Crayon	Apple	75
Magic Slate	Apple	81

Title	Computer (* = version reviewed)	Final Rating
Magic String, The	Apple	46
Make a Match	Apple*, IBM*, Atari	75
Many Ways to Say I Love You	Apple, C64*	69
Mary Marvel . . . Costume Ball	Apple	62
Mary Marvel . . . the Garden	Apple	62
Mask Parade	Apple*, IBM, C64	77
Math and Me	Apple* (128K), IBM, IIGS ($49.95)	78
Math Facts Level 1	Apple	38
Math Magic	Apple*, IBM	53
Math Maze	Apple*, IBM, Atari ($19.95), C64	52
Math Rabbit	Apple*, IBM	78
Math Sequences	Apple	69
Maze-o	Apple	55
Memory Building Blocks	Apple	83
Micro-LADS	Apple	75
Microzine Jr. (Sept/Oct.'88)	Apple	81
Milk Bottles	Apple	39
Money Works	Apple (128K)	76
Monkey Math	Apple*, C64, Atari	49
Monsters and Make-Believe	Apple*, Mac, IBM	71
Moptown Parade	Apple*, IBM*, C64	55
Mount Murdoch	Apple*, IBM, C64	45
Mr. and Mrs. Potato Head	Apple	71
Muppet Slate	Apple	88
Muppet Word Book	Apple	82
Muppets On Stage	Apple*, IBM, C64	73
Muppetville	Apple	87
Music	Apple	59
Music Maestro	Apple*, IBM, C64, Atari	73
My Letters, Numbers, and Words	IBM*, Apple, Atari ST	46
My Words	Apple (64K)	78
Not Too Messy, Not Too Neat	Apple	89
Notable Phantom, The	Apple*, IBM, C64	66
Now You See It, Now You Don't	Apple	79
Number Farm	Apple*, C64, IBM	78
Numbers	Apple	58
Numbers Count	Apple* (128K), IBM, C64	80
Observation and Classif.	Apple	80
Odd One Out	Apple*, C64	74
Ollie and Seymour	Apple	77
Ollie Finds It	Apple	64
Ollie Hears and Sequences	Apple	64
Ollie Remembers It	Apple	64
Once Upon a Time . . .	IBM* (256K), Apple (128K), Mac	59
One Banana More	Apple	34
Ordering/Sequencing	Apple*, TRS80	38
Paint With Words	Apple (64K)	73
Pals Around Town	C64*, IBM, Apple	73
Path-Tactics	Apple*, IBM, C64	69
Patterns	Apple	79
Patterns and Sequences	Apple	72
Peanuts Maze Marathon	Apple*, C64, IBM	46
Peanuts Picture Puzzlers	Apple*, C64, IBM	59
Peter and the Wolf Music	Apple*, C64 ($24.95)	77

Title	Computer (* = version reviewed)	Final Rating
Peter Rabbit Reading	Apple*, C64	79
Peter's Growing Patterns	Apple	73
Picture Dictionary	Apple	53
Picture Perfect	Apple*, IBM	79
Pictures, Letters, and Sounds	Apple	78
Play Together Learn Together	Apple*, IBM, C64	44
Preschool Fun	Apple	44
Preschool IQ Builder I	Apple*, C64, Atari, PET*	38
Preschool IQ Builder II	Apple*, C64, PET, TI	43
Print Shop, The	Apple, Mac, IBM, C64, Atari, IIGS*	85
Puss in Boot	Apple	34
Puzzle Master	Apple*, IBM, C64	79
R.J.'s Switch Progressions	Apple	65
Rabbit Scanner, The	Apple	67
Race the Clock	Apple*, IBM	69
Rainbow Painter	Apple*, C64	80
Rainy Day Games	Apple*, C64, Atari, Mac	83
Read, Write, & Publish 1	Apple (128K)	81
Reader Rabbit	Apple*, IBM, C64, Apple IIGS ($59.95)	71
Reading and Me	Apple* (128K), IBM, IIGS ($49.95)	79
Reading Comprehension: Lev. 1	Apple (64K)	82
Reading Fun: Beg. Consonants	Apple	56
Reading Helpers	Apple (64K)	69
Reading Machine, The	Apple	65
Reading Starters	Apple (64K)	63
Representational Play	Apple (64K)	71
Rhyming to Read	Apple* C64	37
Rosie the Counting Rabbit	Apple	89
Rumpelstiltskin	Apple	43
Run Rabbit Run	Apple	70
Same or Different	Apple*, C64	55
Sesame Street Print Kit	Apple*, IBM, C64, Atari	46
Shape & Color Rodeo	Apple*, IBM, C64	73
Shapes & Patterns	Apple	66
Shutterbug's Patterns	Apple*, C64	36
Shutterbug's Pictures	Apple*, C64	61
Sight Word Spelling	Apple	39
Simon Says	Apple*, C64	80
Size and Logic	Apple	77
Sleepy Brown Cow, The	Apple	89
SocPix	Apple	61
Sound Ideas: Consonants	Apple (64K)	80
Sound Ideas: Vowels	Apple (64K)	80
Sound Ideas: Word Attack	Apple (64K)	72
Sound Tracks	Apple (64K)	74
Space Waste Race	Apple*, Atari, TRS 80	49
Spaceship Lost	Apple	45
Spatial Relationships	Apple	25
Spellicopter	Apple*, IBM, C64 ($29.95)	66
Spelling and Reading Primer	Apple*, IBM, C64	51
Spelling Bee, The	Apple	32
Stepping Stones Level I	Apple, IBM*, Mac	59
Stepping Stones Level II	Apple*, IBM, Mac	58
Stickers	Apple, IBM*, C64	79

Title	Computer (* = version reviewed)	Final Rating
Stickybear ABC	Apple*, Atari, C64	59
Stickybear Math	Apple*, IBM, C64	81
Stickybear Numbers	Apple*, IBM, Atari, C64	64
Stickybear Opposites	Apple*, Atari, C64	73
Stickybear Printer	Apple	43
Stickybear Reading	Apple*, IBM, C64	77
Stickybear Shapes	Apple*, Atari, C64	70
Stickybear Town Builder	Apple*, IBM, C64	80
Stickybear Typing	Apple*, IBM, C64	42
Story Machine	Apple*, IBM, Atari, C64, TI	69
SuperPrint!	Apple*, IBM	62
Surrounding Patterns	Apple*, C64	77
Sweet Shop, The	Apple*, C64	54
Talk About a Walk	Apple	56
Talking Nouns I	Apple (128K)	80
Talking Nouns II	Apple (128K)	80
Talking Textwriter	Apple* (128K), Apple IIGS, IBM	75
Talking Verbs	Apple (128K)	80
Teddy and Iggy	Apple*, C64	78
Teddy Bear-rels of Fun	Apple*, C64	56
Teddy Bears Counting Fun	Apple	32
Teddy's Playground	Apple	80
Telling Time	Apple*, C64, TRS 80, IBM, Atari, Pet	34
This Land Is Your Land	Apple* (128K), IBM, C64	80
Tiger's Tales	Apple*, C64	80
Time Master	Apple	25
Tink's Adventure	Apple*, C64, IBM, Atari	41
Tonk in the Land of Buddy-Bots	Apple*, C64, IBM, Atari	56
Touch & Write	Apple	81
Touch and Match	Apple	65
Touch and See	Apple	61
Toybox	C64*, Apple (128), IBM	56
Tuk Goes to Town	Apple*, C64, IBM, Atari	41
Up & Add 'Em	Apple*, IBM, C64	75
Webster's Numbers	Apple*, C64	67
What Makes a Dinosaur Sore?	Apple	89
What's in a Frame?	Apple	81
What's Next	Apple*, C64	74
Where Did My Toothbrush Go?	Apple	89
Word Factory	Apple	22
Words	Apple	61
Words & Concepts	Apple	80
Words & Concepts II	Apple	80
Words & Concepts III	Apple	80

COMMODORE (124 titles)

Title	Computer (* = version reviewed)	Final Rating
ABC's	Apple* (128K), IBM, C64	80
Adventures of Dobot, The	Apple*, IBM, C64	70
Alpha Build	Apple*, IBM, C64 (cartridge)	56
Alphabet Arcade, The	Apple*, C64, Atari	42
Alphabet Circus	Apple*, IBM, C64	68
Alphabet Zoo	Apple*, IBM, C64 ($20.95)	51
Animal Hotel	Apple*, C64	45
Astro-Grover	Apple, IBM, C64*	41
Best Electronic Word Book Ever!	Apple*, C64	70
Big Bird's Funhouse	C64	49
Big Bird's Special Delivery	C64* (cartridge), IBM, Apple	31
Bike Hike	Apple*, C64	41
Castle Clobber	Apple, IBM*, C64, Atari	56
Charlie Brown's ABC's	Apple*, C64, IBM	64
Color Me	Apple*, IBM, C64 ($34.95)	89
Computergarten	Apple*, C64	27
Copycats: ABC for Micro & Me!	Apple*, C64	48
Counting	C64	60
Counting	Apple*, C64	53
Delta Drawing	Apple, IBM*, C64*	78
Dinosaurs	Apple*, IBM, C64 ($34.95)	65
Dinosaurs Are Forever	Apple* (128K), IBM, C64	80
Dr. Seuss Fix-Up . . . Puzzler	Apple, C64*	70
Ducks Ahoy	C64 (cartridge)	78
Early Childhood . . . Program	Apple*, C64	53
Early Games	Apple*, IBM, C64, Atari	60
Early Learning Friends	C64	71
Easy as ABC	Apple*, Mac, IBM, C64	80
Ernie's Big Splash	C64*, IBM, Apple	59
Ernie's Magic Shapes	C64*, Atari, IBM, Apple	45
Expl. Your World: The Weather	Apple*, C64	51
Facemaker	Apple, IBM*, C64, Atari	54
Fantastic Animals	Apple*, IBM, C64 ($7.99)	70
First Numbers: First Words	Apple*, C64	41
First Steps to Reading	Apple*, C64	43
Flying Carpet, The	Apple*, C64	44
Fruit Tree/Gumball	C64*, VIC 20	28
Fun on the Farm	Apple* (128K), IBM, C64	80
Gertrude's Secrets	Apple*, IBM*, C64 ($29.95)	84
Getting Ready to Read and Add	Apple, IBM*, Atari, C64*	63
Grabbit Factory, The	Apple*, C64	52
Grandma's House	Apple*, C64, Atari	68
Grover's Animal Adventures	C64*, IBM, Apple	76
Hey Diddle Diddle	Apple*, C64, Atari, IBM	47
Hobo's Luck	Apple*, C64	54
Hodge Podge	Apple*, C64, IBM, Atari	51
Holidays & Seasons	Apple* (128K), IBM, C64	80
How to Weigh an Elephant	Apple*, C64	42
I Love My Alphabet	Apple*, C64, Atari	59
Juggle's Rainbow	Apple, IBM*, C64	62

Title	Computer (* = version reviewed)	Final Rating
Kermit's Electronic Storymaker	C64	77
Kids on Keys	Apple*, IBM, C64 ($20.95), Atari	62
Kidwriter	Apple*, C64*, IBM (3.5)	73
Kindercomp	Apple, IBM*, C64, Atari	68
Learn the Alphabet	Apple*, IBM, C64 (cartridge)	56
Learning With Fuzzywomp	Apple*, C64	73
Learning With Leeper	Apple*, C64, Atari	69
Let's Go Fishing	Apple*, C64	36
Letter-Go-Round	C64* (cartridge), Atari	56
Letters for You	Apple* (128K), IBM, C64	80
Lion's Workshop	Apple*, C64	49
Many Ways to Say I Love You	Apple, C64*	69
Mask Parade	Apple*, IBM, C64	77
Math Maze	Apple*, IBM, Atari ($19.95), C64	52
Monkey Math	Apple*, C64, Atari	49
Moptown Parade	Apple*, IBM*, C64	55
Mount Murdoch	Apple*, IBM, C64	45
Muppets On Stage	Apple*, IBM, C64	73
Music Maestro	Apple*, IBM, C64, Atari	73
My Book	C64*, Atari	38
Notable Phantom, The	Apple*, IBM, C64	66
Number BeCi	C64*, VIC 20	29
Number Farm	Apple*, C64, IBM	78
Numbers Count	Apple* (128K), IBM, C64	80
Odd One Out	Apple*, C64	74
Pals Around Town	C64*, IBM, Apple	73
Path-Tactics	Apple*, IBM, C64	69
Peanuts Maze Marathon	Apple*, C64, IBM	46
Peanuts Picture Puzzlers	Apple*, C64, IBM	59
Peter and the Wolf Music	Apple*, C64 ($24.95)	77
Peter Rabbit Reading	Apple*, C64	79
Play Together Learn Together	Apple*, IBM, C64	44
Preschool IQ Builder I	Apple*, C64, Atari, PET*	38
Preschool IQ Builder II	Apple*, C64, PET, TI	43
Print Shop, The	Apple, Mac, IBM, C64, Atari, IIGS*	85
Puzzle Master	Apple*, IBM, C64	79
Rainbow Painter	Apple*, C64	80
Rainy Day Games	Apple*, C64, Atari, Mac	83
Reader Rabbit	Apple*, IBM, C64, Apple IIGS ($59.95)	71
Rhyming to Read	Apple* C64	37
Same or Different	Apple*, C64	55
Sesame Street Print Kit	Apple*, IBM, C64, Atari	46
Shape & Color Rodeo	Apple*, IBM, C64	73
Shape Games	C64*, VIC 20	44
Shutterbug's Patterns	Apple*, C64	36
Shutterbug's Pictures	Apple*, C64	61
Simon Says	Apple*, C64	80
Spellicopter	Apple*, IBM, C64 ($29.95)	66
Spelling and Reading Primer	Apple*, IBM, C64	51
Stickers	Apple, IBM*, C64	79
Stickybear ABC	Apple*, Atari, C64	59
Stickybear Math	Apple*, IBM, C64	81
Stickybear Numbers	Apple*, IBM, Atari, C64	64

Title	Computer (* = version reviewed)	Final Rating
Stickybear Opposites	Apple*, Atari, C64	73
Stickybear Reading	Apple*, IBM, C64	77
Stickybear Shapes	Apple*, Atari, C64	70
Stickybear Town Builder	Apple*, IBM, C64	80
Stickybear Typing	Apple*, IBM, C64	42
Story Machine	Apple*, IBM, Atari, C64, TI	69
Surrounding Patterns	Apple*, C64	77
Sweet Shop, The	Apple*, C64	54
Talking Teacher	C64	76
Teddy and Iggy	Apple*, C64	78
Teddy Bear-rels of Fun	Apple*, C64	56
Telling Time	Apple*, C64, TRS 80, IBM, Atari, Pet	34
This Land Is Your Land	Apple* (128K), IBM, C64	80
Tiger's Tales	Apple*, C64	80
Tink's Adventure	Apple*, C64, IBM, Atari	41
Tonk in the Land of Buddy-Bots	Apple*, C64, IBM, Atari	56
Toybox	C64*, Apple (128), IBM	56
Tuk Goes to Town	Apple*, C64, IBM, Atari	41
Up & Add 'Em	Apple*, IBM, C64	75
Webster's Numbers	Apple*, C64	67
What's Next	Apple*, C64	74

IBM (115 titles)

Title	Computer (* = version reviewed)	Final Rating
1st Math	IBM*, Atari ST	75
ABC's	Apple* (128K), IBM, C64	80
Adventures of Dobot, The	Apple*, IBM, C64	70
Alpha Build	Apple*, IBM, C64 (cartridge)	56
Alphabet Circus	Apple*, IBM, C64	68
Alphabet Zoo	Apple*, IBM, C64 ($20.95)	51
Astro-Grover	Apple, IBM, C64*	41
Bank Street Writer III, The	Apple*, IBM	71
Big Bird's Special Delivery	C64* (cartridge), IBM, Apple	31
Bird's Eye View	Apple*, IBM	73
Bouncy Bee Learns Letters 1.0	IBM	72
Bouncy Bee Learns Words 1.0	IBM	62
Castle Clobber	Apple, IBM*, C64, Atari	56
Cat 'n Mouse	Apple*, IBM	65
Charlie Brown's ABC's	Apple*, C64, IBM	64
Color Me	Apple*, IBM, C64 ($34.95)	89
Come Play With Pockets	IBM	66
Comparison Kitchen	Apple*, IBM	72
Cotton Tales	Apple*, IBM, Mac	78
Creature Creator	Apple*, IBM	62
Delta Drawing	Apple, IBM*, C64*	78
Dinosaurs	Apple*, IBM, C64 ($34.95)	65
Dinosaurs Are Forever	Apple* (128K), IBM, C64	80
Early Elementary I	Apple*, Atari, IBM	27
Early Games	Apple*, IBM, C64, Atari	60

Title	Computer (* = version reviewed)	Final Rating
Easy as ABC	Apple*, Mac, IBM, C64	80
Easy Street	Apple*, IBM, Mac, IIGS	84
Ernie's Big Splash	C64*, IBM, Apple	59
Ernie's Magic Shapes	C64*, Atari, IBM, Apple	45
Facemaker	Apple, IBM*, C64, Atari	54
Facemaker Golden Edition	Apple*, Amiga ($49.95), IBM (3.5)	61
Fantastic Animals	Apple*, IBM, C64 ($7.99)	70
Flodd, the Bad Guy	Apple*, IBM, Mac	70
Fun on the Farm	Apple* (128K), IBM, C64	80
Fun With Letters and Words	IBM	76
Fun With Memory	IBM	77
Fun With Numbers	IBM	59
Gertrude's Secrets	Apple*, IBM*, C64 ($29.95)	84
Getting Ready to Read and Add	Apple, IBM*, Atari, C64*	63
Grover's Animal Adventures	C64*, IBM, Apple	76
Happy Birthday, Pockets	IBM	71
Hey Diddle Diddle	Apple*, C64, Atari, IBM	47
Hodge Podge	Apple*, C64, IBM, Atari	51
Holidays & Seasons	Apple* (128K), IBM, C64	80
Integrated Learning System	Apple IIGS, IBM*, Mac	79
Introduction to Counting	Apple*, IBM, Atari	66
Jack and the Beanstalk	Apple*, IBM, Mac	70
Juggle's Rainbow	Apple, IBM*, C64	62
Kid's Stuff	IBM*, Apple, Atari ST	76
Kids on Keys	Apple*, IBM, C64 ($20.95), Atari	62
Kidwriter	Apple*, C64*, IBM (3.5)	73
Kindercomp	Apple, IBM*, C64, Atari	68
Kindercomp Golden Edition	Apple*, IBM 3.5	70
Koala Pad Graphics Exhibitor	Apple IIe*, II+, IBM	76
Learn the Alphabet	Apple*, IBM, C64 (cartridge)	56
Letters for You	Apple* (128K), IBM, C64	80
Make a Match	Apple*, IBM*, Atari	75
Mask Parade	Apple*, IBM, C64	77
Math and Me	Apple* (128K), IBM, IIGS ($49.95)	78
Math Concepts Level P	IBM	73
Math Magic	Apple*, IBM	53
Math Maze	Apple*, IBM, Atari ($19.95), C64	52
Math Rabbit	Apple*, IBM	78
Memory Master	IBM*, Atari ST	56
Monsters and Make-Believe	Apple*, Mac, IBM	71
Moptown Parade	Apple*, IBM*, C64	55
Mount Murdoch	Apple*, IBM, C64	45
Muppets On Stage	Apple*, IBM, C64	73
Music Maestro	Apple*, IBM, C64, Atari	73
My ABC's	IBM	63
My Letters, Numbers, and Words	IBM*, Apple, Atari ST	46
Notable Phantom, The	Apple*, IBM, C64	66
Number Farm	Apple*, C64, IBM	78
Numbers Count	Apple* (128K), IBM, C64	80
Once Upon a Time . . .	IBM* (256K), Apple (128K), Mac	59
Pals Around Town	C64*, IBM, Apple	73
Path-Tactics	Apple*, IBM, C64	69
Peanuts Maze Marathon	Apple*, C64, IBM	46

Title	Computer (* = version reviewed)	Final Rating
Peanuts Picture Puzzlers	Apple*, C64, IBM	59
Picture Perfect	Apple*, IBM	79
Play Together Learn Together	Apple*, IBM, C64	44
Pockets and Her New Sneakers	IBM	62
Pockets Goes on a Picnic	IBM	61
Pockets Goes on Vacation	IBM	63
Pockets Goes to the Carnival	IBM	68
Pockets Leads the Parade	IBM	75
Primary Editor Plus	IBM PS/2	74
Print Shop, The	Apple, Mac, IBM, C64, Atari, IIGS*	85
Puzzle Master	Apple*, IBM, C64	79
Race the Clock	Apple*, IBM	69
Reader Rabbit	Apple*, IBM, C64, Apple IIGS ($59.95)	71
Reading and Me	Apple* (128K), IBM, IIGS ($49.95)	79
Sesame Street Print Kit	Apple*, IBM, C64, Atari	46
Shape & Color Rodeo	Apple*, IBM, C64	73
Spellicopter	Apple*, IBM, C64 ($29.95)	66
Spelling and Reading Primer	Apple*, IBM, C64	51
Stepping Stones Level I	Apple, IBM*, Mac	59
Stepping Stones Level II	Apple*, IBM, Mac	58
Stickers	Apple, IBM*, C64	79
Stickybear Math	Apple*, IBM, C64	81
Stickybear Numbers	Apple*, IBM, Atari, C64	64
Stickybear Reading	Apple*, IBM, C64	77
Stickybear Town Builder	Apple*, IBM, C64	80
Stickybear Typing	Apple*, IBM, C64	42
Story Machine	Apple*, IBM, Atari, C64, TI	69
SuperPrint!	Apple*, IBM	62
Talking Textwriter	Apple* (128K), Apple IIGS, IBM	75
Telling Time	Apple*, C64, TRS 80, IBM, Atari, Pet	34
This Land Is Your Land	Apple* (128K), IBM, C64	80
Tink's Adventure	Apple*, C64, IBM, Atari	41
Tonk in the Land of Buddy-Bots	Apple*, C64, IBM, Atari	56
Toybox	C64*, Apple (128), IBM	56
Tuk Goes to Town	Apple*, C64, IBM, Atari	41
Up & Add 'Em	Apple*, IBM, C64	75
Writing to Read 2.0	IBM	45

ATARI (43 titles)

Title	Computer (* = version reviewed)	Final Rating
1st Math	IBM*, Atari ST	75
Alphabet Arcade, The	Apple*, C64, Atari	42
Castle Clobber	Apple, IBM*, C64, Atari	56
Early Elementary I	Apple*, Atari, IBM	27
Early Games	Apple*, IBM, C64, Atari	60
Ernie's Magic Shapes	C64*, Atari, IBM, Apple	45
Facemaker	Apple, IBM*, C64, Atari	54
First Letters and Words	Apple IIGS*, Mac, Amiga, Atari ST	74
First Shapes	Apple IIGS*, Mac, Amiga, Atari ST	75

Title	Computer (* = version reviewed)	Final Rating
Getting Ready to Read and Add	Apple, IBM*, Atari, C64*	63
Grandma's House	Apple*, C64, Atari	68
Hey Diddle Diddle	Apple*, C64, Atari, IBM	47
Hodge Podge	Apple*, C64, IBM, Atari	51
I Love My Alphabet	Apple*, C64, Atari	59
Introduction to Counting	Apple*, IBM, Atari	66
Kid Talk	Mac*, IIGS, Atari ST, Amiga	89
Kid's Stuff	IBM*, Apple, Atari ST	76
Kids on Keys	Apple*, IBM, C64 ($20.95), Atari	62
Kindercomp	Apple, IBM*, C64, Atari	68
Learning With Leeper	Apple*, C64, Atari	69
Letter-Go-Round	C64* (cartridge), Atari	56
Magic Melody Box	Atari	59
Make a Match	Apple*, IBM*, Atari	75
Math Maze	Apple*, IBM, Atari ($19.95), C64	52
Memory Master	IBM*, Atari ST	56
Monkey Math	Apple*, C64, Atari	49
Music Maestro	Apple*, IBM, C64, Atari	73
My Book	C64*, Atari	38
My Letters, Numbers, and Words	IBM*, Apple, Atari ST	46
Preschool IQ Builder I	Apple*, C64, Atari, PET*	38
Print Shop, The	Apple, Mac, IBM, C64, Atari, IIGS*	85
Rainy Day Games	Apple*, C64, Atari, Mac	83
Sesame Street Print Kit	Apple*, IBM, C64, Atari	46
Space Waste Race	Apple*, Atari, TRS 80	49
Stickybear ABC	Apple*, Atari, C64	59
Stickybear Numbers	Apple*, IBM, Atari, C64	64
Stickybear Opposites	Apple*, Atari, C64	73
Stickybear Shapes	Apple*, Atari, C64	70
Story Machine	Apple*, IBM, Atari, C64, TI	69
Telling Time	Apple*, C64, TRS 80, IBM, Atari, Pet	34
Tink's Adventure	Apple*, C64, IBM, Atari	41
Tonk in the Land of Buddy-Bots	Apple*, C64, IBM, Atari	56
Tuk Goes to Town	Apple*, C64, IBM, Atari	41

MACINTOSH (23 titles)

Title	Computer (* = version reviewed)	Final Rating
Clock Works	Mac	72
Coin Works	Mac	71
Cotton Tales	Apple*, IBM, Mac	78
Easy as ABC	Apple*, Mac, IBM, C64	80
Easy Street	Apple*, IBM, Mac, IIGS	84
First Letters and Words	Apple IIGS*, Mac, Amiga, Atari ST	74
First Shapes	Apple IIGS*, Mac, Amiga, Atari ST	75
Flodd, the Bad Guy	Apple*, IBM, Mac	70
Integrated Learning System	Apple IIGS, IBM*, Mac	79
Jack and the Beanstalk	Apple*, IBM, Mac	70
Kid Talk	Mac*, IIGS, Atari ST, Amiga	89
KidsTime	Mac	82
Kieran	Mac	70
Match-On-A-Mac	Mac	79
Monsters and Make-Believe	Apple*, Mac, IBM	71

Title	Computer (* = version reviewed)	Final Rating
Once Upon a Time . . .	IBM* (256K), Apple (128K), Mac	59
Preschool Disk 1	Mac	62
Preschool Disk 2	Mac	75
Print Shop, The	Apple, Mac, IBM, C64, Atari, IIGS*	85
Rainy Day Games	Apple*, C64, Atari, Mac	83
Stepping Stones Level I	Apple, IBM*, Mac	59
Stepping Stones Level II	Apple*, IBM, Mac	58
Talking Tiles	Mac (1 MB required)	85

APPLE IIGS (14 titles)

Title	Computer (* = version reviewed)	Final Rating
Easy Street	Apple*, IBM, Mac, IIGS	84
First Letters and Words	Apple IIGS*, Mac, Amiga, Atari ST	74
First Shapes	Apple IIGS*, Mac, Amiga, Atari ST	75
Integrated Learning System	Apple IIGS, IBM*, Mac	79
Kid Talk	Mac*, IIGS, Atari ST, Amiga	89
Math and Me	Apple* (128K), IBM, IIGS ($49.95)	78
New Talking Stickybear ABC's, The	IIGS (512K)	64
Print Shop, The	Apple, Mac, IBM, C64, Atari, IIGS*	85
Reader Rabbit	Apple*, IBM, C64, Apple IIGS ($59.95)	71
Reading and Me	Apple* (128K), IBM, IIGS ($49.95)	79
Talking ABC's	IIGS (512K)	43
Talking Clock	IIGS (512K)	65
Talking Numbers	IIGS	41
Talking Textwriter	Apple* (128K), Apple IIGS, IBM	75

AMIGA (8 titles)

Title	Computer (* = version reviewed)	Final Rating
Beginning Counting	Amiga (512K)	43
Beginning Reading Skills	Amiga (512K)	57
Early Math	Amiga (512K)	43
Facemaker Golden Edition	Apple*, Amiga ($49.95), IBM (3.5)	61
First Letters and Words	Apple IIGS*, Mac, Amiga, Atari ST	74
First Shapes	Apple IIGS*, Mac, Amiga, Atari ST	75
Kid Talk	Mac*, IIGS, Atari ST, Amiga	89
Learning the Alphabet	Amiga (512K)	50

TRS 80 (6 titles)

Title	Computer (* = version reviewed)	Final Rating
Counting Skills	Apple*, TRS 80	40
Jr. Typer	Apple*, TRS 80	41
Language	Apple*, TRS 80	37
Ordering/Sequencing	Apple*, TRS80	38
Space Waste Race	Apple*, Atari, TRS 80	49
Telling Time	Apple*, C64, TRS 80, IBM, Atari, Pet	34

APPENDIX 5: NOTEWORTHY SOFTWARE

Since compiling our first *Survey of Early Childhood Software* in 1984, we are often asked, which programs stand out? Here's our answer. The following programs are ones we've observed children going back to time and time again. They are worthy of note by early childhood educators and parents. The programs are listed by recommended age under each category.

For Language

Animal Alphabet and Other Things by Random House Software, 1986, $29.95, Age: 3-6, Apple
■ Letter recognition, alphabetical order

Child presses a key, e.g., A, to see that letter on the screen. Pressing A again causes the letter to turn into an alligator. Pressing spacebar causes the next letter in the alphabet to appear. There are 26 pictures on each side of the disk. Side 1 covers upper case; side 2, lower case. Very easy to use.

Kid's Stuff by Stone & Associates, 1984, $39.95, Age: 3-8, IBM, Apple, Atari ST
■ Counting skills, letter recognition

Offers three activities accessible by a picture menu. Most notable is the letter recognition activity, where child types in letters of a word, which creates animation and sounds. An entertaining program that provides options for the child.

Fun From A to Z by MECC, 1985, $59.00, Age: 3-6, Apple (64K)
■ Alphabet skills practice

Child uses arrow keys to play three games: Birds — child matches letters. Dots — child completes a dot-to-dot picture by selecting next alphabet letter. Runners — child sees sequence (K,L,M,__,O) and must select missing letter. Management allows selection of upper/lower-case. Well-designed.

Explore-a-Story Series by D.C. Heath & Company, 1988, $75.00 per story, Age: 4-10 Apple (128K)
■ Language experience

Children use mouse, Koala Pad, joystick, or arrow keys to select or move objects, backgrounds, words, or characters in a story. They can also add their own words. Resulting stories can be saved and printed in color. Includes four copies of the storybook. Good design. Fun to use. The story titles are the following:

A Great Leap; A Brand New View; Just Around the Block; Not Too Messy, Not Too Neat; Rosie the Counting Rabbit; The Bald-Headed Chicken; The Sleepy Brown Cow; What Makes a Dinosaur Sore?; Where Did My Toothbrush Go?

For Young Children's Word Processing

Dr. Peet's Talk/Writer by Hartley Courseware, 1986, $69.95, Age: 3-7, Apple
■ Language exploration and skills

Consists of two disks. Disk 1 includes the ABC song, finding and matching letters, and creating and listening to words. Disk 2 is an easy-to-use talking word processor that says whatever is typed, in robotic voice. Uses large letters. Echo speech synthesizer recommended. Stories can be saved and printed.

Kid Talk by First Byte, Inc., 1988, $49.95, Age: 3-10, Macintosh, IIGS, Atari ST, Amiga
■ Language experience

An easy-to-use word processor that will say what is typed. Makes features such as moving text, selecting sizes of type, changing sounds of words, and printing stories easy to use through clear picture menus. Uses built-in speech synthesizer. Best talking word processor available.

Muppet Slate by Sunburst Communications, 1988, $65.00, Age: 5-7, Apple
■ Language experiences

A large-letter word processor with 126 pictures that can be added to the story. Stories can be saved and printed with 10 borders. Not good for long stories. Options allow teacher control. Can be used with Muppet Learning Keys.

Magic Slate by Sunburst Communications, 1984, $99.95, Age: 7-up, Apple
■ Word processing

Easy-to-use word processor with large (20-column) text and picture menu. Effective for experience stories for preschool level. Stories can be saved, printed, and edited. Graphics printer desirable.

For Creating Things

Color Me by Mindscape, Inc., 1986, $29.95, Age: 3-10 Apple, IBM, C64 ($34.95)
■ Drawing, creating

Easy-to-use program. Our youngest children could use this program with success. Requires Koala Pad, mouse, or joystick. Child can draw, select colors, or write. Pictures can be printed in color and saved. Includes book, puppet, and picture disk.

Electronic Crayon Series by Polarware, Inc., 1986, $14.95, Age: 3-up Apple (128K), IBM, C64
■ Coloring pictures

A coloring program with 30 blank pictures per disk. Child moves cursor with mouse, joystick, or arrow keys to fill in sections of a picture with 1 of 16 available colors. Prints in color. Mouse and color monitor recommended. Very easy to use. Prints picture with calendar, banner, or message. Following are the names of each program: Dinosaurs Are Forever, 1988, $29.95; Fun on the Farm, 1986, $14.95; Holidays & Seasons, 1988, $29.95; Letters for You, 1987, $14.95; Numbers Count, 1987, $14.95; This Land Is Your Land, 1986, $14.95.

Mask Parade by Springboard, 1984, $39.95, Age: 4-12, Apple, IBM, C64
■ Creative design of masks and other cut-out objects

Child can design and print masks and other cutouts. The design part requires choosing the components of the mask (eyes, nose, etc.). Easy to print, once printer is set up. Pictures can be saved on disk. No reading required.

The Print Shop by Broderbund Software, 1987, $49.95, Age: 6-up, Apple, Macintosh, IBM, C64, Atari, IIGS
■ Creation of printed materials

An easy-to-use printing program that allows the creation of greeting cards, signs, letterheads, or banners. Includes 120 graphic elements. Includes 6 envelopes and 20 sheets of colored paper. Four Print Shop Graphics Library disks can be purchased separately for $24.95. Prints in color with selected printers.

For Matching, Counting, and Problem Solving

City Country Opposites by Random House Software, 1986, $29.95, Age: 3-7, Apple
■ Word meanings through context

Presents and illustrates 20 antonym pairs. Child uses left and right arrows to alternate between pictures illustrating antonyms, e.g., push/pull. Easy to use. Good level of child-control. Includes scenes from city and country environments. Limited content.

Counting Critters 1.0 by MECC, 1985, $59.00, Age: 3-6 Apple (64K)
■ Counting and early math concepts

Five games on one disk. Child uses arrow keys and number keys to match numerals from 1-20, match sets with numerals, create a set corresponding to a given numeral, and use numerical order to fill in a dot-to-dot design. Clear graphics and sounds support content. Allows teacher modification.

Observation and Classification by Hartley Courseware, 1985, $35.95, Age: 3-5, Apple
■ Classification skills

Three activities. Child selects which object is different from others, which is the same size as one shown, or which belongs to the same class as a group shown, e.g., "all animals." Teacher options allow control over sound, movement of cursor, and number of plays per game. Child selects own difficulty level.

Math and Me by Davidson and Associates, 1987, $39.95, Age: 3-6, Apple (128K), IBM, IIGS ($49.95)
- Shapes, patterns, numbers, and addition

Twelve activities covering shape matching, number recognition, patterns, numerical order, and addition with objects or numbers. In each activity, child uses mouse (optional) or arrow keys to select 1 of 4 boxes in a multiple-choice format. Good design and graphics. Good range of content. Talking version for the IIGS gives verbal feedback.

Number Farm by DLM, 1984, $32.95, Age: 3-6, Apple, C64, IBM
- Counting skills

Six entertaining games present multiple counting experiences. Feedback is effective. One game presents counting in a unique way by having child count sounds. Provides good number practice.

Easy Street by MindPlay, 1988, $49.95, Age: 4-8, Apple, IBM, Macintosh, IIGS
- Classification, matching, and counting

Using the arrow keys, joystick, or mouse, child moves a boy down a street past various storefronts in search of special objects. "Challenge Upgrade" feature offers a wide range of challenges. Optional speech synthesis makes the program easier to use (Echo speech synthesizer).

Estimation by Lawrence Hall of Science, 1984, $34.95, Age: 4-6, Apple
- Estimation of length, area, & time units

Offers three activities with estimation skills: Choo-Choo — child guesses when a train is over an arrow by pressing spacebar. Junk Jar — child estimates area. Bugs — presents units of "bugs" for child to estimate a line's length. Simple reading required.

Math Rabbit by The Learning Company, 1986, $39.95, Age: 5-7, Apple, IBM
- Counting, matching sets, addition, subtraction

Enjoyable activities: child uses arrow keys, spacebar, and RETURN to count using a number line and musical scale; to match numerals; to match a set of objects or a math problem to a given number; to solve math problems to create number patterns; and to match sets of objects, numbers, and math problems. Four levels of play.

1st Math by Stone & Associates, 1986, $39.95, Age: 4-8, IBM, Atari ST
- Addition & subtraction equations, patterns

Four well-designed activities: Equations — child enters answer for equation to see answer animated. Construction — child sees equation and types answer to build a scene. Freight Depot — child uses arrow keys or joystick to load answers onto truck. Patterns — child selects next pattern element. Adult menu offers control over content.

Stickybear Math by Weekly Reader Software, 1984, $39.95, Age: 6-9, Apple, IBM, C64
- Counting, addition, and subtraction

A 20-level math program that keeps names, levels, scores, and types of problems for up to 25 children. Automatically tracks and adjusts difficulty level. Content ranges from counting to three-digit subtraction with borrowing. Includes poster and stickers. Animated graphics illustrate problems.

For Fun and Variety

Muppets On Stage by Sunburst Communications, 1984, $65.00, Age: 3-6, Apple, IBM, C64
- Counting, letter recognition, colors, stopping and starting

Three games: Discovery, Letters, and Numbers. Provides experience with letters, colors, numerals, and number. Well-designed. Is effective in giving child control. This is the program that comes with the Muppet Learning Keys, although it can be used with a regular keyboard.

KidsTime by Great Wave Software, 1987, $49.95, Age: 3-8, Macintosh
- Letters, numbers, matching, writing, music

Five games in which child uses mouse to play a piano, record and play back melodies, match letters or pictures, use or create dot-to-dot pictures, find letters on the keyboard in upper or lower case, or write stories and have them read back using Macintosh's built-in speech. Nice range of activities. Good child-control.

Ducks Ahoy by Joyce Hakansson Associates, 1984, $34.95, Age: 3-6, C64
- Timing, logical reasoning skills

A game in which children move a boat through canals to pick up ducks. Timing and selection of the best route to avoid a moving obstacle are required to collect all the ducks. Entertaining music and graphics. Joystick required.

Rainy Day Games by Baudville, 1985, $29.95, Age: 4-up, Apple, C64, Atari, Macintosh
- Memory practice

Contains three card games on one disk: Concentration, Old Maid, and Go Fish. Child uses mouse, joystick, arrow keys, or Koala Pad to move cards. Three difficulty levels offer a range in content. Well designed. Offers good level of child-control. Up to three players can play against the computer.

Stickybear Town Builder by Weekly Reader Software, 1984, $39.95, Age: 6-9, Apple, IBM, C64
- Map skills

Using joystick or arrow keys, child makes a town by placing 1 of 30 buildings on an empty map. The child can then drive car to find buildings in a matching game or to find hidden keys in the town. Towns can be saved. Joystick and color monitor recommended.

APPENDIX 6: GLOSSARY

Definitions are given here for *Survey* terms or computer terms that may be unfamiliar to the reader.

BASIC — Acronym for Beginners All-purpose Symbolic Instruction Code. A language often used with microcomputers, using word-like commands rather than numerical codes. A relatively easy language to learn.

Branching — The capacity of a program to adjust its level of challenge to match the child's performance, an important component of Computer-Managed Instruction (CMI). For example, if the child performs a task poorly, the program automatically presents a simpler task.

Chip — A tiny silicon surface containing a computer circuit.

Computer literacy — Familiarity with the parts of a microcomputer and some measure of programming skill.

Computer-Managed Instruction (CMI) — A capacity of a computer program that allows a teacher to set up individualized activities. This often includes the ability to sort, print, and automatically update performance records of children who use the program. (See Branching.)

Cricket speech synthesizer — An attachment for the Apple IIc computer. Plugs into the modem port of the computer. Equivalent to the Echo IIb speech synthesizer. Made by Street Electronics Corporation. Costs about $100. (See Echo speech synthesizer.)

Cursor — A symbol, such as a dash or box, that marks on the screen where the next keystroke will occur.

Disk — See Floppy disk.

Disk drive — The mechanism into which the disk or diskette is inserted. Makes the disk rotate as on a record player.

Divergent — See Open-ended.

Drill and practice — A program design that provides repeated practice with specific skills or concepts. Frequently involves answer checking, performance feedback, or chances to review missed problems.

Echo speech synthesizer — A computer attachment that permits computer output to be spoken. Plugs inside the computer. Requires special software that takes advantage of speech capability. Costs about $100. Made by Street Electronics Corporation. (See Cricket speech synthesizer.)

Embedded reinforcements — A program's pictures or sounds that relate to and work with the content, rather than being merely entertaining or attention-getting.

Floppy disk — A vinyl disk, coated with magnetic material, on which computer programs can be recorded for storage. Also called diskette.

Freeware — See Shareware.

Graphics — The pictorial part of a program presented on the screen. Often animated and in color.

Hardware — The physical equipment that makes up a computer system, such as the monitor, computer, keyboard, printer.

Icon — A picture or symbol that stands for a word. Often used in menus to make a program usable by nonreaders.

Imagewriter — A printer designed for Apple computers. The Imagewriter II can print in color if it has special ribbon.

Joystick — A computer attachment. Moving the joystick handle up, down, left, or right makes an object or cursor move in corresponding directions on the screen. A button on the joystick may also be used to stop or start action or pick up an object.

K — An abbreviation for Kilo, or thousand, usually referring to a computer's memory size in bytes. A 64K computer, for example, has 64 thousand bytes of memory. A byte can be roughly translated as one alphabet character.

Key experiences — The learning objectives of the High/Scope Curriculum. Approximately 50 guideposts for planning classroom activities and evaluating learning progress.

Koala Pad — A book-sized, touch-sensitive pad that allows information to be entered into the computer by drawing with a stylus or finger on the pad. Mostly used for drawing.

Light pen — A pen-shaped attachment sensitive to the light of the computer's TV display. Can be used to "draw" on the screen or to point to and select objects or areas on the screen.

Load — To copy a program's instructions from a disk or tape into the computer's memory.

LOGO — A computer language that uses a combination of simple instructions and graphics. Commonly used to introduce programming procedures to children.

Memory — An ability of a computer system to store information for later retrieval.

Menu — A list of a computer program's choices displayed on the screen.

Microcomputer — A desktop-sized computer with many of the capabilities of larger computers.

Monitor — The video display device attached to most microcomputers. Like a television screen without a channel tuner.

Mouse — A handheld computer attachment whose movement (left, right, up, or down) on a desk moves objects or a cursor in corresponding directions on the screen. A button on the mouse may also be used to stop or start an action or pick up an object.

Muppet Learning Keys — A separate keyboard that plugs into a joystick port. Contains numbers 0-9 in left-to-right order and letters in alphabetical order, plus eight color keys. It requires specially designed software. Produced by Sunburst Communications, it costs about $100.

Open-ended — The quality of computer programs, such as word processing, programming, and drawing programs, that allows many different results to be produced.

Paddles — A computer attachment with dials that can be turned to move an object or cursor on the screen. Similar in operation to knobs of an Etch-a-Sketch game.

Password — A word or code that allows a child to use parts of a computer program, or gives access to his or her stored files.

Peripheral — An attachment to the computer, such as a keyboard, monitor, printer, mouse, or speech synthesizer.

PowerPad — A large (12″ by 12″) touch-sensitive graphics tablet that plugs into the Apple II, IIe, or IIGS computer (not the IIc). Often used with picture templates that can be laid over its surface, allowing children to press pictures to enter answers into the computer. Also called WonderWorker. Produced by Dunamis, Inc., it costs about $200.

Program — An organized set of instructions, written in a computer language, that makes the computer perform a specified task. Programs are referred to as "software."

Programming — The process of giving the computer instructions. Several programming activities exist for children, e.g., for drawing — "Delta Drawing" and "LOGO"; for programming the movements of a face or object — "Facemaker," "Creature Creator."

Pull-down menu — A visual method of making on-screen selections. A mouse is used to move a pointer to an icon or word. Clicking the mouse then causes a related list of options to appear.

Shareware — Software that you are encouraged to copy and give to others at no cost and on a noncommercial basis. A message is included in the program, with the address of the producer, asking for a contribution if the user finds the program of value. Also called freeware.

Simulation — A program that models a real-life situation, such as the operation of a lemonade stand, the flying of an airplane, or the exploration of a volcano. Simulations are frequently designed to allow children to practice skills or concepts in a lifelike situation.

Single switch — A computer attachment. Has a single button or switch that can be used to enter responses into the computer. Commonly used in special education settings. Produced by Developmental Equipment, Inc.

Slotbuster II — A card for the Apple IIe that includes a modem, a clock/calendar, and a speech synthesizer that will say anything that can be printed. Costs around $230.00 and is available from RC Systems, Inc.

Software — The information that controls the computer. This information is usually stored on an electromagnetic medium such as a disk or tape. See Program.

Spell checker program — A program that checks the spelling of word processor stories. Some include such features as a built-in thesaurus, a list of optional spellings, or the ability to add words to the dictionary.

Touch Window — A touch-sensitive transparent screen that fits over a computer monitor, allowing information to be entered into the computer by touching screen images with a finger or stylus. It requires specially designed software. Produced by Personal Touch Corporation, it costs about $200.

Tutorial — A computer program, or part thereof, demonstrating a process or skill, such as matching objects one-to-one, with provisions for children to model or try the same process or skill on their own.

WonderWorker — See PowerPad.

Word processing program — A program that enables a child to use the computer to write, as with a typewriter. Word processing programs usually have additional features, such as ability to edit, save, and recall written material; ability to reformat written material; and ability to choose print style.

ABOUT THE AUTHOR

Warren Buckleitner has been
an educational consultant and computer specialist at the High/Scope*
Educational Research Foundation
in Ypsilanti, Michigan, since 1984.
A national speaker and workshop
leader, Mr. Buckleitner trains parents,
teachers, and college educators in
successful techniques for using computers with young children. Identifying
an unmet need through his training
and speaking engagements,
Mr. Buckleitner developed the
HIGH/SCOPE SURVEY OF EARLY
CHILDHOOD SOFTWARE in 1984.
This publication is now in its
fourth edition.